Life Without

Life Without

The Wrongful Conviction of
Sandy Shaw

Sandy Shaw

Dan Gleason

BLOOMSBURY ACADEMIC
NEW YORK · LONDON · OXFORD · NEW DELHI · SYDNEY

BLOOMSBURY ACADEMIC

Bloomsbury Publishing Inc, 1359 Broadway, New York, NY 10018, USA
Bloomsbury Publishing Plc, 50 Bedford Square, London, WC1B 3DP, UK
Bloomsbury Publishing Ireland, 29 Earlsfort Terrace, Dublin 2, D02 AY28, Ireland

BLOOMSBURY, BLOOMSBURY ACADEMIC and the Diana logo are trademarks of Bloomsbury Publishing Plc

First published in the United States of America 2025

Copyright © Sandy Shaw and Dan Gleason, 2025

Cover design by Sally Rinehart
Cover image Courtesy of the Library of Congress

All rights reserved. No part of this publication may be: i) reproduced or transmitted in any form, electronic or mechanical, including photocopying, recording or by means of any information storage or retrieval system without prior permission in writing from the publishers; or ii) used or reproduced in any way for the training, development or operation of artificial intelligence (AI) technologies, including generative AI technologies. The rights holders expressly reserve this publication from the text and data mining exception as per Article 4(3) of the Digital Single Market Directive (EU) 2019/790.

Bloomsbury Publishing Inc does not have any control over, or responsibility for, any third-party websites referred to or in this book. All internet addresses given in this book were correct at the time of going to press. The author and publisher regret any inconvenience caused if addresses have changed or sites have ceased to exist, but can accept no responsibility for any such changes.

A catalog record for this book is available from the Library of Congress.

ISBN: HB: 979-8-8818-0280-6
ePDF: 979-8-8818-6028-8
eBook: 979-8-8818-0281-3

Typeset by Deanta Global Publishing Services, Chennai, India
Printed and bound in the United States of America

For product safety related questions contact productsafety@bloomsbury.com.

To find out more about our authors and books visit www.bloomsbury.com and sign up for our newsletters.

Dan Gleason
This book is for Mom, Dad, Patty, Peggy, Mark, and Bridget; for Joe and Amber, and my childhood brother/best friend, the late Denny Mallette.

Sandy Shaw
My effort and contributions to this book are dedicated to the memory of the big-hearted rock of my life, my mother, Connie Jean Fosteson Shaw (March 14, 1953–March 8, 2016).

Contents

1 High Anxiety: Seeking a Pardon 1
2 Turbulent Beginnings 5
3 Battle Scars 7
4 Sweet in Small Doses 9
5 The One that Broke the Camel's Back 11
6 My Bridge to Sin City 13
7 Things We Lost in the Fire 15
8 Beware of an Enemy Reconciliation 19
9 "Who You Want to Live With?" 21
10 Dysfunction: The New Normal 27
11 Kidnapping Us Back 29
12 Vegas: Doorway to Disaster 31
13 Sixth Sense 33
14 Neon Wilderness 35
15 Enter Troy Kell 37
16 Rescuing Baby Nicole 39
17 Kidnapped... Again 43
18 I Already Got a Sister 45
19 The Last Kidnapping 47
20 The Truce 49
21 Grandma's Sobering Moment 51
22 Big Trouble at Rancho Circle 53
23 Virginia's Fatal Decision 57
24 Triple Homicide 61
25 Alex's Grand Plan 67

26	Aftermath	69
27	The Night Terrors	71
28	Psychotic Intrusions and Lowlife Friends	73
29	Halloween Fiasco and Back to Dad's	77
30	Another Shooting	81
31	Enter "Cotton"	83
32	Fighting Off a Rapist	87
33	The Stalker: Prelude to Murder	89
34	Cotton's Murder	93
35	A Nightmare, but Not a Dream	101
36	Booked for Murder	103
37	Clark County Jail	109
38	Five-Day Circus	113
39	On Hold	131
40	Welcome to the Rest of Your Life	135
41	Lockdown in the Fish Tank	139
42	Breaking Point	143
43	What to Do With Me	145
44	First Day in the Yard	149
45	Monica	151
46	Wall of Noise, Den of Violence	153
47	Facing a Predator	155
48	Ordeal in the Prison Kitchen	159
49	Just a Bar of Soap	163
50	Return of My Jailhouse Stalker	169
51	Sheila's Ordeal	171
52	First Appeal and Varela's Contrition	175
53	Changing My Tune	179
54	Appeal Denied!	183
55	Bitter Winter and off to Reno	185
56	Troy's Troubled Life	189
57	The Annabelle Hall Situation	191
58	Sold Down the River	195

59 Our Escape Plan 199
60 What Happened in Between 205
61 Shakopee Prison and Troy Kell's Fate 211
62 Fighting for a Parole 215
63 The Mob Cop and 2002 Pardons Hearing 221
64 The Mystery Packet 225
65 Big Win at the Pardons Board 229
66 2007 Parole Hearing 231
67 On Parole: Forever 233
68 Last Visits With Dad 239
69 Back to Prison 241
70 A Week of Sorrow 245
71 Judgment Day 249
72 The Morning After 257

Index 261
About the Authors 267

1

High Anxiety
Seeking a Pardon

June 28, 2022. Las Vegas, Nevada.

It is not yet 9:00 a.m., but the temperature outside the Regional Justice Center of the Nevada Supreme Court is climbing steadily toward the predicted high of 112.

I'm sweating it out at the defendant's table inside the railed barrier separating the trial area from the public spectator benches, waiting for the hearing to start. I fidget but try to appear calm. I'm a bundle of nerves, but I'm trying to appear confident. I'm somber but inwardly terrified.

I made sure to dress conservatively and professionally for what I'm praying is my life-changing hearing. Fifteen years I've been trying to get this hearing for a crime that happened thirty-five long years ago, when I was a fifteen-year-old kid.

I picked out a smartly cut black pencil skirt, hemmed just below the knee, a white blouse, and small, gold, circular earrings. My 2-inch heels elevate me to 5 feet 8 inches. My hair has been blonde since I was a kid, but not long back I colored it brunette to hide the gray creeping in. I have blue eyes and a light-complexioned face I got from my Irish, French, and Norwegian ancestors. That face is fifty-one now. My soft features contradict the hard life I've lived.

I've always looked younger than my years and I'm fortunate I still do. Even in the TV footage from the preliminary hearing when I was fifteen, I looked much younger. But nothing I see in the mirror or what folks notice when I pass them on the street suggests I'm a convicted felon who spent twenty-one years in prison for murder. Or that at fifteen and barely into puberty, I was the youngest female ever incarcerated in an adult Nevada prison. Not an honor anyone in their right mind covets.

It's intimidating to look up at those Pardons Board members. They're on this wide, elevated judges' bench way above me. They're exalted and I'm just some nobody way down here. Nine of them make up the Nevada Board of Pardons, about to hear my case and determine how I'm going to live the rest of my life.

My entire fate is in the hands of seven Nevada Supreme Court justices in spooky black robes; also Nevada attorney general Aaron Ford in his trademark bow tie. Traditionally, because attorneys general represent the state, they usually vote no.

Governor Steve Sisolak runs the show, nattily dressed in a cream-colored business suit. In a pardons hearing in Nevada, the governor's vote is the most important of all the members. While a five to four majority is needed for a pardon, the governor's vote has to be among them. In fact, if eight members of the board vote yes and the governor votes no, the pardon is denied. Yet, his yes vote alone will not be enough to grant the pardon. It's just that his no vote is a deal-breaker for the petitioner. I take some comfort in his soft, kind face as he glances over at me, and I pray he is sympathetic to my case.

All the board members stare intimidatingly down at me, and I stare nervously up at them.

I have to calm my nerves, so I sneak a glance over my shoulder for supporters who've come to speak for me. I spot my two younger half-sisters, Leah and Nicole, and my brother Shane, who smiles and gives me a thumbs-up. My stepfather, Mike Flanery, a rock who stuck by me all those years, is with my niece Jocelyn, Nicole's kid. It's Jocelyn's sixteenth birthday, but she chose to come here to stand up and plead for me. Then I notice three friends who are also going to speak on my behalf.

My mother, who stood by me steadfastly and gallantly all those years, died six years ago. God I wish she had lived to see this day, even just to know I'm getting this chance.

The judges' faces are stern, gruff like schoolmarms. A few of them are shuffling papers, what must be reminder notes and questions to ask me, maybe to trap me with. What do they see when they look at me? Do they see a little girl trying to survive a fractured family? Or a thirteen-year-old witness to a triple homicide in her best friend's house, who went through a long hell with PTSD and emotional lockdown?

Maybe they see a confused fifteen-year-old kid who didn't realize she was getting mixed up in a murder that would shock the city and for months be tabloid fodder for the Las Vegas press. Me, I hope they see a survivor, a woman who lost the best years of her life locked in prison through the prime of life, but who has tried never to play the victim card and has never given up. Someone who now just needs a break to, at long last live a normal life.

A newspaper columnist wrote when I made parole: "How Sandy Shaw got into this predicament, and how she handled it after that was equal parts tragic and inspirational." That truly sums it up.

I'm getting more nervous by the minute, wondering how they're going to grill me. I hope they don't ask me to recount the worst memory of my life: the night I was pushed to the ground after the first shot rang out. The night Billy yelled, "Get him now, Troy, get him now!" The night I got up and started running, after Troy shot twice more, thinking they would shoot me, too. The night I ducked for cover behind desert scrub knowing Troy Kell had just shot James Cotton Kelly dead.

I was three months shy of sixteen then, but it was the fourth murder I'd seen in two years.

Come on, I'm thinking. *Get this thing started*. I'm good one-on-one or talking to a few people, but I've always been terrified getting up in front of a group and speaking. My mouth gets dry, and my hands and knees shake; it's awful. Performance anxiety, I have been told. So, I really dread having to step up to the podium and make my case for my unconditional pardon. But I got no choice. I'm hoping I get through it without looking like a bungling idiot.

It's taken fifteen years of trying just to get to this hearing. I had it on the docket last year, and they postponed me for a year. And there's no guarantee it's going to turn in my favor. Odds are long because to win a full pardon, I had to have the vote of five of the nine board members, with one vote being from the governor himself.

I woke at daybreak after an unsettling sleep, tossing and turning, getting up to drink water three, four times. I managed to calm myself on the drive to court, but now I'm getting rattled, waiting on a long delay to hook up the Carson City Zoom feed, as there are officials there in the state capitol who must witness it, and some witnesses who might speak from there. So, while the board members use the lull to read through notes, I start sweating, and my hands begin to shake. I'm really scared. I grab a tissue to blow my nose and wipe my watery eyes, but wouldn't you know it, they placed the tissue box just out of my reach. And there's no way I'm going to get up and walk around this table and telegraph to the judges and everybody in the courtroom how crazy nervous I am.

To calm myself, I close my eyes and slow my breathing, a trick I learned fifteen years ago that worked when I won parole. So, with my eyes shut, my mind drifts back to fading memories and dark moments of my life.

Memories no member of a Pardons Board can likely fathom.

2

Turbulent Beginnings

My first memory ever, I'm three years old, lying next to my mom on my childbed in our Minnesota trailer. She was fighting to catch her breath because she was terrified of the beating my dad, Mike Shaw, was about to give her—as soon as he got that flimsy door open.

July in the little town of Wadena, Minnesota, was sticky hot, even more so inside that mobile home because we had a busted swamp cooler. Mom protectively draped one arm across my back, but she was the one who needed protecting. Her hand felt clammy on my neck and her long, skinny legs dangled off my small bed. She'd startled me when she rushed into the bedroom and locked the door behind her, seconds before Dad started pounding on it.

He called her to come out and face him. "Don't you try to hide from me, you *bitch*. Come on outta there."

Mom whispered stuff in my ear. "Don't be scared, honey. It's okay. We're gonna be okay." But there wasn't anything she could say to drown out Dad's yelling as he hammered on the thin plywood door. The scary world on the other side of that door seemed to suck all the air out of the room.

Our single-wide trailer was isolated in the middle of a thick patch of piney woods just outside Wadena. In the spring and early summer, the sweet smell of pine and wildflowers filled the air. There were upsides to living isolated way out in the woods in a town of five thousand. But there were downsides, too—nobody heard Mom's screams, nobody called the police, and nobody came to her rescue when Dad started punching her.

I would bawl when he beat on her. Afterwards, she'd tell me, "He just gets mean when he drinks, honey. He's got bad memories he's tryin' to drink 'off his mind. And it ain't working." That explanation didn't register in my three-year-old brain. He could be a sweet prince to me and my little brother and then turn into the Big Bad Wolf with Mom.

(Later, in seventh grade, I would read Robert Louis Stevenson's *Dr. Jekyll and Mr. Hyde* and think of my father).

After a long, edgy silence, Dad pounded on the door again and hollered. "Connie . . . you come on out and finish this GOD-damned CON-versation!" From experience, I knew "finishing a GOD-damned CON-versation" meant she was about to get the hell knocked out of her. Sometimes her bruises would take weeks to fade away. She'd cake on a lot of makeup and tell Grandma Marie she tripped or banged her cheek on a cabinet door. Grandma Marie had quit believing those lies.

Mom was little more than a girl herself. She just turned twenty-one. She was a rail-thin 5 feet 3 inches, fair-haired, fair-skinned, and had big blue eyes. I've seen the pictures from when she was in high school. Centered between her high cheekbones was this Scandinavian nose her high school friends told her was the perfect shape for her face. But by the time she ended her marriage to Dad, her nose would be crooked slightly to the left for the rest of her life.

I tried to focus on Mom's labored breathing and the squeaking of our old table fan, rather than the monster outside my door. But Dad's earsplitting shout drowned out everything else: "Bring your *skinny* ass outta there or I'm comin' in!"

3

Battle Scars

At this point, my dad, Mike Shaw, was twenty-seven. I would later learn his heavy drinking was his way to numb the painful bad memories he brought home from Vietnam. When the bottle let him down, he moved his attention to my mom to take out the brunt of his anger.

He was only 5 feet 7 inches, but he was wiry, strong, and scrappy. He was a hard worker, laboring outside in the sun and wind on his family farm outside the one-stoplight hamlet of Bertha. Bertha, with a population five hundred, was thirteen miles down the road from Wadena. The farm work had toughened him physically, but the horrors of battle had turned him inward.

Sleepy Wadena pulled its shades up when the summer brought an influx of tourists who came for fishing, camping, and recreational boating on 14,000-acre Otter Tail Lake, a half-hour west of town. Other than farming, Bertha was mostly a bedroom community for people working an hour away in either Brainerd or Alexandria.

Most of the 126-acre Shaw farm was sown with corn and soybeans, but they also raised hogs, chickens, dairy cattle, and a few horses. Mike was one of ten original siblings—two had died in childhood. Every Shaw kid and both parents pitched in to make the farm give them a living.

Then, during his senior year in high school, he and a buddy quit school and took off on an adventure, running out of money in Kalispell, Montana, where they found jobs as ranch hands. At twenty, in 1967, Dad volunteered for the US Army draft at the height of the Vietnam buildup. Assigned to the 1st Cavalry, he got shipped off to war on the last day of 1967. He went on twenty-five combat missions and got promoted to E5 Sergeant during his twelve months in-country.

On the absolute worst day of his life, his outfit got pinned down by artillery, then encircled and overrun by North Vietnamese Regulars. The fighting was fierce, and his outfit was outflanked, outnumbered, and outgunned. Screams filled the air as his buddies got slaughtered, their innards scattered across a wide expanse of tall green grass in a big field stained dark with blood.

Dad took multiple shrapnel hits before six Huey helicopters swooped down—he called them "avenging angels." They came in low with this deafening roar of whirring blades and machine gun fire. The choppers landed near the edge of the field and whisked dad and a handful of other survivors away from certain death.

Like many combat soldiers who lived through the horrors of war, he marched back home with a darkness in his heart. He returned to Bertha with the Bronze Star for valor and the Purple Heart for his wounds—and even though the term Post-Traumatic Stress Disorder hadn't yet been coined, he brought that back, too.

After Vietnam, he went back to work on the family farm. He liked the hard work because it kept his mind on what was under his nose and not over his shoulder. Hard work kept him busy five days a week, but when Friday nights rolled around, bad memories haunted him and boredom overtook him. He found refuge in beer joints and dive bars fifteen minutes up Highway 71 in our town of Wadena.

It was in Wadena he met my mom, Connie Fosteson.

4

Sweet in Small Doses

I've seen pictures of my mom in high school. She was a skinny seventeen-year-old junior at Wadena High when she first set eyes on Mike Shaw. Skinny though she was, my aunt said she attracted a lot of boys she knew in school and had a reputation for being wild. She was the middle child of Bill and Marie Pronovost Fosteson, who owned the Red Otter Supper Club out on Otter Tail Lake. Their dining room and bar raked in big money from late spring to early fall when tourists flocked to the lake to fish for sturgeon, northern pike, walleye, and largemouth bass. Grandpa Bill and Grandma Marie's customers were folks who enjoyed soul-stirring sunset views of the lake from their restaurant tables and heavy drinking in the Red Otter bar.

Grandpa Bill was of Norwegian descent, tall and slim—6 feet 2 inches, maybe only 160 pounds. He was fun-loving but serious when it came to hard work. Grandma Marie was short, dark-haired, and full-blooded French. They were both functioning alcoholics who worked as hard as they drank—which was tirelessly. When Mom was a teenager, their drinking drove her to the solace of the streets, such as they were in Wadena, small-town safe, but where a girl could find trouble if she was of a mind to, and Connie Fosteson was often of a mind to.

After seeing Mike Shaw around town, Mom told her girlfriends he was "a handsome little devil," so they bet her five bucks she couldn't get him to ask her out. She would come to regret winning that bet.

At first, she found him witty and charming. His wisecracks made her laugh. She once told me he was "sweet in small doses." Their first date was fun and led to more dates. She now and then asked him about the war, but he'd go mute or change the subject, so she quit asking.

In 1970, after her junior year, he got her pregnant. Grandpa Bill and Grandma Marie, like Mike's folks, were devout Catholics, and she was terrified to tell them. She considered getting rid of me, but luckily for me, abortions weren't legal yet in Minnesota. They were legal in New York, though, and Mike offered to fund her trip and pay for the abortion. But he gave her another option: get married and have the baby. And that's what they did.

As a result, I entered my turbulent life one bitter-cold night in January of 1971. Mom wanted to name me Stephanie or Heather, pretty names I would've liked, but Dad lobbied for Sandy, honoring a wild mustang he and his brothers never could tame. Like a Native American, my name would have a story behind it, long before it got publicly stained with other monikers.

By the time my brother Shane came along a year later, Dad's sunny, witty facade had disappeared into a beer bottle. At first, when he would come home loaded and high, he would just slap Mom around some, but it wasn't long before he was fist-whipping her.

When the emotional walls closed in on him, he now and then disappeared, sometimes for days or weeks, once for a whole month without bothering to phone us. Because he would leave Mom without money, she started waitressing at Grandpa and Grandma's supper club and had to hitch rides to work in the dead of winter when it was cold as Jesus and the wind stung her face like needles. She would get friends to babysit me and Shane when she had to work.

Dad would always show back up, sooner or later, unannounced, offering no explanation, no apology. He was never home long before his temper boiled over, like that night she took shelter in my bedroom.

5

The One that Broke the Camel's Back

After nearly half-hour of nagging Mom to come out of my bedroom, Dad went dead silent for like a minute and then he exploded, kicking open the plywood door. Scared the hell out of me. He rushed in and grabbed Mom. I will never forget his wild eyes when he grabbed her by the hair. She screamed and kicked and flailed, but no way she could stop him. He was a drunken madman.

My infantile mind believed if I could just hang on tight enough, I could save her. So, when he dragged her out of the room by her hair through the narrow hallway, little did he know he was dragging me with her. I squeezed both arms tightly around Mom's legs and got bounced along the floor all the way inside our small bathroom.

Once in there, Dad yanked Mom to her feet and started punching her face. He landed a roundhouse right, flush on her nose. It sounded like when somebody cracks a walnut open with a hammer. Blood gushed from her nose and spattered down onto my hair and face. I wiped my cheek, saw blood on my hands, and screamed, sure I'd been hurt.

His last punch was head-on with her jaw. I watched her knees buckle, then he let go, and she just crumpled to the floor like a sack of potatoes. He looked down, and for the first time realized I'd been in there all that time. His eyes went wide. He tried to speak, but it came out in a drunken grunt. He staggered sideways into the wall, then stumbled out of the bathroom and out the trailer door. He likely headed for some dive bar to get absolution.

I was still on the floor when Mom struggled to her feet and stuffed tissues up her nose to stop the bleeding. She patted me on the head and convinced me I wasn't hurt, then washed my cheeks and hair before cleaning up her own bloodied face. That's how she was. Her kids came first. She got dressed and called a taxi, and Shane and I went with her to the emergency room at the Tri-County Hospital.

While Mom got treated for a broken nose and multiple fractures of her cheek and jaw, a gentle night nurse sat with me and Shane and would now and then say, "There, there, it's okay."

Sometime in the wee hours, Dad staggered back in the door and left for work next morning without even an "I'm sorry" to Mom. Soon as he was gone, she phoned Grandma Marie to drive us all to the courthouse. With her nose bandaged, her right cheek swollen, and her right eye blackened, Mom filed for legal separation and got a restraining order. It would be the end of the marriage, but not the end of the trouble he would cause us.

6

My Bridge to Sin City

Served with separation papers and the restraining order, Dad moved back to the family farm. I missed his hugs but not how he treated Mom. He sent her money monthly—he was good about that—and she continued waitressing at the Red Otter. She bought a used Chevelle that sounded like the crack of doom when it started; it shot blue smoke out the tailpipe, but it got her where she needed to go.

The next year, 1975, when I was four, my grandparents sold the Red Otter to retire to San Diego. But they never got there. On the way, they stopped in Las Vegas and liked it so much they bought a house and settled there. Their decision would alter my destiny. Mom kept working at the Otter, though once the leaves dropped and tourists left, her tips dwindled from folding money to pocket change.

She hired the teenage son of a friend to babysit me and Shane when she was at work. The boy's parents nicknamed him Buzz because of his close-cropped butch haircut. But the nickname suited him even more because he got stoned every time he came over.

Me and my brother ran around that trailer like two wild ponies while Buzz smoked his marijuana and watched TV. To quiet us down, he started forcing us to take big puffs from his joints and inhale the smoke. We would sit on the floor and stare at the TV like little zombies. He threatened us with bodily harm if we ever leaked a word to Mom about the marijuana, so we never ratted him out.

The same year, Dad found a good-paying roofing job six hours away in Plover, Wisconsin, population ten thousand, a hundred miles west of Green Bay. Being Catholics, my folks put off their divorce, but the separation agreement worked out just as well.

His visits with my brother and me were restricted to Wadena, and the terms were that he couldn't be drinking. I was never scared of Dad because he was always gentle with me and Shane. He wasn't an affectionate guy, but I often wondered how he could be so sweet to me and beat the living shit out of my mom.

He would drive down on Fridays and take us to the family farm, where I would run all over the place, petting horses and playing with the family's German Shepherd, "Duke," and pet wolf, "Sheba."

My folks were getting along okay from a distance—but none of us knew he was plotting revenge against Mom for kicking him out. It wasn't long after I turned five that he saw his chance and took it.

7

Things We Lost in the Fire

It was a frigid March night. Mom had the faucets dripping to keep the pipes in our trailer from freezing. That afternoon, out my window, I watched the north wind sway the tops of the tall pines and heard the wind whistling through tiny cracks in the seams of our trailer. The woods were thick with Eastern white pines, elm trees, oaks, and maples. Patchy snow from the hard Minnesota winter had almost all melted, but the ground was still like cement.

I pleaded to play outside, but because it got below freezing, Mom made both of us play indoors. She wanted to keep us underfoot to take advantage of two straight days off to clean.

I was five years old then and because we lived way out in the boonies, my playmates were usually my little brother, my German Shepherd puppy, Angel, and my imagination. I so adored Angel, the rescue puppy Mom got me for my fourth birthday. I cherished giving her cuddles and belly rubs, and she loved getting them. Angel was rambunctious and cute and tagged under foot like my shadow.

Early that afternoon, Mom and Shane were napping, but I wasn't sleepy. I played with Angel, convinced she understood everything I said as she looked at me with her big puppy eyes. I found myself humming the birthday song: *Happy birthday to you, happy birthday to you . . .*

I got an idea to bake a pretend cake in my bedroom. For Angel. From under the bathroom sink, I fetched five rolls of toilet paper and took them to my bedroom. Mom warned me never to play with matches, but I knew where they were and couldn't have a birthday cake without candles. I stood on a kitchen chair and fetched a candle and matches.

In my bedroom, I folded several sheets of toilet paper and stacked them high to look like a cake, then put a candle on the top. I figured out how to light it, and while kneeling on the floor, I sang to Angel, "Happy birthday, to you . . . happy birthday to yooooou . . . happy birthday, dear Angel—"

And just like that—*whoosh*—the toilet paper caught fire. Angel darted from the room.

I froze, staring at the flames. Mom smelled the smoke and rushed into the room. In her panicked and groggy state, she grabbed a pillow and tried to beat the fire out. That just fanned the flames, and they spread faster, jumping to the curtains and quickly engulfing the room.

Mom knew how fast mobile homes burned—because they had a confined space, very little drywall, and very few wall boards. So, when the walls had caught fire, she grabbed me and Shane and rushed us both outside into the bitter cold with blankets around us. She dashed back inside and called 911 to summon firemen, then ran back outside to get us away from what was now a burning mess of plywood.

Just as the fire truck roared up, the heat kicked out the front window next to the door. The firemen worked fast, hooking their hoses up to a hydrant on the street. I stood numb, wrapped in my blanket, the heat from the blaze toasting my face. I realized what I had done and started bawling. Mom, wearing a parka and holding Shane with one hand, pulled me close and hugged me with her free arm. "You didn't do it on purpose, sweetie. Anyway, it's just *stuff*. We ain't hurt. We're gonna be okay."

The crackling fire spit out charred hunks of the trailer as I rubbed tears off my cheeks. Then my heart sank to my stomach. *Oh, my God. Angel! Where's Angel?* I tugged Mom's coat sleeve. "Momma. Where's Angel?"

In a rush to get us out of there, Mom had forgotten about the puppy. ". . . I don't know, honey. I—I think she maybe got out when I opened the door. That's likely what she did."

"Yeah, but where *is* she?"

"Prob'ly in the woods. That's what dogs *do* when they're scared. They hide."

In a panic, I hollered "Angellll" over and over. When she didn't come out of the woods, I broke free from Mom and sprinted toward the trailer. A fireman grabbed my arm and stopped me. "Whoa there, little lady. You can't go in there."

I pointed at the trailer. "My puppy's in there and I—"

Mom had hoisted Shane above her shoulders and came and yanked me back from the blaze. Then she locked both of us in the car. The firemen could not save the trailer or any possessions. Everything we owned, other than the clothes on our backs, had gone up in flames—and I knew my little puppy was likely dead. No matter what Mom told me and kept telling me all the way to the motel that afternoon, I knew it was my fault.

I cried myself to sleep that night.

Mom kept saying Angel escaped to the woods, but she would one day admit she was hoping the smoke had killed Angel before the fire got her.

The next day, an old high school friend of Mom's offered to put us up until Mom could figure her next move. I wouldn't let up about Angel, so the morning after the fire, Mom drove me back out to the burned-out trailer and we both called into the woods for Angel. I yelled as loud as I could, over and over. Then reality hit me: if Angel were alive, she would have come to me from the woods when I called her.

As I stood there dazed with grief, the odor of burned-out embers stinging my nose, looking at the smoldering ashes of what had been the only home I had ever known, I asked Mom if they let dogs into heaven. She crouched down, eyeball to eyeball, and put her arms around me. "Sure, they do, sweetie. What kind of crummy joint would God be running if he didn't have no dogs? Nobody'd want to go in."

I watched the white ashes from the trailer swirling into the cold air toward the tops of the trees, convinced those ashes were Angel's soul heading for heaven.

Our family had lost all their belongings, but the fire would cost us much more. My dad would make sure of it.

8

Beware of an Enemy Reconciliation

With all of us cramped into her friend's house, Mom decided our best move was Minneapolis. More opportunities there and she had long wanted to leave Wadena. Just before she moved, Dad called her at her friend's place and surprised her with an offer. "Sorry 'bout that fire," he said. "Things are tough, I know. Look here, I can help you some till you get on your feet."

"Oh, yeah? How so?"

He said, "I can take the kids off your hands, just till you get a little more change in your pockets. Soon as you're ready, come get 'em. Whenever ya want."

Mom liked the offer but she had learned to distrust him. "Okay, let me mull it over. I'll call you, one way or the other."

Then two days later, her car quit on her and she had to get a mechanic to tow it. She had reached her tipping point and called Dad to take him up on his offer. "Don't you forget, it's *temporary*," she warned him. "I get things squared around, you bring the kids back here. Fair enough?"

"You got a deal," he promised.

That weekend, Dad drove six hours from Plover to Wadena, picked up me and Shane and put one hundred eighty dollars in Mom's hand to pay her car mechanic. She was touched.

Soon as her car was fixed, she drove to Minneapolis and found a job right away, tending bar at a high-end restaurant with way better tips than the Otter. She found a two-bedroom apartment in a nice part of town, and when she got a little ahead, she was about to call Dad and ask him to drive us down. But one night around closing time, when she was polishing beer glasses, some stranger in a fancy suit appeared at the bar.

"Excuse me, ma'am, but are you Mrs. Connie Shaw?"

She stopped polishing a glass and nodded. "Yeah, that's me . . . I know you?"

He smirked and handed her a manila envelope with papers inside. "This is a present from your husband." Then he sauntered out the door, whistling.

When she read the papers, her mouth dropped open. "That *fucker*. Who's he calling an *unfit Mother*!"

Dad had hired a lawyer and filed a motion in a Minnesota court to get legal custody of us. He claimed Mom was unfit because she should have watched me closer so I wouldn't play with matches. That was a load of crap, but he'd found his chance for revenge.

Mom wanted to kick herself for falling for his con. Grandpa Fosteson told her she should've learned from the ancient Greeks to avoid an enemy reconciliation. She couldn't afford a lawyer and didn't want to ask Grandpa for money. She thought she'd fight it on her own. I wasn't sure what was going on, but I kept asking Dad when I could move back with her. And he'd just say, "We'll have to see."

9

"Who You Want to Live With?"

That was about when Mom met that loser, Bill Lynch. He was a tall, slim, smooth-talking ex-con. Up around 6 feet 3 inches, coal black eyes, a head of long, thin dark hair, and who would lie if it was handier to tell the truth. Bill was always primping his long hair and checking it in the mirror. He was a regular in the bar where she worked, and she was lonely and started filling her void with Bill.

They had been dating for a month when she found out he'd done hard time for burglary and theft—first in Florida and then in Minnesota. She got in his face about it, but he played it down—foolish mistakes, he said. All behind him now, he said. Was a changed man, he said.

Mom weighed the risk, but because Grandma and Grandpa were alcoholics, she had grown into a rescuer. She was sure she could fix Bill Lynch, who was a comfort to her. So, they moved into an apartment and he paid his share of the bills with part-time jobs, until such time, he swore, he could find a solid job and get back on his feet. Truth be known, he'd never been on his feet. He was a born thief and con man.

The custody hearing in Wadena neared and Mom hadn't hired a lawyer. On the day of the hearing, she drove three hours to Wadena from Minneapolis. By this time—and I had no idea—she was pregnant with Lynch's baby. If that news came out in court, there was no way she would win custody. Lucky for her, she wasn't far enough along that her bump showed.

I rode down from Plover with Dad the day before and spent the night at Grandma and Grandpa Shaw's. I was in the courtroom with Dad's brother Doug. Mom also had a brother named Doug. One other thing they held in common, I never had much use for either of them.

Mom walked into court late, catching her breath, and the judge checked his wristwatch and frowned. I was so happy to see her, I smiled and blew her a kiss, and she blew one back.

Two long tables faced the judge. Dad and his lawyer sat at one table, and Mom sat at the other. Dad took the witness stand first and fibbed about how Shane and I had come to live with him. "Connie called me after the fire, all upset, darn near begging me to take them kids." I knew it was a lie because I was on Mom's lap when she took the call, and I heard it all. But he kept fibbing. "She said she just couldn't deal with 'em, everything going on, finding a place to live and what not."

I wanted to blurt out it wasn't true, but I was afraid to get yelled at by somebody for speaking out of turn.

Mom slammed her hand on the table and yelled so loud it echoed through the courtroom: "That's a damn *lie* and you know it. I—"

"Stop it, Mrs. Shaw," the judge cut her off. He wagged his finger like a school teacher. "You will get your turn to testify."

Dad told the judge he always made sure matches were out of reach of his kids, but the night I started the fire they were where they always were, and all I needed was a chair to stand on and get them. "That's one reason she's an unfit Mother," Dad said. "That fire never should've happened." He had never hidden those matches where I couldn't find them. They were always in the same place.

I wanted to jump up and yell to the judge, *"Stop. It's my fault. Not hers. I knew where they kept matches. I started the fire."*

The last thing Dad told the judge was, "I figured it out these last couple months—them kids are way happier with me."

Not so. I was every bit as happy with Mom. My life hadn't changed much either way.

When Mom took the stand, she squirmed in the chair. "Look. I got a steady job, okay? I mean, a *good* job. And I always make sure them kids have babysitters when I'm at work and I spend quality time with 'em. When I'm not working or cleaning or cooking for 'em, I'm spending time with those kids."

That was the God's truth.

She sucked in a breath and dabbed her eyes with a tissue. "I know Mike and I are still legally married, but if some learn-ed somebody or other would just read that separation agreement." Then she raised her voice. "He signed that paper. The kids are to live with *me* and he gets 'em weekends. Didn't anybody *read* that? Far as I know, it's *legal*. So, I don't understand why we're even in a courtroom."

Mom paused to clear her throat then spoke again. "Mike Shaw made a habit of beating the hell out of me. No sugar coating it, Judge. He'd work me over so bad I had to cover bruises with makeup, for days. Now and then, he'd go over the hill and disappear, one time a whole month." She pulled in a long breath and let it out. "Supposed to be providing for us, and I had no inkling where he was. So, I don't know how he can sit there straight-faced and say *he's* fit and I'm not."

The judge was a chunky, silver-haired man with reading glasses on the bridge of his nose. He rubbed his chin. "Can you produce evidence of his physical abuse, Mrs. Shaw?"

Dad's lawyer chimed in, "Your honor, there's no record of Mr. Shaw ever being violent toward Mrs. Shaw. No police report, no arrest. Police were never called about any domestic disturbances. The separation papers state 'irreconcilable differences' and that it's a *trial* separation."

The judge turned to Mom. "Well? Did you file a police report about the alleged assaults, Mrs. Shaw?"

"Why do you figure I had to get a restraining order? Wasn't anything *alleged* about my broken nose and my wired-up jaw."

"Did you bring a copy of that restraining order, ma'am?"

"No. I'd have to hunt it up. At the courthouse. It's filed there, trust me. I drove all the way up from Minneapolis this morning to get here. Check the hospital records here in Wadena and you'll see. They treated me for a busted nose and a fractured jaw. Wasn't any first-time thing either."

The judge exhaled, then he scolded her again. "Look. I don't want to seem insensitive. But you had plenty of notice about this hearing to gather evidence to help your case."

I was mad at the judge for being mean to her.

Then Dad's lawyer got up again. "If your honor pleases, I checked the hospital report and Mrs. Shaw never said *anything* about her injuries being the result of violence."

Mom shot him the stink-eye. "Yeah, well, I told a nurse all about it. You think maybe I slipped on a patch of ice, middle of July, busted up my nose and jaw?"

The judge waved her off. "I'm not saying you were not a victim of violence, Mrs. Shaw. I'm not calling you a *liar*. I would never suggest that. But in court, you must have documentation. We don't operate on hearsay."

Dad's attorney interrupted again. "If it pleases the court. Mrs. Shaw, under her own free will, handed over her children to their father. We contend it was *she* who asked *him* to take the kids. It's just her word against his. There is no proof that she didn't ask him. There are no records of that phone call."

Of course, I knew better.

Then Dad's lawyer cross-examined Mom, peppering her with questions like if she ever got drunk and slept around. "Are you now cohabitating with a man in Minneapolis?" the lawyer said.

I had no idea what "cohabitating" meant but it didn't sound good.

"Well, yes, I did move in with a man. So what? Whose business is it?"

The judge told everyone he wanted a short recess. He came back a little later and slid his reading glasses back down on the bridge of his nose. "This case is filled with he said/she said." He took a breath and leaned forward. "I understand both of the Shaw children are here in the courtroom today." He pointed in my direction. "Are these your children, Mr. Shaw and Mrs. Shaw?"

Dad and Mom both answered yes.

"And the little girl is the oldest, am I right?"

Mom replied, "Yes, Sandy. She's five."

The judge then asked Uncle Doug to walk me up to the witness stand and have a seat in the witness chair. I wondered if I was in trouble. I was nervous. He made me put my right hand on a Bible some guy was holding and swear to tell the truth. Then the judge asked me, "What is your name and how old are you, young lady?"

"I'm Sandy Marie, and I am five." I was jiggling around in that big chair.

"Is your father good to you—is he nice to you?"

"Oh, sure and so is my momma. They're both nice to me and to Shane." I looked at my dad. "Just not nice to each *other*."

"Has your father ever been mean to you while you've been staying with him, or to your little brother, other than normal, you know, *discipline*?"

I shook my head. "He's never been mean to me, just to my Mom."

The judge paused to ponder it. "I'm going to ask you a very important question, Sandy, and I want you to tell me the truth, best you can."

I clenched my fists, scared he'd ask a question and I wouldn't know the answer.

"Which of your parents would you rather live with? Your father or Mother? I mean, if you *had* to choose?"

I couldn't believe he asked me a question like that. Who asks a little kid to choose between her parents when she loves them both? Mom rolled her eyes at the judge.

I stared at that judge a long time and finally said, "Both of 'em! I wanna live with *both* of 'em. In the same house. Like my aunts and Uncles and Grandmas and Grandpas do."

The judge shrugged and nodded, then told me I could get down off the chair. Uncle Doug walked me back to my seat.

The judge removed his reading glasses. "Ladies and gentlemen, I am going to retire to my chambers. I hope to have a decision in a few minutes."

A short while later, he returned with a notepad in hand. He took his seat and cleared his throat. "After careful consideration, the court awards custody to Michael Shaw . . . Based in part on his steady income and other variables, including providing the children a safe, stable home."

Poor Mom looked like somebody had pulled a plug and let all the air out of her. I wanted to run up and hug her, but Doug had a grip on my hand and I couldn't. I was sad for her, for me, for Shane.

Mom's brother and some friends were in the courtroom muttering, mumbling, and grumbling. Her brother said loud enough for the judge to hear, "That son of a bitch." I didn't know if he meant Dad or the judge.

The judge held up his hand. "Respect this court, sir. We are still in session." Then he turned to Mom. "Mrs. Shaw, you will have visitation rights . . . every other weekend, and we will work out holiday visits. You said you reside in Minneapolis now, correct?"

Mom took out a tissue and blew her nose with a loud honk. "That's right. I work at a nice restaurant and I make good money. It's real steady." She kept talking, but the judge had grabbed a stack of papers and was reading them, ignoring her like she wasn't even there anymore.

Before she left, she gave me and Shane big love hugs, then wiped away my tears with her fingertips and kissed my cheek.

She'd tell me sometime later that, despite the court-mandated visitations, her plan was to get some money ahead and take the case back to court. Then during her long drive back to Minneapolis, she said screw the court. Come hell or high water, by hook or by crook, she'd get me and Shane back.

10

Dysfunction
The New Normal

I started kindergarten in Plover, and midway through the year, Mom gave me a new sister, by Bill Lynch, named Nicole. On a weekend visitation, she brought Shane and me to Minneapolis to meet Bill and little Nicole. I adored that baby, but I didn't take to Bill. I wasn't sure why. A gut feeling.

I really missed Mom, but I was doing okay with Dad in his double-wide in a Plover mobile home park. Three comfy bedrooms, a huge kitchen, a front yard, and a gigantic wooden deck. The park was chock-full of kids, so I had tons of playmates.

I liked school because I started reading. I liked science and health most, got straight A's, and always asked questions. My questions sometimes wore Dad out, but he said he was glad I took to school with the same fire he did not.

At least once a week in the winter, he took us snowmobiling, and in warm months on picnics and to the lake. He was sure trying to be a good dad. He took us to the Bertha farm a good deal where I learned to ride horses. Even though I was mad he pulled a fast one on Mom, he worked to make sure we enjoyed life with him. But he was still drinking, and I was the one who often had to get him a beer can from the fridge. At least he wasn't beating the shit out of anybody.

One issue was Dad worked an early morning to late evening shift on a roofing crew and would sometimes even hit up the bar before coming home. He would leave us with a drunk babysitter named Bernice. A bony-faced, gravel-voiced old souse whose eyes always sagged low and made her look old and sad. She was in her late forties but looked sixty.

She was a gin drinker—Gordon's London Dry Gin. Mom said Gordon's was cheap stuff that alkies drink. Bernice would guzzle that poison till she passed out. On a few occasions, she would pass out on our couch, and Shane and I would go wait under our front porch for our dad to alert him, but he always seemed to shrug it off. It was hard to figure why he didn't find it odd we were usually outside waiting for him when he got home so late at night.

Then came Christmas, 1978. Second grade, nearing my eighth birthday. Dad finally caught on to Bernice and fired her, thank God. It was right about then Mom phoned him and asked if she could fly me and Shane to Las Vegas to visit Grandma and Grandpa Fosteson. Dad said he could use a break from us and figured Grandpa Bill and Grandma Marie deserved to see us. "How long you thinking?"

"Couple weeks, tops," she said.

"I got no problem with that."

I was excited to see my grandparents and ride on a plane. So, Mom drove three hours to Plover on a Friday and took us back to Minneapolis to be ready to leave for Vegas with her the next day. I had no way to know what was up her sleeve.

11

Kidnapping Us Back

I sat on the edge of Mom's bed that morning, watching her dart all around the room like a dervish, packing this and that for the trip. Now and then, she'd stop and catch her breath.

"You okay, Momma?"

"I'm hunky-dory, honey. But you need to get a move on. We got a plane to catch. I want you and Shane ready to go."

"We won't be late. You said three o'clock and it's only nine-thirty. We got most all day."

"Don't sass. Get yourself ready." She saw me pout and said, "Sorry I snapped, sweetie. Look. I'm kinda jittery this morning. Too much coffee."

"I already got all my stuff in my suitcase. Where's Bill?" Bill had left the house on an errand the night before.

"Don't you worry about Bill," she said. "He had to go out of town. Just go make sure Shane's ready."

On the twenty-minute cab ride to the airport, Mom kept checking her watch, even though it was two hours to flight time. I couldn't understand why she was so jittery.

I was nervous when the plane roared down the runway, but once it got airborne, I relaxed. I loved looking down on the world from my window seat. It was only a one-hour flight to O'Hare Field, Chicago, where we had a two-hour layover and a plane change.

Mom called Dad collect from there. She had the receiver in one hand and cradled Nicole in her free arm. I could hear Dad talking.

"So, you're changin' planes in Chicago? Everything alright?"

"Everything's just swell," Mom said. "I just want to let you know, you conniving *prick*, we're about to hop a flight to Vegas and we *are not* coming back. Not *ever*. I'm moving these kids there with me, and if my luck holds, you won't see 'em again! And that judge in Wadena, you tell him to kiss my ass." She slammed down the phone.

So, this was no vacation. We were moving to Las Vegas. I didn't mind it, though I would miss Dad and my school friends.

On the long flight to Las Vegas, I got a window seat and Shane was in the middle, right across the aisle from Mom and Nicole. Mom looked relaxed for the first time all day, her seat reclined and a chilled martini in her hand.

I'd have to make new friends, but that didn't worry me. I was good at that. I was excited to be around Grandpa Bill and Grandma Marie again and to enjoy winters Mom said were as mild as springtime in Plover.

Gazing out the airplane window through wispy clouds below to a world in miniature, I couldn't wait to discover the paradise Mom described. "It's all gonna be velvet," she promised. "Nothing but velvet."

12

Vegas
Doorway to Disaster

Those mountains framing Las Vegas on the east and west were pretty, especially with the orange skies at sunrise looking east and at sundown looking west. I had seen pictures of deserts and expected those giant cacti and big rust-colored sand dunes like big pillows. But I was disappointed Vegas was flat, ugly. barren sweeps of dirt and scrub and sagebrush. But when the sun went down, oh, how all that changed. The flashing downtown neon and the bubbling lights from the Strip hid all the ugliness and made me feel like I was living under a gigantic, magical, electric dome. Lights and mirrors, that's what it was, just lights and mirrors.

In January 1979, I turned eight and resumed second grade at my new school, Howard Wasden Elementary, west of downtown and north of the Strip. Within the first several days, I became fast friends with another second-grader, Jessica Mallin. She was tall, smart, and pretty, with long, shiny dark brown hair. She had all the nice things I did not and was as rich as we were poor. She readily shared those nice things with me, but that wasn't why I made friends with her. I enjoyed her company, and it seemed to me she needed more friends.

Jessica's dad, Stanley Mallin, had made gobs of money developing casino hotels like Caesar's Palace and Circus-Circus, but he and her mom were now divorced. He was quiet and even-tempered, nothing like my dad. He had a new wife, and we would stay at his house sometimes. I liked him right off. He had met Jessica's mom, Virginia, when he had a business in Atlanta. She was petite, dark-eyed, and pretty and she had an enchanting southern drawl.

Jessica told someone years later she liked me because I was outgoing, fun, and easy to be around. One day, I wouldn't be.

While my family scrimped by, Jessica's lived like royalty inside the twenty-four-hour guarded gates of Rancho Circle, the city's most elite neighborhood. I shared her privileged life with desert sunset horseback rides from her private stables and got invited on family vacations to five star resorts.

Jessica liked making decisions, and I was fine with that. I was easygoing, never the pushy type. We often had sleepovers at each other's houses, and whenever I was at hers, my mom was comforted that the gated community was a guarded fortress.

I will always consider Jessica the best friend I ever had and will continue to wish her nothing but happiness

But I would come to curse the day I met her.

13

Sixth Sense

Mom moved us into what became a family compound in North Las Vegas. Her older brother, Doug, lived in an apartment right around the corner from Grandpa and Grandma Bill and Marie's house. Our apartment was next door to Doug's. I didn't like him. He had a mean streak and a loud mouth, and his foul language made me uneasy. But Doug Fosteson was a prince compared to Bill Lynch. Mom had sold her car right before she left Minneapolis, and Bill drove his car to Vegas with a lot of Mom's things. He showed up a few days after we got there. My mother had such a great work ethic, and just three days after we got to Vegas, she landed a job as a cocktail waitress downtown at the Golden Nugget. It was good money.

Bill Lynch had promised her he would find a steady job, but he seemed in no big rush. He always made excuses. He circled a lot of things in the want ads, but never went on any actual job interviews. The big lazy bastard would slouch down into a soft living room chair and stare at the TV most all day. Often, he'd crack open a beer soon as he finished breakfast. When Mom wasn't around, he'd make snotty remarks to me and Shane, then pretended he was kidding.

I saw through him long before Mom did.

One day, not long after Jessica and I became friends, he said, "I heard you got a little rich friend. How 'bout you introduce me to her Daddy, and I hit him for a loan. I'll give ya 10 percent."

That made me mad. I got up in his face. "Mind your own business, Bill Lynch. It's nothin' to do with you."

Even our dog didn't take to Bill. Mom adopted a rescue mutt, friendly to everyone but him. Bill would call the dog, but the dog would just stare at him. "Dog doesn't take to me," Bill grumbled one day. My first-grade teacher in Plover had said animals sense things about people that most people don't. She was right, at least when it came to Bill. He had Mom fooled, but the dog was onto him.

It wouldn't be long before everybody in the family felt the same about Bill as that dog did. He would be gone soon, but it would not be a pleasant goodbye.

14

Neon Wilderness

Dad made it clear he wasn't happy about being suckered, but with us kids gone, he could at least drink out in the open again. Meanwhile, Grandpa Bill and Grandma Marie were hitting the alcohol even harder than they had in Wadena because they had more free time. On the upside, they were not mean drinkers like Dad; they laughed and got silly when they got a few in them and would regularly take what Mom called "afternoon beer naps."

Despite my family's quirks and flaws, I liked having them around.

I was mesmerized by the bubbly nighttime neon and adored the colorful Caesar's Palace fountain. It was like a gigantic, twenty-four-hour carnival. Grandpa Bill explained how a dead Roman emperor supposedly served as a spiritual guide at Caesar's, leading poor dumb bastards to the gambling tables where they lost all their money. He said it was a bad idea for people who lived in Vegas to gamble because they'd likely go broke.

"You don't gotta worry about me, Grandpa," I assured him. "I got no money."

Up against Las Vegas, Wadena and Plover were gloomy and boring. In Vegas, from my bedroom window, I could listen to happy music blaring from a popular nearby nightclub. Life seemed exciting and promising, though I didn't realize it was mostly just made of plastic. When the clouds were low enough to pick up the downtown neon, I would gaze out my bedroom window and dream of the storybook future I would never have.

15

Enter Troy Kell

One lovely spring morning, in my first year in Vegas, I went bike riding with Shane. An older boy whizzed past me on his bike and nearly ran me off the sidewalk. "Hey, watch it, road hog," I hollered. "Ya own the sidewalk or what?"

The boy turned around and chased me, but he was laughing and I laughed too as I pedaled away. Was all in fun. He caught up and curbed my bike. "Didn't nobody tell you little girls shouldn't say snotty stuff to big boys?" He was smiling.

I was still laughing, and then we started chatting. He introduced himself as Troy Kell. A lanky ten-year-old, three years older than me, lived just a few houses down from us. He would become a sort of neighborhood protector for me, Shane, and other younger kids in the neighborhood. He said he considered himself like an Indian warrior, and his friends were his tribe, and it was his duty to protect them.

I soon introduced Troy to Mom, and because his dad was really strict, he liked hanging out at our place. He was mannerly and always said yes ma'am, no ma'am, please, and thank you. Mom often asked him to stay for lunch or dinner, and one day he asked her was it okay to call her "Mom." She thought that was sweet. "Of course you can call me Mom."

Troy's parents were divorced, and he lived with his Dad, who grounded him a lot, sometimes for little things that would get other kids a minor scolding. Once, because he was restricted for some minor thing, I had to pedal over on my bicycle and toss his birthday present to him over a wall into his backyard. I felt sad for him. Even after we moved out of his neighborhood, I kept him as a friend, and so did Mom. For years to come, he would send Mom a card and flowers every Mother's Day.

Even after he went to prison for murder.

Since Vegas was a lot more dangerous than little Wadena, Mom was especially protective of me. She didn't want me going anywhere without an adult, but Troy could charm her, and she'd let me go with him. He once said to her, "Mom, you don't *ever* have to worry about Sandy when she's with me. Nothing bad will ever happen to her when I'm around."

A day would come when Troy's promise would send a chill down my mother's spine. Mine, too.

16

Rescuing Baby Nicole

After a few months in Vegas, Bill Lynch and Mom were at each other's throats; their tiffs evolved into shouting matches—but never anything physical, like with Dad. Bill had promised to pitch in to help support the family, but he never made the effort. He was just mooching off Mom.

The final straw came when Mom found out he had slipped back into his felonious ways and burglarized a Firestone tire store. He was fencing tires all around town. She confronted him and ordered him to move out. "If I never see you again," she promised, "it'll be way too soon."

Knowing Mom's mind was made up, Bill packed his things and loaded them into his car one Saturday morning. In the trunk and the back seat were five tires he had yet to fence.

After he took the last of his things to the car, Mom flopped down on her bed, feeling more relief than regret. She had closed her door and failed to spot him sneak back into the apartment and grabbing Nicole from her crib. He would have gotten away if I had not been in the kitchen fixing peanut butter-and-jelly, and I would probably never have seen my sister again.

I spotted him heading for the door and screamed, "Momma, Bill's taking Nicole!"

"That sonofa*bitch*!" she shouted from the bedroom. I could hear her knock the phone off the night table, then shortly crying out into the phone, "Dad, get over here. Goddam Bill's tryin' to kidnap Nicole."

I knew I was the only one standing in the way of Bill taking Nicole from us. As he neared the door, I rushed at him and grabbed his free arm.

He spun around and shoved me to the floor.

I got back on my feet and jumped on his back, hoping to slow him down till the cavalry rode in. I clung tight to his neck, and he was calling me every cuss word he'd learned in prison. He finally shook me off, and I landed so hard on the floor it felt like somebody had hit me in the back with a ball bat. But I got up. I ran at him and was about to jump him again when he slammed the big steel door on my foot. Mom was in the kitchen now, fumbling through a drawer trying to find a weapon as Bill was headed for his car. There was no time to wait. I hobbled outside after him, screaming at him to stop. Nicole was bawling.

Bill moved good for a big man and in one smooth, continuous motion, he opened the car door, slid in, and sat Nicole in the passenger seat. Then he pulled the door shut for his getaway.

But as he fumbled to find the right key, I pounced. Through the rolled-down window, I grabbed hold of his long locks with both hands, anchored both feet on the car door for leverage, and used all my weight to yank on his hair. His scream was loud as a factory whistle.

"You nasty little *bitch*." He took a full swing with his fist and grazed my forehead just as Mom came flying out the door with a claw hammer.

I was so relieved to see Uncle Doug and Grandpa Bill speeding around the corner of the building. Tall, lanky Grandpa Bill and short, stocky Uncle Doug, galloping full speed into battle.

Mom closed in with the hammer just as I lost my grip on Bill's hair. He was about to stick the key in the ignition when Doug pushed Mom out of the way, pulled the car door open, and yanked him out.

Grandpa and Uncle Doug soon wrestled Bill to the ground. Doug used his knees to pin him and yelled, "Goddamit, Bill. We can do this the easy way or the hard way. But you *ain't* takin' that kid."

Bill Lynch snarled. "Fuck yourself, Doug!"

Doug started punching him and Grandpa dropped to his knees and joined in. While they pummeled Bill, Mom was still focused on the fight, her claw hammer cocked. I saw my chance and slipped around the other side of the car, jerked open the passenger door, and scooped Nicole up in my arms. I made a wide loop around the front end of the car to avoid the fray and handed Nicole off to Mom.

When Grandpa and Doug were done with Bill, he had a split lip, a bloody nose, a bruised jaw, and a shiner swelling under his left eye. With his face all bruised and his pride all banged up, he held a handkerchief against his nose and climbed back into his car. He revved the engine hard, and as he shot out of there, his tires smoking from burning rubber as he held his middle finger high out the window and disappeared from our lives.

Doug lit two cigarettes and handed one to Grandpa. Mom, holding Nicole, quivered from adrenaline. Shane was outside now, too, trying to figure out what he had just missed.

Mom wrapped one arm around my shoulder and pulled me close. "Here's our little hero," she smiled down at me.

When she recounted to Doug and Grandpa how I battled Bill to keep him from leaving with Nicole, Grandpa gleamed. "Well, how 'bout that! Won't nobody ever get one over on *this* little gal." He laughed. "She's tough as a two-dollar steak."

I extended my arms, and Mom lowered Nicole down. I was glad Grandpa was proud of me, but I didn't think I had done anything special. I did what I thought anybody would. I took Nicole inside and eased her down into her crib and watched over her till she was asleep.

As for Bill Lynch, he would do more prison time in Nevada and later in California. Over the years, he tried contacting Nicole, but she would have nothing to do with him. She would keep the family name of Shaw, and one day, years later, she got an official letter that he had died.

She donated his body to science.

17

Kidnapped . . . Again

It was nearing Christmas, 1979. Shane and I were playing with kids up the street when a strange car pulled to the curb and a familiar voice called out, "Hey, you kids."

I looked up wide-eyed. It was Dad in a taxi. I ran to the curb to greet him, Shane right behind me. "Hi, daddy. Watcha doin' here?"

"Hop in, both of ya. Tell ya all about it."

We did as we were told. I got in the front seat and Shane got in the back. Before I could ask again what he was doing in town, he made a hard U-turn and sped the other direction from our house.

I said, "Hey, where we goin'?"

"A surprise," he said. "You'll see."

In twenty minutes, our taxi was pulling up to the main terminal at McCarran Airport. He said, "You two are goin' back to Wisconsin with me. That's the surprise."

"No, no, I don't wanna go back there" I pleaded. "I live here and I like it. I love you, daddy, but why don't you just move here, up the street from us?"

"Because I can't. Besides, the court order says you're to come back home with me. And if your momma doesn't go for it, she'll get arrested."

There was no such court order, but I didn't know that and I swallowed that story.

"You don't want your mom to go to jail, do you, angel?"

Shane piped in. "I don't wanna go neither, daddy. I'm on a pee-wee football team."

"You can play peewee football in Plover," Dad growled.

Dad called Mom from the airport and said he was taking us back with him. "Revenge is sweet and turnabout is fair play." Then he slammed down the receiver.

By the time airport police officers got the alert, we were already airborne with a tailwind to Milwaukee.

When I got to Dad's house in Plover, Cindy—a slim, sort of pretty seventeen-year-old—was there. I'd met Cindy long before Dad. She lived in the trailer next to us and would always invite me over to hang out with her and her daughter, who was a baby then. And now, she sat on Dad's couch with her now toddler, Candy. "Hi, Sandy. Remember me?"

I thought, *who in hell is this woman staying here, hardly any older than me?*

I hoped she didn't think she was going to be my mom. I was just fine with the one I had. Being back in Plover was bad enough, but no way I would play nice to this stranger who was only eleven years older than me and thirteen years younger than my cradle-robbing dad—this woman who seemed intent on bossing me.

18

I Already Got a Sister

Mom went to a lawyer, but he said there wasn't a thing she could do since we were out of state. And he brought up the Minnesota custody thing—said it would be tough to reverse a judge's decision. Said he'd look for a loophole.

I was resigned to being in Plover for God knows how long. I celebrated my eighth birthday there right after starting second grade, second semester. I had leftover friends from the last time, but I tried to keep ties with old ones in Vegas.

I grudgingly accepted my life in Plover, and Cindy was okay except when she'd suggest Candy was our little sister. I'd say, "I already *got* a little sister. Me and Candy aren't related."

Winter turned to spring, and I finished second grade with straight A's. Dad wanted us to have fun, so our summer was filled with hikes and picnics along the Wisconsin River and at Lake Pacawa Park. By now, Dad let us talk regularly to Mom on the phone. When he was out of earshot, Mom would always assure me she was working on a plan to get us back. She asked me to be patient.

Then, right around Christmas, she came up with her bold plan.

By then, the honeymoon phase of Dad and Cindy's romance had faded. He would belittle her or criticize her for the slightest things, repeating the same pattern he did with Mom. Soon as he would get a few drinks in him, he'd start arguments with her. One night, Dad pushed Cindy down the stairs. I was right next to her and watched it all. She broke her tailbone and was lucky she didn't break her neck.

Needless to say, I wanted out of there, and Mom was about to put her scheme into action.

19

The Last Kidnapping

Mom took a week off work in the middle of January and made the long, hard drive to Wisconsin. She slipped in under the cover of darkness and checked into a motel on the outskirts of town. The next morning was Saturday, but Dad worked Saturday mornings. Mom phoned and Cindy answered. She was used to Mom's regular calls and held the phone out to me. "Sandy, it's your mother."

I was excited as always to talk to her but wondered why she was whisper-shouting. "Sandy. Now, you listen up. You wanna come back and live with me in Vegas, doncha?"

"Oh, boy, do I *ever*."

"Okay. Here's the plan. You get Shane, you both bundle up and walk down to the end of the street—the entrance to your mobile home park. Ya follow? I'm at a pay phone just a block from the park. I'll pick you up, and off we go back home. And I mean for good this time."

I kept nodding because Cindy was a nosey-parker and within earshot of me. "Yes, mom. Yeah, that would be really nice."

"Don't make like anything's wrong," Mom warned.

To throw Cindy off her gait, I said, "Yes, I'll be a good girl, Mom. I'm behavin', I promise. . . . Love you, too. . . . Bye."

Then I found Shane in his room and told him to put on his coat. "Don't say *nothin'*, Shane. Don't ask me nothin'. You just follow me and do just what I say."

Cindy was in the kitchen when we got to the front door. I called out, "We're goin' outside to play."

Cindy shouted back. "Take Candy along."

"Naw, not this time," I hollered. "We're gonna play with big kids. She wouldn't have no fun. We'll come get her in a while. Okay?"

As we neared the entrance to the trailer park, I spotted Mom's car with the motor running and the passenger door wide open. I grabbed Shane by the hand. "Come on, little brother. We're goin' to Vegas." We sprinted for all we were worth to the open door and we jumped in. Mom was wearing a wide grin.

With a cigarette dangling out the side of her mouth and a tank full of gas, she sped down Highway 51 south out of Plover. Four hours later, we crossed the Iowa border on Interstate 80 and stopped at a diner. She knew Dad's shift had ended at 3:00 p.m. So, she called him from a pay phone.

Cindy answered and handed him the phone. "Mike, it's Connie."

"Kids ain't here," he said. "They went outside to play and they're not home yet. I was about to go look–"

"This is a courtesy call, Mike, so's you won't worry. They're safe here with me. We crossed the Iowa line on our way back to Nevada. . . . *Checkmate!*" She hung up and off we went.

The day after getting back to Vegas, Grandpa Fosteson told Mom, "I'm tickled they're here, Connie, but these kids are gettin' bounced around like a couple cue balls. For their sake, you and Mike better work this out. All legal."

Dad's revenge game was over, but if I had 20/20 hindsight, I would have stayed in Plover, put up with Cindy, put up with Dad's drinking, and never again set foot in Nevada.

20

The Truce

Dad phoned Mom a few days after she returned to Vegas and admitted she had worn him out. He wanted a truce. "I'd like for them kids to come visit me some, but we'll make it legal, so if you don't trust me, if I pull a fast one again, you go ahead and have me jailed." He said he had a life in Plover and admitted his motivation for stealing me and Shane both times was to get revenge for throwing him out.

They agreed we were old enough to decide who we wanted to live with. So Dad honored his word and signed papers from both a Nevada court and a Wisconsin court, giving Mom full legal custody. He also got the Minnesota court order repealed. Their new agreement was he had visitation rights and an obligation to pay reasonable child support. We'd spend summers with Dad and go to school with Mom.

I was glad to be able to visit Dad without him having to steal me to do it.

The following Christmas vacation—I was nine, and Shane was eight—he and I spent a two-week holiday in Plover. But just before I left, I was on a bike ride in the desert and found a litter of abandoned kittens someone left in a box. With Grandpa's help, I took them to a non-kill shelter, but kept one for myself—a fluffy, precious, light gray kitten I named "Strawberry" because she was so sweet.

Dad had bought a really nice three-bedroom house on River Drive, kind of the silk stocking district of Plover. It was cozied among a thicket of tall pines and spruce trees, and he had a beautiful view of the Wisconsin River. He even okayed me bringing my kitten on the trip. Dad was screwed up from his past traumas, but he was truly a generous soul with a big heart. He even arranged a cat carrier for the plane ride.

After the fourth night, I woke, unable to find Strawberry anywhere in the house. I called and called for her. Cindy finally fessed up—she had put Strawberry outside the night before. "It kept meowing, getting on my nerves."

I was concerned; the temperature had dropped to freezing.

I couldn't find Strawberry anywhere outside. Then Cindy started her car to leave for work, and there was a horrible yowl from under the car hood. Cindy cut the engine and opened the hood, and there was what was left of poor little Strawberry, oh my god, chopped into hunks and pieces by the fan blade. Her blood was all over the engine block. When Cindy had put her out of the house, Strawberry had crawled up under the car, seeking the engine's warmth.

Cindy tried to say she was sorry, but it kept coming out all wrong.

I plopped down in the snow and bawled, tears running cold down my cheeks.

"I'm sorry, Sandy. I'm so, so very sorry. I didn't know—"

I didn't answer her and refused to speak to her the rest of my stay. She had vaulted to the head of my shit list.

A few nights after Cindy murdered Strawberry, Dad and Cindy got into a screaming match in the upstairs bedroom. I went to the bottom of the stairs just in time to see Dad shove Cindy. He sent her tumbling to the bottom of the steps, and she landed with a hard *thud*. She didn't move for several seconds, and I was worried she was dead. I had no idea what to do when he exploded like that. He could have just as easily broken her neck.

Cindy came to, rubbed her neck to make sure it was okay, then mumbled cuss words. Dad retreated into the bedroom.

When I woke the next morning, Cindy was asleep on the couch with a comforter pulled over her and a bruise the size of an apple on her right cheek.

And so, my dysfunctional childhood continued. I was happy to get on that plane and fly out of there.

21

Grandma's Sobering Moment

Once home, my dysfunctional life at least went back to "peacefully" dysfunctional. Mom was pleased, despite all the early turmoil, that my brother and I seemed headed toward normal. Her big worry was Grandma and Grandpa Fosteson would drink themselves into early graves. Mom had a sit-down with them, and they agreed with everything she said, but they kept right on hitting the bottle like a punching bag.

Then fate interceded with Grandma.

One night, after downtown shopping, Grandma Marie stopped in a bar for one drink that turned into six. On the way home, seeing double, she swerved between lanes.

A few blocks from her house, way over the speed limit, she made a turn too late and too wide. The car jumped a curb onto the edge of a sidewalk. As she tried to hit the brakes, her foot slipped off and mashed the gas pedal. The car sailed through the air and crossed the lawn in front of an apartment building. She blacked out just as her car slammed into the side of the building, buckling the front end. The impact shattered a bedroom window, and the shockwave knocked a little girl out of her top bunk bed, face first onto shards of broken window glass.

When Grandma came to, squad car and ambulance lights surrounded her. Out of the corner of her eye, she saw a young girl on a stretcher, her face covered with blood as medics toted her to the ambulance.

Grandma luckily could afford a good lawyer. Following her felony DUI conviction, she got no jail time, but the judge ordered her to a rehab center and Alcoholics Anonymous meetings. She would never take another drink for the rest of her life.

Grandpa kept drinking full bore, pedal to the metal. But now he had a designated driver.

A few years later, when I was twelve, I was at a softball game with Mom, cheering on her boyfriend Mike Flanery's team. In line at the snack stand, I struck up a conversation with a curly haired girl my age. We chatted a bit, and when she walked into the light, I saw the awful crescent-shaped scar on her cheek.

"None of my business," I said. "And I'm not bein' mean or nothin', but I'm wonderin' how you got your scar."

The girl frowned then sighed. "Aw, some dumb old drunk woman crashed her car into the side of our apartment, right where my bedroom was. Flung me clean off my bed, and I landed on busted glass from the window. Cut me awful. But the doctors say my scar will go away some day."

"Musta been horrible." I cringed. "It's good your scar's gonna go away." I patted her on the shoulder. When I got back to my bleacher seat, I nudged Mom. "You ain't gonna believe this, Mom, but I just met Grandma's victim."

22

Big Trouble at Rancho Circle

It was Saturday, September 23, 1984. I woke that morning to howling wind blowing dust around. By late morning, the gusts calmed and it turned out to be a gorgeous fall day. The sun glimmered warmly down over the whole valley and flooded the streets with sunshine. I'd done cheerleading for Shane's football game that morning. I grabbed a change of clothes and my pajamas, and Mom drove me to Jessica's for a sleepover.

When Virginia divorced Stanley, she got the house, a ton of alimony and child support, and custody of both daughters. Jessica's older sister, Jennifer, was now out of college and had a job in California. Virginia was still relatively young and ripe for romance when she divorced Stanley. She soon started dating Hungarian expatriate Alex Egyed, and eventually the two got married.

Alex had escaped Hungary during the failed 1956 revolt against the Soviet Union. He spoke with a thick Hungarian accent, but his English was fluent. He came to America penniless, determined to succeed, and he damn sure did. He made his fortune launching a chain of variety stores in Philadelphia. He moved to Las Vegas in the late seventies to open more stores, then sold his share of the company and became a partner in MISCO, a booming Las Vegas cable TV company.

Alex was a few years older than Virginia, balding but 6 feet 2 inches and in good physical shape. He had a closet full of pricey Italian suits and shoes and was a romantic. When they were first married, he would leave love notes around the house for Virginia. On the night of her first birthday as his wife, he hired musicians to serenade her outside their bedroom window.

But the saying "fires that burn brightest burn out fast" applied to Virginia and Alex—especially Virginia. After the first year, Alex became controlling, smothering, and suspicious. Virginia soon realized marrying him was a blunder and shared that with several friends and with Jessica, who shared it with me. The more she pushed Alex away, the more he smothered her and tried controlling her. Things got to the point that Alex moved out for six months but had recently sweet-talked his way back into the house and was trying to rekindle the fire.

But that fire had been banked for Virginia. She was no longer in love with him, but the problem was he was still in love with her and obsessed with her. On the day of my sleepover, he was to move out the next morning and head back to Philadelphia to wait for the divorce decree.

When Mom dropped me off, I didn't know Alex was moving out, but it wasn't a big shock. Even though I'd gotten along good with him, I'd heard a bunch of their squabbles, and Jessica had shared a lot of stories with me.

The gate guards recognized Mom's car and waved us in that day. All the Rancho Circle security guards were either off-duty or retired Las Vegas PD. who were serious about their jobs and ever on their toes. If someone didn't live inside those gates or couldn't prove they had business there, no way they got in.

Jessica's home was near the back of the community, a big ranch-style house with a long driveway, located off a circle, and one of the first homes built in that swanky community. From an aerial view, the entry resembled a stick on a lollipop.

The day was normal for Jessica and me. Her German maid, Dah, cooked for us and conferred with us. She was the one who took Jessica and me out about town if we ever needed anything. But this day, while Alex was out running errands, Virginia had said she was relieved it would be his last night in their house. Eventually, saying, "Girls, we're going to Nina's the rest of the day. You can have just as much fun over there as you can here."

Jessica made a pouty frown. "Why Nina's?"

"Because that's where I'm going, and you two are going with me and this isn't negotiable." She pointed at Jessica. "Alex will be back in a while, and he will start another damn argument, and I'm done with all that. So, girls, let's go."

Nina Schwartz was forty and one of Virginia's best friends. They looked strikingly similar, both petite and pretty, with dark hair cut about the same length. Nina's ex-husband was one of Alex's business partners at MISCO. Nina said she had pegged Alex for a phony the first time she met him and kept that no secret from Virginia. So, when trouble first erupted, Nina pleaded with Virginia to get out of the marriage.

In Nina's kitchen that day, she and Virginia chatted while Jessica and I jabbered and listened to music in another room. When I asked about Alex, Jessica said, "They fought like alley cats all week. Was awful. Tell you more when Mom can't hear us."

Virginia had brought a fancy formal dress to Nina's to wear to a political fundraiser that night at Caesar's Palace. Nina and her boyfriend, sixty-six-year-old Jack Levy, a real estate agent who owned jewelry shops in the Riviera and Sahara hotels, would go with her. So would their friend, fifty-two-year-old Betty DiFiore, a mother of two and a doctor's ex-wife. Betty managed a Sak's Fifth Avenue store in the Fashion Show Mall and had a sweet disposition. Alex had wanted to tag along, but Virginia nixed it. Jessica told me he had pouted for days about it.

Dusk was about to blanket the horizon when Virginia dropped us back at Rancho Circle. She spotted Alex's Porsche in the driveway and let us off at the curb. "I'd rather not go in there," she said. We got out, and Virginia left for Caesar's.

Once inside, I heard Alex's voice booming from his phone in the master bedroom. His door was closed, and we didn't want to interrupt him, so we made peanut butter-jelly sandwiches and went to Jessica's room. We watched television, listened to music, and gabbed about all sorts of teenage stuff.

Then around 9:00 p.m., Jessica's personal phone line rang in her bedroom. Alex was calling from right down the hall in the master bedroom. He asked us to play a game of Backgammon with him, and when Jessica hung up, her brow furrowed in confusion. "Why did he phone and not just walk down the hall and ask?"

I agreed it was strange.

We played one game of Backgammon with him. Alcohol was heavy on his breath, and I spotted an empty wine bottle on the nightstand, next to another open bottle with just a tad gone. His speech wasn't slurred, but his eyes were red and watery, like he'd been crying.

When the game ended, Alex said he would be leaving early in the morning and would never return. He sounded so forlorn I felt bad for him. He said he had errands to run, so we walked him to his car to say goodbye.

We stayed up for about another half-hour, then cut the lights, looking for a peaceful night's sleep.

There would be nothing peaceful happening the rest of that night.

23

Virginia's Fatal Decision

Turns out Alex's only errand was a trip to Caesar's Palace to antagonize Virginia. This was how I heard it later, secondhand from Nina and others:

By the time he found Virginia, she and her friends were in a cocktail lounge, and he came in boiling with rage. She was at a table with Betty, Nina, Jack Levy, and two male friends Alex didn't know. He wobbled toward their table.

Virginia glared hard at him "What the *hell*, Alex?"

"I want to talk. . . . I want to . . . reconcile."

"Jesus, Alex. We've talked, and we've talked, and we've talked. I'm talked out."

"In *private*. I want to talk in private."

"No, Alex. I got nothing more. Nothing. Whatever you have to say, say it to everybody or leave."

Alex scowled at Virginia, his cheeks flushed deep red. "Virginia, anyone ever tell you, you are *trash*?"

One man at the table said, "Hey, now, fella, that's uncalled for. Why don't you just—"

Alex kept his eyes fixed on Virginia. "You can dress up fancy, but underneath, you are *trash*." He pointed at her, his voice so loud now everyone in the lounge heard him and customers mumbled. "Trailer trash from Georgia," he roared. Then he gave the once-over to everyone at her table. "And the rest of you—you're all trash, too. Nothing but *trash*. Trashy people traveling in a trashy pack."

The bartender came out from behind the bar holding a nightstick that got Alex's attention. He pointed toward the exit. "*You!* Out. *Now.*"

Alex turned and left, cussing as he went.

"God, I'm just so awfully embarrassed," Virginia apologized, catching her breath. "I'm so sorry, y'all."

Jack Levy shrugged. "For what? You didn't do anything. *He* did."

She shook her head. "I'd hoped this last day would be—I don't know. . ." She let out a sigh. ". . . Uneventful."

An attorney friend of Nina's piped in, "Virginia, for god sakes. That man is off the rails. If I were you, I would *not* go home tonight."

Nina lit a cigarette with the butt of the one she was about to douse in the ashtray. "He's right, 'Ginia. You stay at my house tonight. That man isn't stable. I don't think he ever *was*."

Another man chimed in. "Nina's right. You said he leaves in the morning, right? So go to Nina's and wait him out."

Virginia rested her forehead in her hands. "Okay, okay. You guys are right. I'll stay at Nina's till that son of a bitch is out of my house, out of and gone. But I *have* to get Jessica and Sandy out of there. I am *not* leaving those girls in *that* house with *that* man."

"It's fine." Nina patted Virginia's shoulder. "Get the girls. I got plenty of room for everybody at my place."

They all stuck around the bar and chatted till around 11:30 p.m. and came up with a plan. For safety's sake, someone would ride with Virginia and go into the house with her to get me and Jessica while somebody else would follow behind Virginia for backup. Betty DiFiore volunteered to ride with her, and Jack Levy and Nina would follow them in Jack's car to Virginia's house and wait in the driveway.

As they approached Virginia's long driveway in their two-car convoy, Nina mentioned to Jack how oddly dark the outside of the house was. "This place is always lit up with lawn lights and porch lights. Looks spooky."

Jack laughed. "Maybe Alex got so pissed he forgot to pay his light bill." He kept his Mercedes coupe close to Virginia's back bumper as they eased up to the house and parked in the driveway near the garage. Virginia got out and told Jack and Nina to wait in the car while she and Betty fetched me and Jessica. They'd try to be out in a jiffy.

As Jack and Nina waited in the dark, he turned up the radio and found music he liked as Nina put out one cigarette in the ashtray, then lit another.

Jack shook his head. "God, Nina, I swear those cigarettes are gonna be the death of you."

But her chain-smoking was about to save her life.

24

Triple Homicide

I nudged Jessica awake just after midnight. "I'm hungry. You?"

Jessica rubbed her eyes. "Yeah. Let's make soup."

We heated soup in the kitchen microwave and just before taking our bowls to Jessica's room, the doorbell startled us. Jessica eased carefully up to the peephole and peered into it. "Gee-*suz* H. It's *Mom*." Jessica opened the door and spotted Betty standing right behind Virginia. "Hey, mom, ya lose your key?"

Virginia looked all around and seemed fidgety, nervous, and scared. Betty stood close to her. "So, where is he?" Virginia said.

"Prob'ly asleep," Jessica replied, "if the doorbell didn't just wake him."

Virginia put one hand on Jessica's shoulder and the other hand on mine. "Go grab some clothes, gals. You're gonna spend the night with me at Nina's."

Jessica frowned. "Ah, Mom, we're beat. We don't wanna go anywhere. We just wanna eat our soup and go to sleep."

Virginia squinted. "Don't argue with me, young lady. Just get some clothes and let's *git*."

Betty put her arm around Jessica's shoulder and turned to Virginia. "I'll help 'em get ready. You wait here."

The doorway into Jessica's L-shaped bedroom wasn't visible from her large dressing room, where we were getting dressed under Betty's watchful eyes. I was groggy and moved slow. "Come on now, don't linger, Sandy," Betty prodded. "You need help, honey?"

"No, ma'am, I'll hurry." I slipped into my shorts and pullover t-shirt.

Betty moved her hand in a swirly motion. "Speed it up, girls. Alex made a big scene at Caesar's. We don't need him waking up from his drunken stupor."

I bent down to tie my laces as Betty continued, "You won't believe what he did—"

And then a sound. A *grunt*. From somewhere down the hall. I paused, then looped my last lace and raised up.

Betty kept on. "He starts calling all of us trash and he—"

Thump, thump, thump. Somebody was in the room and running across the carpet. Right toward us. Then, in full stride, Alex appeared around the corner—in a brown robe, arm extended, pistol in hand.

It all happened so fast.

Betty was still in mid-sentence when Alex yelled, "You *stupid* sons of bitches," as he fired point-blank into the side of her head. Her brain matter flew through the air as she fell dead on the carpet like a rag doll.

The room was a blur. I screamed. Bits of Betty had splattered all over my legs and stuck to my face and hair. I wanted to run. Nowhere to go. *Help me, God.* I froze. Jessica was behind me, gasping.

Alex took a step forward and pointed the gun toward Jessica. Then, he turned toward me, the barrel so close, the sulfur smell of gunpowder filled my nostrils. I stared into his bloodshot eyes and a face so flush-red he looked like the devil. My skinny legs wobbled like spaghetti and my pounding heart hit my rib cage.

I knew I was about to die. The crazy son of a bitch was going to kill us all. I closed my eyes and screamed from the pit of my lungs.

But instead of pulling the trigger, he suddenly backed up a step. His face scrunched up like he was confused. Then he turned and sprinted out of the room, the smoking revolver dangling from his hand.

"The bathtub." Jessica's breathing was uneven. "Gotta hide."

I shook my head no. "He'll find us there. Let's get in the shower."

"C'mon." Jessica gripped my hand and tugged me with her to the bathtub. A bad idea but I got in, sunk low and hunkered down. I felt sweat coming off my face and down my neck. I prayed. I waited. I worried. Then I heard a loud gunshot. Like it came from the kitchen. I shot Jessica a glance, but we were both too terrified to speak. It would turn out to be the shot Alex fired point-blank between Virginia's eyes. She had been out cold already—he had evidently pistol-whipped her before he charged in and murdered Betty.

My whole body shook and I started whimpering.

Jessica whispered. "Shush. He'll hear you."

Outside in the driveway, as Nina would recall, she held her watch up close to the burning ash of her cigarette to check the time. "What's taking them so darn long? C'mon, Virginia. Let's get the *hell* out of here."

Jack said, "Women *can* piddle." They had the radio up loud and had not heard gunshots. But Alex must have peeked out a window and spotted the second car. The driveway was wrapped in darkness, but he saw Jack's car and somebody inside it.

Nina had just ducked down to look for her matchbook behind the front seat. That model Mercedes coupe had no backseat, just a small storage area. As Nina rose partway up, out of the corner of her eye, she noticed a shadowy figure walk out the front door. In the dark, she mistook Alex's robe for a dress and thought it was the housekeeper.

But before she rose all the way up, she realized it was Alex and spotted the gun in his hand.

It went down in a split second, too fast to warn Jack. Alex was ten feet from the rolled-down driver's side window as he fired. The bullet struck Jack in his temple and killed him instantly.

Nina slid down flat as she could and closed her eyes, waiting to die. But to her surprise, she heard the patter of his slippers trotting back toward the house. When the door slammed, she raised up. Because Alex had fired from so far away, he hadn't noticed Nina scrunched down in the seat. Her chain-smoking wasn't the death of her after all; it saved her life.

Alex's undoing was leaving Nina alive. She sat up, trying to breathe. She could see Jack was dead. In one continuous motion, she opened the driver's side door, shoved his body onto the driveway, and got behind the wheel. She started the car and slammed it in reverse. The burning rubber squealed, then she cut the wheel and stepped on the gas, hell-bent down Rancho Circle toward the safety of the gate guards.

The sound of the car roaring away must have alerted Alex he had left a witness alive and was boxed in.

From inside Jessica's bathtub, we heard the tires peel and the car speed away. "Gotta be Alex," I said, wiping thick sweat off my forehead with the back of my hand.

Jessica nodded and whispered, "Makin' his getaway?"

I climbed out of the bathtub first, with Jessica right behind me, and we moved with great caution through the bedroom and past Betty's corpse. Jessica clicked off the light switch on the way out, and we ventured into the pitch darkness. I could still hear my heart pound.

Jessica hung back at the edge of the kitchen—there was one dim light on in there. I tiptoed gingerly through the dark toward the long foyer. I muffled my scream when I was right on top of Virginia's body in the large space between the kitchen and foyer. I almost stepped right on her. There was enough light to glimpse the bullet wound in her forehead. Her eyes were wide open, staring up at me like she was pleading for help. I jumped back, spooked, hoping Jessica wouldn't see her dead mother. I rerouted her toward the living room where we peered out into the dim light. In the driveway, we spotted a body, curled up motionless. We had no idea who.

"My God. Who is *that?*" Jessica said.

"Alex?" I said. "Playin' possum. We go out there—*boom*. We're dead."

Then I heard somebody moving inside the house, so we both darted for the master bedroom. It was dark, and we crawled under the king bed to hide. Confined under there, I whiffed an odor like copper. Good God, that smell was Betty's blood and brains stuck in my hair. I gagged, but I held the bile in so I wouldn't throw up and make a noise.

We both stayed under the bed, sweating it out till I mustered enough nerve to crawl out and pull the phone down under the bed with me. I dialed 911. A dispatcher answered and peppered me with questions: *"Is the killer still in the house? How many people hurt? How many dead? You hiding in a safe place?"*

I spoke just above a whisper. "Lady, I can't keep talkin'. He could hear me. Please, please, just get cops here. Fast!"

The dispatcher said someone had already phoned in the emergency and squad cars and ambulances were on their way. We didn't realize Nina had stopped at the gate and the off-duty cops called it in.

The dispatcher wanted me to stay on the phone and kept saying, "You're gonna be okay, honey. You're gonna be okay. You're gonna get through this. Stay on the phone with me. Don't you hang up."

The wail of distant sirens got louder as squad cars and an ambulance thundered down Rancho Circle. Just then, the dispatcher said, "They should be pulling up any second. Is there a way out—a side door, a back door, maybe a window?"

Jessica was listening and yanked on my arm. "The garage. Come on!"

When the sirens were right on top of us, we both pulled in a deep breath and sprinted through the living room. I was scared Alex would see us and pick us off before we could get to the garage.

Once inside the garage, Jessica slammed the door and locked it behind her. We scrambled for the garage door and yanked and tugged till it raised up. Flashing blue lights swarmed around the yard and lit it up like an arcade. A blinding spotlight hit my eyes and a bullhorn called out, "Put your hands above your heads. Walk out slow. Do *not* run."

We both ignored the bullhorn. We figured Alex could be hiding outside somewhere and shoot us. We raced past two EMT's kneeling over Jack Levy's body and ran into the waiting arms of police officers. We were safe, and thank God, we were alive.

Two cops had their pistols drawn, trained on the front door, and a third cop was positioned behind a police cruiser, pointing a high-powered rifle with a telescopic sight at the house. A couple other officers had maneuvered around the back to cover the other exit.

If Alex was still in there, he was trapped.

An EMT draped blankets around us and the cop with the bullhorn hollered to the EMT, "Shooter's still in that house. For chrissake, get these kids into a squad car."

As I was about to get into the back of the police cruiser, I glanced over at a woman in a cocktail dress standing next to a Mercedes coupe. Nina had driven the car back to the house after the police had come.

But she so resembled Virginia, it spooked the bejesus out of me. My eyes got wide—I was positive it was Virginia's ghost. Then, as we walked closer on our way to the police cruiser, I realized it was Nina, staring blankly down at her shoes, her pretty cocktail dress spattered with her dead lover's blood.

I got one last look at the house as it hung crooked in the rearview mirror when the squad car drove us to the safety of the police precinct. There, we would get grilled for hours and would find out how Alex took the coward's way out, ending his life with a bullet to his brain. Hours earlier, I might have cared, but now I had no pity for him.

On Monday, a reporter from the *Las Vegas Sun* newspaper would write that what was most shocking about these murders is they occurred within the guarded gates of the safest neighborhood in Las Vegas. Goes to show, you never can tell.

25

Alex's Grand Plan

I would later see a copy of both the coroner's report and the police investigator's report. The police removed the four bodies, then investigators scoured the property. They found an empty wine bottle on Alex's nightstand along with another bottle more than half empty. An autopsy determined he was legally drunk when he went on his rampage. His .38 Smith & Wesson revolver was untraceable, likely bought off the street, like he'd planned to kill Virginia. Four bullets were fired, and two remained in the chamber.

Even more telling, they found a briefcase in his Porsche stuffed with cash, mostly big bills, and containing his recently updated Hungarian passport. Hungary—a Communist Bloc country then—had no extradition treaty with the United States. Alex also wore a sweat suit under his robe, and investigators figured he'd readied himself for a fast getaway.

Based on all the evidence, the chief investigator for the district attorney's office, a guy named Beecher Avants, determined it *wasn't* an outburst of rage. Alex had planned it—if he couldn't get Virginia to take him back, he meant to murder her and anyone else inside the house. Jessica and I would be collateral damage. Avants also speculated Alex planned to board a morning flight to the east coast then a connecting flight back to his native Hungary. If he had made it there, he would have totally got away with it. If he had shot Jack Levy point-blank and seen Nina in the car with him, we'd probably all be dead.

26

Aftermath

My nerves were totally haywire. I just wanted to go home, hug Mom tight, get under a hot shower, and get all the awful dried blood off me. But the cop in the squad car said we had to go to the precinct and answer questions.

Two homicide cops at the station told us Alex blew his brains out in the kitchen before they could get to him. One bullet that entered his switchboard. They also told Jessica her mother was dead, something she had already figured out.

The detectives let me wash some blood off my face and hands but not out of my hair. They gave me a cold soda and escorted me into an interrogation room and took Jessica to a different room. The detectives had tape recorders, and somebody had fetched more cold sodas and junk snacks from the vending machine for me.

The room was long and narrow, and the hot lights liked to blind me. The table was the size of a small picnic table with four uncomfortable metal folding chairs.

The detective said my mom was on her way, then he became business-like and serious. "There's stuff we gotta know, Sandy." He switched on the tape recorder and asked me to tell him every detail I could pluck from my brain from the time Mom dropped me off at Jessica's till we escaped.

I had to pause a few times to gulp soda because my throat and mouth were like sandpaper. At one point, I stopped and sobbed. The detective shut off the recorder. He was patient and gentle but relentless. He made me go through the timeline three times, and I understood why he had to do it, so I wasn't mad at him. It was nearing three-thirty in the morning when he switched off the recorder and I signed a typed statement.

Mom was alone in the waiting room, wearing a worried look when I came out, like she wanted to cry for me for what I'd been through. She said Jessica just left with her dad and his wife.

This night would drive a wedge between me and Jessica, ending our long and close friendship. She would live with her dad and stepmom through the rest of middle school and high school until she left for college in Washington DC. I would be in prison two years by the time she started college.

When I spotted Mom, I ran to her as fast as my shaky legs would carry me. She hugged me all the way out to the car, then as she was leaving the precinct parking lot, for some crazy reason, I plopped down on the floorboard, hyperventilating. Mom flipped her lit cigarette out the window and pulled to the curb. "Good lord, child! What's goin' on?"

"I gotta hide."

"From *what*?"

"Alex."

"*Alex!* Christ, didn't you hear? The cops said that crazy bastard killed himself in his kitchen. He is *gone*, honey. Dead as in *d-e-a-d*. He can't hurt you."

I was biting hard on my bottom lip and trying to catch my breath. "Yeah . . . I know, I know. Don't make no sense, but I'm scared he'll come find me and kill me."

27

The Night Terrors

I hunkered on the floorboard the whole way home. Once safely inside the house, I made double sure the doors were locked, then took a long, hot shower with Lava soap to scrub the caked blood off my body and out of my hair. I watched bits of Betty's brain wash down the shower drain, and all I could say was, "Jesus, Christ almighty." It made me want to vomit, made me want to cry. To cry for poor dead Betty, to cry for poor dead Virginia, to cry for whoever the dead man was, sprawled in that driveway. And for me and Jessica for what we'd gone through.

Mike Flanery was living with us now and working a night shift tending bar at the Maxim, where he had met Mom. Mom phoned and told him everything. He said he'd find a way to get off early. He was always a kind and caring soul who has stayed in my corner my whole life.

After my shower, Mom gave me a tablespoon of brandy to calm my nerves. It helped. Then I crawled into bed, physically and emotionally wrung out. I fell into an uneasy sleep, but about an hour later, I woke up scared and went to Mom's room and nudged her.

"What is it, honey? You alright?"

"Can I crawl in with you? I'm still real scared."

She pulled the covers back, and I got in next to her. A couple hours later, at first light, my own primal scream woke me. Mom switched on the nightstand lamp. I was sweating and disoriented. "Oh God, Mom, I just had an awful dream. Alex was chasing me, and he looked exactly like the devil. If I hadn't woken up, I don't know what he woulda done."

Mom draped her arm around my shoulder. "Whoa, now, honey. You had an awful night, and you just woke from a bad dream. You go on back to sleep. Alex can't hurt you now, not ever. I promise you it'll get better. Just give it a couple days, let your head clear, and you'll be fine. You'll see."

She meant well and I so wanted to believe her. But Alex would find ways to hurt me, even from his grave. I would not be okay in a couple days, a couple weeks, or even a couple years. My life was not about to get better; it was about to get worse. Horribly worse.

28

Psychotic Intrusions and Lowlife Friends

I didn't go back to school for days after the murders. Jessica had enrolled in a school across town, near where she was living now. I figured it would be good to go back to school because I would be in my element, and it would distract me from the lunacy making a home in my brain.

So, there I was, sitting at my desk, reading my social studies book, and I spotted somebody out of the corner of my eye. I looked up and, great God almighty, it was Alex. How could that be? Standing there, gun in his hand, pointed at my head. I screamed loud as I could. I knew the son of a bitch was dead, but yet, there he was. Then I looked again, and he wasn't there. I was so humiliated I jumped up and ran from that room and out of that school. After several blocks, I sat on a city bus bench, hyperventilating. When I regained composure, I called Mom to come get me.

I told her what happened, and she looked at me cockeyed. Back then, I didn't know a psychotic intrusion from a Popsicle stick. I just figured I'd gone nuts. Everybody in my classroom who had witnessed my behavior would have agreed.

And that was the last time I ever attended Gibson Middle School.

Mom didn't know I'd started ditching. She would drop me off at school, but I'd go in the front door and right out the back to meet fellow ditchers. I started hanging out with them. Like most of them, every morning when I left home, I had it in mind to get high.

There were older kids in the group, some with drivers' licenses and access to cars. So, sometimes we would go for a fun day to Lake Mead or take a ride up to Mount Charleston to enjoy nature and get wasted.

Eventually, I got booted out of Gibson Middle School for ditching, then I registered at Rancho High School using my grandmother's address. But I got kicked out of Rancho for ditching, and they sent me to Washington Continuation Junior High, an alternative school for the marginally fucked up. I eventually got the heave-ho from there, too—also for ditching. But at Rancho, something horrible happened that set back the small progress I'd been making.

Periodically, as I made a gradual descent into temporary psychosis, Alex would appear live and in color right before my eyes, like a movie. Mom finally had enough and sent me to a shrink. She could only afford one session at a hundred bucks a pop. Looking back, the State of Nevada should have paid for counseling for a kid going through such trauma. Today, the Nevada Victims of Crime Program pays for all counseling sessions for a minor in that kind of distress. But back then, Mom and I were on our own.

She sent me to this psychiatrist named Jurowsky—not sure the spelling. He was an older man, probably in his sixties. At one point, as I poured out my heart, I caught him checking his watch, like he had someplace better to be. I realized I was just another square on his appointment calendar.

When the hour ended, he told me in so many words: shit happens, deal with it. Then he wrote me a prescription for Valium. It would help me sleep, he promised. It was the only time I saw him, but it had given me the idea that medication was the answer, and when the Valium ran out and I couldn't get more, I took the short hop to street drugs, from weed to LSD, uppers and downers, and alcohol. I was convinced drugs would tunnel me out of my madness.

Jessica and I got together one more time, but I just couldn't be around her because her very presence triggered psychotic intrusions with Alex and awful panic attacks, but I never told her that. She also didn't like the new friends I'd made, the lowlife ditchers, so it was okay by her, I'm sure, I didn't come around anymore. Part of me felt lousy about it. I'd just lost my best friend of half my young life.

Frightened to spend a night alone, I was still sleeping in Mom's bed. I often wondered how my life would have turned out if I hadn't gone to Jessica's for the sleepover that night. I wish to hell I hadn't. But life doesn't give us do-overs, and I might as well wish for a sack of Jack's magic beans.

29

Halloween Fiasco and Back to Dad's

By fourteen, I was one rebellious child, after having always minded my mother and been a responsible little kid. Now, I would sneak out, stay out late, and even got an ignition key to her car. I would drive around when she would ride to work with Mike, since they both worked at the Maxim and sometimes worked the same shifts. In my current mental state, I was a tornado blowing all over the streets of Vegas, my mom's biggest pain in the ass. I still helped around the house and babysat my siblings—three of them now counting baby Leah—mom and Mike Flanery's baby. But I was hanging with a creepy crowd and getting high all the time. I am sure I would never have gone this route had I not been traumatized seeing those murders.

The day before Halloween, 1985, a friend called and told me about a Halloween shindig in Lone Mountain, out in the desert. A keg party with loads of teenagers sounded like tons of fun to me. I wanted to go, but I would be stuck babysitting baby Leah, who was three months old.

Foolish is as foolish does, and so I got this really dumbass idea. I wrapped Leah up and took her to the car, and accompanied by my friend, Tara, off we all went to the party. I was so short I took a throw pillow to sit on so I could see over the steering wheel.

I sped down the freeway like a thrill driver, pedal to the metal. I cut across three lanes of traffic at the last moment to make the exit. People I'd nearly hit were shaking their fists, blowing their horns, and flipping me off.

I was thinking, *Those people need to lighten up before they give themselves a heart attack.*

Baby Leah was a big hit at her first Halloween party. Everybody was coming up and koochie-cooing her. "Awwwww, ain't she cute?" "Let me hold her." "She's so precious." Several kids passed her around, cradled her, and commented how absolutely darling she was.

It seemed to me like all innocent fun. Then finally, the bewitching hour came for me and I had to get my ass and Leah's little ass home.

And then, holy mother of pearl, I couldn't find my car key. *Shit. This can't be. No, no, no!*

I looked through my purse four or five times, and no car key. It wasn't in my pockets. Then I checked to see if I'd left it in the ignition. Nope. I knew then I'd dropped it somewhere in the desert brush.

Tara and I got kids with flashlights to scour the wide expanse of desert where we'd been partying. I again checked the inside of the car, on the floorboard, the seat, in between the seats, everywhere. Nothing.

Seven of us combed through the whole area on our hands and knees then inch by inch where I'd parked the car. We even looked underneath it. It was no use. That car key had pulled a disappearing act.

We'd looked for an hour, and I knew Mom and Mike were likely home from work. So I panicked and got two boys to drive Leah home to my house. But I was scared to go, so I stayed over with Tara for the night.

That morning, I called Mom. She came and picked me up, got me food, and when we got home, she told me to take a shower and pack. My plane was leaving at three o'clock that afternoon for Wisconsin.

"This was the final straw, Sandy," Mom said. Dad had agreed to let me come live with him and Cindy. Frustrated and feeling out of options, Mom hoped he could manage me better than she could, maybe straighten me out. But what she didn't realize, and what I didn't realize, I was suffering from Post-Traumatic Stress Disorder, and years later a shrink would tell me I was "mildly psychotic" back then. That afternoon, I was in the air headed for Wisconsin.

Dad put me in school in Plover, ninth grade in the regular high school. I went to school every day, and dammit, I did try, but I was still a bad mess.

And there was still the bad blood between me and Cindy over killing my kitten Strawberry.

Cindy was still trying to boss me around, no matter how much I asked her to stop. "I want to see that room of yours clean, Sandy . . ." or "You need to get in there and do those dishes . . ." or "You're wearing too much makeup."

Then one day, she got up in my face and yelled at me. She gave me a little shove, and I gave her a harder one back. She slapped my face, and I backed up. She slapped me again, and I doubled up my fist and knocked her right on her ass. She got up cussing, and I hit her four or five more times, and then the fight was over. When Dad got home, he was as pissed as he was disappointed. "I gave you a chance up here," he hollered, "and you start a goddam *fight* with my wife."

"I didn't start—"

"I don't wanna hear no more," he growled. He got on the phone and called Mom and said he couldn't handle me and was sending me back COD. I didn't last a month up there.

I was relieved to be getting out of Plover and going back to Vegas and all my so-called friends, but if somehow I could have stuck it out, kept my mouth shut, just ignored Cindy's bossy ways, I likely would have never ended up in trouble. But "*if, if, if.*" And if my Aunt Minnie had a mustache, she would be my Uncle Fred.

30

Another Shooting

There's that saying, wrong place, wrong time. But things happening to me seemed more than just bad luck. I was becoming a magnet for murder and violence. I read a statistic: if you witness a murder, you are three times more likely to witness a second one than people who have never witnessed a first one. It sounds crazy, like the voodoo root lady put a curse on me—but it makes as much sense as any other explanation. The law of magnetic attraction, they call it. Or like the Buddhists say, "You are always where your thoughts are taking you." Mine must have been taking me down the highway to Hell.

When I returned from Wisconsin, I registered at Rancho Middle School/High School. I was actually, at long last, experiencing a little emotional breakthrough, a crack of light at the end of what had been a deep dark tunnel. I was going to class daily and those psychic intrusions had stopped. Every now and then I would have a panic attack, but I carried a paper sack in my purse that quickly stopped the hyperventilating.

I did quite well in the first semester, really good grades again. Then, in January, start of the second semester, I was outside school waiting for Mom to pick me up. Directly across the street stood a girl named Yvette, also waiting for her ride. I didn't know her well, but I'd seen her around, always waiting over there for her daily ride, and a few times, we chatted small talk.

She was a tall, pregnant, sixteen-year-old African American girl who had recently broken up with her boyfriend. I was lost in thought when I suddenly heard a speeding car roar up, slam on its brakes, and stop at the curb. It was a yellow Corvette with smoked windows. I glanced over and saw a young man open the door and jump out.

Yvette saw him, too, and darted the other direction. The guy caught her from behind and shot her point-blank in the side of her head with a .22 pistol. Then he ran to his car, jumped in, and sped off. I memorized his license plate and told a boy over near the door to run in and get the principal's office to call an ambulance.

Then I ran across the street and cradled Yvette in my arms and kept saying, "Don't die, don't die, please, don't die." Very soon, an ambulance pulled up and EMTs came and took over. "Is she gonna make it?" I pleaded. They didn't answer. They got her up on a gurney, put her inside the back of the ambulance, and quickly had her hooked up to an IV and had an oxygen mask on her.

I talked to the police and gave them a description of the car, the shooter and his plate numbers. They caught him in less than an hour. It turned out to be Yvette's twenty-year-old ex-boyfriend, Raymond Jones. A policeman got me a wet rag and got the blood off my hands. Then, after they left, I found myself standing frozen, like I was in a trance. I was holding a bloody rock and staring blankly at it when Mom pulled up.

I prayed long into the night for Yvette. Thank God, both she and her baby pulled through. The shooter would get sentenced to twenty years in prison, and if I remember right, he did most of it.

Whatever emotional progress I'd made went down the crapper. Within a few days, I found myself having one of those psychotic intrusions again, a term I wouldn't hear till years later; I just called them "daymares." I stopped going to class, so Mom enrolled me in Washington alternative school for troubled kids. I would eventually get expelled from there, too. For ditching. Damn, I used to love school. I couldn't understand it. I couldn't understand any of it.

I didn't know it at the time, but I didn't have much of my childhood left to enjoy.

31

Enter "Cotton"

It was early February, 1986, when I first encountered James Cotton Kelly. "Cotton" was his middle name, the name he wanted people to call him. I had just turned fifteen a few weeks earlier and was at The Speedway arcade one night with my friend Tina Wilson.

Circus-Circus Casino owned the arcade and had an entrance from the hotel. The casino built it as a babysitting option for out-of-town gamblers to dump off their kids so they could go lose all their money at the tables. But the place also got popular with us locals. That night, it was packed with teenagers and the room was filled with loud clangs and beeping noises from all the arcade games.

Tina and I were playing Pac-Man and, while I was in the bathroom, some grown-up Canadian dude came up behind her and hit on her. He was gone when I came back from the john, but she didn't tell me about him till we were outside and about to go home—when we got to the parking lot outside the exit. She sprang his offer on me: he would buy us beer if we would ride around with him and show him the sights. He told her he was twenty-four, but I learned later he was shading his age a couple years and was probably twenty-two. He said he was a tourist in town a few more days. I told her it was spooky, a grown-up man hitting on young teenage girls in a kids' arcade. The only adults who ever came in there were the chaperones and the people who worked there making change for the machines. It didn't take a genius to know he was trolling.

Then Tina put me on the spot. "I wanna go, but I don't wanna if you don't go."

That little voice inside my head said, *No, don't.* "Nah, I gotta be home soon. Before Mom gets off her shift. Besides, I don't wanna ride in a car with some adult man we don't know. What if he's a serial killer or rapes girls?"

Tina put on a pouty face and whined, "Naw, he wasn't no rapist. He was real nice. Anyways, we always do what *you* wanna do, Sandy. For just this once, can't we do one thing *I* wanna do? Heck, I kinda like the guy."

The fool I was, I didn't listen to that warning voice. I relented just as Cotton pulled up in his white 1984 Chrysler LeBaron convertible. He had the top up on this chilly night and he flashed a wide grin as he pushed open the passenger door to motion us in. He was a husky guy, broad-shouldered, up around 6 feet, with a round face, dark eyes, and wavy, shoulder-length hair. Not bad looking, just not my type. But evidently Tina's.

I got in the back seat, and Tina got in the front and scooched close to him. He was chatty and again said he was twenty-four. I was nervous and didn't want him getting any ideas, so I said, "Yeah, well, she's fourteen and I'm barely fifteen, case you didn't know."

He adjusted his rearview mirror to see me better. "Doesn't bother me if it doesn't bother you. Age is just a number."

I wanted to say, "Not according to the police," but I kept quiet. He pulled into a minimart, bought two six-packs of beer and a six-pack of wine coolers, then drove up Las Vegas Boulevard. As Tina pointed out landmarks and famous casinos, Cotton acted excited. "Oh, wow, there's Caesar's," he said. "Just look at that fountain." He was acting like a kid, first time at the circus. He pulled in and drove slowly past the fountain to get a better look.

"Oh, look. The Flamingo," he exclaimed, slowing down to get a better look. "The casino that launched the Strip. Bugsy Siegel's place. Man, oh, man."

After my second wine cooler, I dozed off, and when I woke, the car was racing through the dark, south down Highway 93. "Hey, mister, where are you taking us?"

Cotton glanced at me through the rearview. "I can't go back home without seeing Hoover Dam, now can I?"

"I'm not going to no *Hoover* Dam. Take me home. My Mom's gonna skin me."

Tina chimed in, popping her gum. "Aw, fer chrissake, Sandy. Loosen it up."

Cotton paid me no mind. Like I was no longer there. Just sped up and kept going south down the desert highway, nearly an hour, all the way to the dam. He parked on the Arizona side by the spillway to get to the observatory. He turned around and looked at me. "Me and Tina, we're gonna go for a little walk. You okay here for a bit?"

He didn't give me a chance to answer, but it was obvious he wanted to be alone with Tina. The two of them got out and went on what I figured was a romantic stroll, somewhere they could neck and pet and maybe more, leaving me in the car alone. I didn't trust being alone way out here with some stranger. I'd been jumpy about that kind of thing ever since that night at Jessica's.

After about twenty minutes, I said the hell with it and got out of the car. Luckily, I had enough money for the pricey cab fare home. I knew there were payphones around the observation area, and I called a taxi. They said it could be an hour, and I said I'd walk to the main highway and wait.

I stood there shivering on the side of Highway 93 for almost two hours before the taxi got there. I don't know what happened with Tina and Cotton because I never saw his car leave. And I never talked to Tina after that, not until many years later. When she came to prison.

Daylight was breaking when the taxi dropped me off at my house. Mom was waiting up, worried and angry-eyed. I explained what happened, and when I said Cotton had parked on the Arizona side, across the state line, she wanted to have him arrested for kidnapping. But I waved her off. "Forget it, Mom. He's just some Canadian tourist and I'll never see him again."

But little did I know, he wasn't a tourist and I would see him again eight months later, and it put the wheels in motion for my terrible fate.

And his.

32

Fighting Off a Rapist

In spite of all my ditching, I somehow managed to pass ninth grade, and I would be able to enter tenth grade at Western High School in the fall.

One miserably hot day that summer, the thermometer well up over a hundred, I was headed home near the end of the day. The heat seared my skin, and a hot wind kicked up dust devils and scattered tumbleweeds around next to a housing development where a vacant lot was a shortcut to my house.

About halfway across the lot, I felt eyes on me and glanced to my right. There was this boy glaring at me. I knew him as Randy, an older boy about to go off to college in the fall. Up around 6 feet and slim, he would have been a decent-looking boy if his eyes weren't so close to his nose. I saw him hop across the fence into the vacant lot, and then I heard him trotting behind me. I spun around just as he grabbed me and pushed me down to my knees.

"Hey! What the hell?" I hollered.

He was strong enough to hold me down, and the next thing, he was unzipping his pants. "Little Shaw girl," he said, "you are going to suck me off before I go off to school."

I couldn't believe it. "The *hell* I am," I shot back. I thought fast. "If you put your thing in my mouth, I swear to Jesus and all the saints I'll bite it off, and you won't have *no* fun at college or nowhere else, never."

I hoped that would scare him off, but he grabbed me by the hair in the back of my head and pulled me toward his crotch. That's when I somehow managed to free my right arm and punch him hard as I could directly in his nuts. He doubled over and moaned, and I jumped up and ran like a scared rabbit. I got hung up trying to climb the fence near the sidewalk at the end of the lot as he gained on me. I scrambled over the fence, stood in the middle of the street, and flagged down a motorist and when the motorist stopped, Randy ran away. The man was very concerned about me, took me to the nearest police station, and walked me inside. Once there, still trying to catch my breath, I filed a report and called Mom.

I figured that rat bastard belonged in jail, and maybe me going to the cops would save other girls from getting jumped. But when it was all sorted out, a cop told me and Mom, "It's just your word against his."

I said, "Ya mean you're not even gonna *arrest* him for that?"

The cop shrugged apologetically. "Got no proof, no witness." I wondered if they had checked Randy out and discovered he was from a well-to-do family and we were unconnected nobodies. In any case, Randy went off to college, free as a sparrow, and I became that much more traumatized. I could only hope Karma would exact justice on him one day, that the next girl he tried that on would stab him.

It wasn't the last time local police couldn't help me. The next time would ultimately cost me twenty-one years of my life and lead to a murder.

33

The Stalker Prelude to Murder

One late August day in 1986, I approached the McDonald's on the Strip, and there was Cotton Kelly standing outside the entrance. The same man I told Mom back in January not to report to the cops because I'd never ever see him again.

That Mickey D's was a teenage hangout, and kids were standing around in the blazing heat, chatting, joking, and smoking. Cotton was in a t-shirt and jeans and had two boys with him, one black and one white, neither likely more than twelve years old. I was shocked to see him but not so shocked that he was hanging around with little boys and was trolling a high school hangout.

I was with Stacy Buhman, a girl I'd just met when we registered for tenth grade at Western High School. She was my age, kind of a tough type who wore too much makeup and ratted her hair. I hoped he didn't notice me, but he grinned wide and said, "Hey, I remember you, You're Tina's friend Sandy."

I tried to get past him and through the door, but he stepped in front of me. "Look," he said. "Sorry if I got you in trouble with your mom that night. How 'bout you let me make it up to you—take you on a date?"

I squinted hard. "I'm not goin' on no *date* with you. I'm not interested in you, and I'm a kid and you're an adult, so why don't you just move out of the way?"

I managed to get around him and inside the door, but Stacy stayed outside. I didn't realize he offered her ten dollars to give him my number. Stacy said,

"Fuck, I'll play Cupid for ten bucks." He gave her the ten, she gave him my number, and my fate and his were in motion.

No sooner did I get home, my phone started ringing. It was Cotton. He told me he got my number from Stacy and how he got it. He again asked me for a date. I tried to be polite, yet very clear I didn't want anything to do with him. I hung up, and shortly the phone rang again. This time, he explained he was starting a Las Vegas lifestyle magazine and offered me a hundred dollars to pose naked on the hood of a Corvette in front of Caesar's Palace for a cover shot.

I couldn't believe what he just said. "Are you *nuts*? Mister, I'm fifteen years old. What the *hell* is your problem? I'm not gonna pose naked on any Corvette or anywhere else." This time, I slammed down the receiver really hard. But he called me back five more times that night, and I kept hanging up.

He called again the next morning. I told Mom what was going on and asked her to screen my calls. But he called and told her he was a school friend and gave her a phony name and got me on the phone.

He called me daily, and every conversation was about sex. I was annoyed at first, but by now I was angry and scared. I wondered, how can I get this guy to leave me alone?

A couple nights later, getting ready for bed, I spotted the outline of a face peering through my bedroom window. With the lights on, it was hard to see whose face it was. I screamed for Mom, then ran to the front door and looked outside after hearing a car start and zoom off. As it vanished into the night, I got a glimpse of what looked like a white convertible and knew it was Cotton's car. This had gotten way too creepy and way too scary, and it had to stop.

Mom took me to the police station to have him arrested or get a restraining order. But the police sat us down and explained there was no law in Nevada that somebody couldn't follow somebody else around—as long as they didn't harm the person.

"If he hurts your daughter," the cop told Mom, "that's different. We can arrest him. But until then . . . "

I was upset, but there were no stalking laws on the books in any state in 1986. After some murders, California passed the first state stalking law in 1990, and six years later Congress passed a federal stalking law. In Nevada today, the first stalking offense is six months in jail; aggravated stalking is two-to-fifteen years in prison. The federal law carries up to five years in prison, and if the stalking leads to death or injury, the offender can get up to twenty to life.

But in 1986, it was, "let me know if he hurts you."

This guy Anthony was my best friend, and if he had been around, I could have gotten his help with Cotton. But he'd just been sent to a boy's home in Elko. Anthony and I had been in the wrong place at the wrong time. We went to juvenile hall because someone we were with threw a rock through a steakhouse window. The police arrested Anthony and me as we were walking up the street to my house. I was ordered to ten days in juvenile hall and got released, while Anthony went to the boy's home. A really shit deal for him.

Still, I needed protection and asked a couple boys I knew from school. They all declined, so out of desperation, I turned to my childhood protector and friend, Troy Kell. Even though we didn't live in the same neighborhood anymore, he kept in touch with Mom and me. He'd been in some trouble and had spent a few months in juvenile jail out of town, I think for petty theft, but I don't remember.

I called him at his house and told him the whole story. "Jesus, what's wrong with the fucker?" Troy said. "Look, I'll kick his ass. Then he'll leave you alone. How's that?"

Ever since the murders at Jessica's, I'd wanted to steer clear of violence, but I was sure nothing short of slapping Cotton around would run him off.

It was late September, and the nights were finally cooling down, and he was still calling me regularly. I'd been in high school three weeks and Cotton had been stalking me a whole month. I didn't understand how he could be so persistent, how somebody could keep saying "no," and he could keep pushing it.

But with Troy's help, I was sure that trouble would be over. But that's when Troy threw a wrench into it. He told me I had to be involved. "I can't get in a fight out in the open, where the cops might see it," Troy explained, pacing around in his house as he puffed a cigarette. "You got to get him somewhere out in some secluded place."

"*Me*?" I said. "*I* got to get him somewhere out in the boonies?" I was wide-eyed with shock. "I don't wanna get nowhere near him."

"I've thought it over, Sandy. Either you do that or it's no deal." He stopped pacing and plopped down on his couch. "Cops catch me fighting, they'll put me right back in the juvie jail. I can't handle that."

"But, Troy, I don't—"

He pointed at me. "Sandy, I ever let you down? Ever? In your life?"

"No, but I'm scared he—"

"Either we do it my way or I'm out," he insisted. "He still callin' ya?"

"Yeah, three, four times a week."

"Next time he does, you take a date with him?"

"Do *what*?" My mouth dropped open.

"Tell him you'll go out with him but we'll figure a reason to stop and pick me up. Then we'll go somewhere out in the sticks and I'll smack him around and he'll get the message loud and clear. Then you're free of this shithead. Forever."

"Okay, look. I don't want to watch no fight," I said.

"Ya don't have to watch. You just walk away before it starts and I'll meet you after."

I sat there and stared at the fiber designs in his carpet. Finally, I said, "I guess I got no choice. Isn't no other way out."

"Not if it's me that's gonna do it."

I took a deep breath. "Okay, okay. We'll do it your way."

The wheels were in motion now, and fate was about to end one life and ruin three others.

34

Cotton's Murder

It was Monday, September 29, 1986. A pleasant early fall day where the sun bathed the streets on my block bright orange. Then a cold front came through just before sunset.

As darkness fell, I opened the front door partway to slip out unnoticed, about to meet a man on what would tragically be the last night of his life. Mom spotted me and called out from the living room, "Hey, where you headed?"

"Minimart, Mom. Get some snacks and stuff, maybe hook up with a friend a while."

"Young lady," she called back, "you be back no later than 8:30. I *mean* it. You gotta sit for Shane and your sisters. I and Mike got tickets to see Hank Junior at the Sahara."

It was nearing 7:00 p.m. and already dark. "Yeah, Mom. I know. I'll be back in time. Promise."

I walked warily across the lawn to the sidewalk, glancing up at the stars. The sky was clear, but it was chilly, so I'd worn my white, winter-lined agora jacket. As I gazed up at a fading crescent moon, I took a breath that sort of hiccupped—like a thousand butterflies had just been turned loose in my stomach.

I was nervous. I was hesitant. I was scared.

And now, I stood staring down the spooky, dark street for a pair of car lights that part of me hoped would not appear. Couldn't he just forget about me and bother somebody else?

I twirled my purse around, trying to seem calm and cool so Cotton wouldn't think something was up. My right hand was heavily taped with gauze. I had accidentally but conveniently punctured it on a hanging nail while bouncing around in a friend's Jeep the day before, heading down from Mt. Charleston. A perfect excuse to get Cotton to take me to meet Troy—the story being he had prescription meds I needed.

Suddenly, I spotted Cotton's 1984 white Chrysler convertible closing in, illuminated in and out under streetlights. Moving slowly. Like some prowling cat.

I sucked in a big breath and walked in his direction. I had warned him not to pick me up in front of my house. Mom would have chased him off with whatever weapon was handy because she was hopping mad how he had been harassing me.

And now he was about to pick me up, and Troy was about to beat him up for what he had done. It's not what I had wanted, but it had come to that.

When I got in his car, my heart was slamming against my rib cage so hard I wondered if he could hear it.

He wore a clean, white t-shirt with a gold Corona beer logo, jeans, and white sneakers. He was chatty and upbeat and had a suggestion: "I got a new stereo. We should go to my apartment, listen to music, order a pizza."

"Oh, no, you don't. You agreed we'd go to a *public* place. That was our deal." I showed him my bandaged hand. "Cut it bad on a nail. We gotta go meet up with my friend first, okay? This guy Troy, he's got antibiotics. I can't let this get infected 'cause we don't have money to go to the doc."

"Yeah, okay," he sighed. "Where?"

"Circle K, not far away. I'll show you the turns."

He drove past the Circle K on Jones Boulevard and my stomach tumbled because Troy was nowhere in sight. *Jesus!* Did he blow me off? And if so, now what? I was panicked that Cotton might take me to some out-of-the-way place and I'd have to fight him off. I suddenly wished I'd never set the plan in motion. Where the hell was Troy? I stalled for time; I talked Cotton into circling the block twice more, and on the second loop, there was Troy, under a streetlight, waving when he spotted me with my head leaned out the window. "*There* he is. That's him!" I tried not to sound as excited and relieved as I totally was.

Cotton pulled over to the curb.

But there was a surprise waiting. Troy wasn't alone. He had a guy with him, about Troy's age, some beanpole who towered over five-foot-ten Troy. A half-empty bottle of Southern Comfort dangled from the beanpole's hand. Both he and Troy were dressed in black leather jackets and black leather gloves. Their getups seemed ridiculous. I would have laughed if my stomach wasn't doing barrel rolls from anxiety, because they looked like they were in costume for a masquerade party as matching burglars.

I leaned forward so Troy and his friend could get in the back seat. Troy sat behind Cotton, reached around, smiled wide, and shook hands with him.

"I'm Troy. Friend of Sandy's."

Beanpole hesitated, then said, ice cold, no smile, "Billy. Friend of Troy's."

I turned around. "Hi, Billy. I'm Sandy."

"Yeah, I figured that out."

I stared into Billy's eyes and got the willies. He had a long, thin face that framed a pair of cold, dark eyes, sunken under high cheekbones. I suddenly pictured a bony-faced Charlie Manson.

Cotton pulled away from the curb and drove north on Jones Boulevard. "So, you got some healing meds for our girl?" Cotton spoke without turning around, kept his eyes straight ahead but drove slowly, waiting for Troy's directions.

"Medicine's at my Ma's," Troy assured him. "Just up the road a bit. I'll run in and grab it and then you can just drop me and Billy back off at the Circle K, if ya don't mind."

"Sure thing," Cotton said.

Troy directed him on a few turns, and soon we were headed east on Racel Street, a desolate stretch of road framed by desert—not a single house or living thing out there in those days. Then Billy pushed his knee hard into my seatback—the agreed signal Troy and I had worked out.

"Hey, would you pretty please pull over," I begged. "I gotta pee real bad."

Cotton obliged, pulling off the road a few yards into an open space surrounded by scrub brush. I got out and walked south, in the direction back toward town, listening to the scrunch-scrunch of my shoes in the desert dirt. The deal with Troy was I didn't want to see the fight because I'd seen enough violence at Jessica's to last forever. Now Troy just needed to do his thing, maybe with a little help from his new sidekick Billy, and my life would be back to whatever version of normal it had been.

Well, I got maybe fifty yards when Billy came trotting out. "Hey, Sandy. Hold on a sec."

I spun around, wondering what the hell. Troy and Cotton were standing outside the car, chatting away like they were old buddies.

"What?" I asked.

"Pretend ya hurt your leg." Billy glanced back over his shoulder toward Troy and Cotton.

"My *leg*? What for?"

"'Cause I need to get Troy out here to talk."

"Let's just forget about this," I said. "I don't want you guys to beat him up. Let's just all go home. But I'll ride home from the minimart with you and Troy. I don't trust Cotton."

But Billy didn't seem to be hearing what I was saying. He hollered back toward the car. "Hey, Troy. C'mon out here. Sandy needs help. She fell—hurt her leg."

Troy ran toward us, and after a few seconds, Cotton followed in a fast trot. I plopped down on a huge rock, doing like Billy ordered me, rubbing my ankle and wincing. I'm thinking, okay, they aren't going to fight, and I'm just going to call it off and go home right now.

Just then, Cotton reached out and grabbed my left arm to pull me up, and a loud pistol shot barked right next to my ear. I was pushed to the ground again. *What the—?* I didn't see who fired it, but I sure as hell knew the sound of a pistol.

Billy called out, "Get him now, Troy. Get him *now!*"

Then *bam-bam-bam*. Three more shots rang out and my instincts kicked in. Scared out of my wits, I jumped up off the ground and bolted. My mind raced as I sprinted away toward the car, thinking I was going to get shot, too. Memories of Rancho Circle flashed through my mind as time sped up into fast motion. I wasn't sure I really knew where I was at that point. I kept crying out, "I'm going to be sick!"

Billy, right behind me now, yelled, "Don't worry about it. You'll be okay, you're going home."

"*Jesus* Christ. Jesus *H.* Christ." Those were the only words I could choke out of my throat. "I'm gonna be sick." It started to become clear. What in God's name just happened and what had I got myself into? I glanced back, saw Cotton's body, flat on the ground, not moving. Cotton, Jesus . . . he's . . . dead.

Half crying, I yelled, "*What* did you just do, Troy?" Troy was just a few yards behind me now, but he wouldn't answer. "Dammit, Troy—why'd you shoot him? Where'd you get that gun?" I hadn't seen the gun, but I'd clearly heard it. Where was it? Did he ditch it?

Troy wouldn't answer, just shrugged and looked blankly at his shoes while I stood numb with shock.

At the car, Troy grumbled when he opened the driver's side door. "Aw, shit. Damn keys are in his pocket. I 'member he stuck 'em in there." He paused and looked at me. "Sandy, you go out there and get his keys."

"Screw *you*. No way I'm goin' out to no dead body and get no damn car keys from somebody's pocket. It's your mess. *You* do it." My voice was raspy because my throat was bone dry from fear and anxiety.

"Whatever," Troy shrugged. Both of them jogged back to Cotton's body. It suddenly hit me, I'm a witness. Shit, they might kill me, too. Troy won't, but I don't know a thing about Billy and I don't trust him. I took off toward some bushes and ducked down, out of sight.

Soon, Billy called out, "Sandy? Hey, *Sandy*. Where the *fuck* are you?" There was a long pause before he called out again. Then he spooked me when he appeared right behind me. Like a vampire. "What the goddam hell you doing? C'mon, dammit. We gotta git."

He had hold of my arm as he walked me to the car, like he thought I might run away. Billy drove and I rode in the back seat alone, sick to my stomach, scared out of my skin, and freaked about riding in a dead man's car. At first, nobody talked—the murder hung heavy in the air among us. All of a sudden, Billy had a wallet in his hand. He took something from it and flung the wallet out the window, far into the desert.

"Ain't no wallet," Billy said, "they won't know who he is, right?" It was Cotton's wallet.

"Dammit, Troy. Why did you shoot the guy?" I pleaded, listening to my own cracking voice. "You could've just beat him up, like you said you'd do.

Jesus Christ, you didn't have to kill the guy." My breathing was labored and I thought I might throw up.

Troy still wouldn't answer, just looked straight ahead. Then Billy turned around and stared at me with those stony eyes. "Look here, Sandy. You tell the cops, you could end up out there right next to Cotton. You follow me?"

I believed he was serious.

Then Billy suggested whoever got caught first had to take the blame.

Hell no. I had *nothing* to do with any of this. But I didn't speak out. In fact, nobody said another word until Billy pulled into a gas station, low on fuel. He ordered me to pump the gas, giving me five dollars to pay inside.

It was deadly silent the rest of the way to my house.

As I got out, Troy tried to comfort me. "Call ya later, okay? Check on how yer doin'."

I nodded but didn't answer. I slogged to the door and opened it to see Mom and Mike on the couch, all dressed up for the concert.

Mom said, "Oh, good, you made it back in time." Then she stared hard at me. "Geez, you look real pale, honey. You coming down with something?"

"Nah. I'm fine, Mom."

She looked closer. My face and hands were scraped up from when I got pushed down in the desert, and my white jacket was dirty. "You have cuts on you," she said. "What the—"

"Some crazy girl jumped me in the alley on the way back from the store. She shoved me down."

"Jesus."

"It's okay. I'm fine. I'm not hurt. You guys go enjoy Hank Junior. Ain't nothing for you to worry about."

I babysat Shane and my two sisters—eight-year-old Nicole and baby Leah, barely a year old now. I mostly stared blankly at the TV the rest of the night, numb, my emotions disconnected from reality. I took Shane into a room and told him everything. He was shocked. I made him swear never to tell a soul, and to this day he never has.

Troy called later, said they'd dumped the car somewhere behind a nursing home and hoofed it to the Circle K to get his car. I thanked him for checking on me, but I didn't want to talk to him. Maybe not ever again.

I took a sleeping pill from Mom's medicine cabinet, and soon after they returned from the concert at the Sahara, I crawled into bed. Even after the pill, I tossed and turned a long time before drifting into a restless sleep—praying I'd wake to find it was all a bad dream.

35

A Nightmare, but Not a Dream

A shaft of bright sunlight came through my window curtain and woke me at first light. I sat up on my bed and seemed to remember something horrible had happened. But what? Then I clearly envisioned Alex shooting Betty DiFiore. And the police quizzing me. It was so real, like it had really happened the night before. My mind accepted that it was the morning after the Rancho Circle murders.

Then I washed my face, and my brain fog lifted. *Jesus, that was two years ago.* I opened the curtain a few inches and looked out. I now remembered hearing gunshots and seeing gunpowder flashes. And it hit me that Troy shot Cotton Kelly last night. Shot him dead.

Or did he?

That's how scrambled my brain wires were on that morning and with the PTSD that had a hold of me. It truly seemed like I had dreamed it. I dearly wanted it to be a dream.

I phoned Dave Fletcher, one of the friends I had asked to fight Cotton and who had turned me down. Dave asked if I needed a ride to school. I told him I wasn't going to school, but I did need a ride somewhere. I waited till he got there to tell him what I thought had happened the night before, and so he drove me out to Racel Street. The wind was blowing dust when he pulled off the road, close enough to spot Cotton's dead body right where Troy had murdered him.

Neither Dave nor I got out of the car. I thought I was going to throw up but I held it back. Dave sat there, holding onto the wheel, his mouth open, staring at the corpse. He would look at me and back at Cotton's body, over and over.

"Let's get out of here," I said, and he drove off, swearing he would never tell a soul, but advising me to go right to the cops. "You're a witness. You don't tell what you saw and you protect those guys, cops might figure you were in on it."

That's exactly what happened. I should have listened to Dave, but I couldn't put Troy in danger. He was my friend all my life, a guy who'd watched out over me from the time I was six years old. I just couldn't.

Dave remembered seeing Cotton hanging around the McDonald's on the Strip a time or two, so he had known who he was even back when I had asked Dave to fight him. He took me home. I needed to sort all this out in my haywire brain.

Yes, Troy killed him, but I felt guilty for asking him to help me. I just couldn't understand why he'd brought a gun to a fight or why he used it. Cotton would have been no match in a fight with Troy and Billy.

I could never go to the police, even though I had figured I had nothing to fear because I hadn't killed anyone and hadn't wanted Cotton dead. But my mind kept scrambling facts—and fantasies kept bleeding into reality. Plus, the kids I'd run with the last few years preached that when it came to the cops, you keep your yap shut. In the end, my sense of loyalty outweighed my common sense and would end up costing me everything.

I didn't talk to Troy again till we were both in county jail. But a few days after the killing, when Dave Fletcher was at my house, I got a call from Billy Merritt reminding me to keep my mouth shut. It sounded like a threat. Fletcher listened on the kitchen extension, but years later, he would be confused and say the call came from Troy. Troy would have never threatened me or hurt me, not for any reason.

But I had no idea what beanpole Billy was capable of.

36

Booked for Murder

October 4, 1986, five days after Troy shot Cotton.

I was home looking out after my brother and little sisters around 7:00 p.m. Mike was asleep because he worked the graveyard shift. Suddenly, I heard the pounding at the front door. It was so loud I almost jumped out of my skin. I called out, "Who's there?"

"Police," a gruff voice called back. "Las Vegas homicide. We need you to come to the door."

My heart took a tumble, and I froze in my tracks. I knew why they were there. I imagined my house being surrounded by cops with guns drawn, like at Jessica's that night. I drew a breath and opened the door just a crack and peeped out. One man was tall and willowy with a great big nose. He stuck his badge in my face and an ID identifying him as Detective Joe McGuckin. He said, "Are you Sandy Shaw?"

I tried to say yes but no words came out. I nodded.

"We need you to come to the station to talk." His partner stood behind him, arms folded, saying nothing. They were both plainclothes cops.

"Can I get my shoes and purse?" I asked.

McGuckin said yes, but he and his partner followed me inside and walked a few steps behind me to my room. As I slipped on my shoes, I asked if it was okay if I told my little brother so he could tell Mom where I was or let my stepdad know once he woke up.

McGuckin squinted at me. He was scary-looking. "No! You need to get in the car with us. Right now."

Their car was unmarked and had a blue light under the dash that plugged into the cigarette lighter in case they needed to stick it up on the dash and turn it into a cop car.

I was scared as they drove me to the precinct. I wished I had water. It was a warm night, and my throat was bone dry. None of us spoke during the ride to the station and that silence was intense.

At the police station, they took me into a small room with a bright overhead light that shone directly in my face when I sat down. There was a single, small table and three metal folding chairs. I asked for water. McGuckin said, "Not right this minute. We'll get you some in a bit."

He straddled one of the metal chairs and leaned so close I could smell he'd had clams for dinner. "Here's the situation and why you're here. We found the body of a man out in the desert. We think he's a Canadian named James Kelly, and we have reason to believe you killed him."

"Whoa!" I said. "Hold on! You got some bad information, mister." I had no idea where they got the idea I'd killed him. Maybe they had arrested Billy or Troy and those guys blamed it on me.

Those detectives kept telling me, over and over again, I had murdered someone, and I kept saying, over and over again, "Fuck you. You're crazy. I didn't kill anybody. I don't know what you're talking about."

I didn't know it was illegal for them to interrogate me without a parent or guardian with me. I didn't know shit about anything when it came to this. But they must have known they were breaking the law. They kept interrogating me and playing good cop/bad cop with me. McGuckin played bad cop. The other guy would leave the room and McGuckin would say I was going to prison and I was a murderer. I just stayed cocky and kept telling him to fuck off—I didn't kill anybody. And it was the God's honest truth.

Now and then his partner would come in and McGuckin would leave. The other cop was sweet as molasses, like he was all concerned about me. He brought me bottles of water. Then he would leave and McGuckin would come back and scare the shit out of me. This went on for hours, until the collar of my blouse was drenched in sweat.

Finally, I gave them a story: I'd been hitching, and these two guys I didn't know gave me a ride in a Cadillac and told me they'd killed some guy. It was a stupid story, but I wasn't thinking clearly.

Finally, at the end of four hours under that hot light, they told me cops at another precinct had arrested Troy and Billy, and Billy had signed a formal statement giving all of us up. By then, they had called Mom. When they told her they had me at the station house regarding a murder, Mom said, "Oh, God no. Don't tell me that poor kid witnessed *another* murder."

McGuckin told her, "No, ma'am. She's no witness. She's being *arrested* for murder."

I was sitting there, my stomach in knots, when I heard the distinctive *clickety-click-click* of Mom's high-heels coming down the hallway toward me.

Soon as she walked into the room, I said, "Mom, I didn't do it."

She reached out and hugged me. They left the two of us alone for a half-hour. I told her the whole story, exactly how it happened. She already knew of it some of from the past few days. She'd known I was not okay, and I was asking her questions, but I had pretended they were for someone else—the old "I know this friend who told me" crap. Mom was supportive. She said whatever I decide to do—to spill all the beans on Troy, or whatever—she was one hundred percent on my side. Mom had her flaws, but loyalty was never among them.

After she left, they booked me for felony murder. I didn't even know what that was. I didn't sign anything. I was mostly wondering how they found Cotton's body and knew it was him since Billy had thrown his wallet in the desert a good mile away. I wondered if Dave Fletcher had betrayed me.

But I soon found out. When they were questioning me, I had Stacy Buhman's Social Security card in my purse, for a reason I don't recall. When they said they were taking me to jail, I handed the card to the good cop and asked, "Can you make sure this girl gets her card back? She needs it."

McGuckin was sitting there with us, shook his head, and said with a crooked grin, "I don't know why in hell you care about *her*. She's the one dropped the dime on you." I was totally bewildered because I had never told Stacy a word about Cotton getting murdered.

The night before, though, she and I had got into a fight. We'd been waiting to cross the street at Las Vegas Boulevard and Sahara when a guy in a car at the light started yelling at Stacy, saying she fucked up his car. She shook her fist and yelled, "Fuck you! I'll *kill* you."

I have no idea why I reacted the way I did. Maybe because I had held my emotions in for the two years since the Rancho Circle killings. I must have been like a ticking time bomb waiting to explode. When she yelled, "I'll kill you," a switch inside me flipped. "Why's everybody want to kill everybody?" I said, and I slugged her.

I hit her so hard I knocked her down. She got up off the sidewalk swinging and missing. Then I beat her ass all the way down the street. I barely remembered doing it. When I finally stopped, she wiped blood off her cheek and said, "You'll be sorry for this, you dirty fucking bitch." And she ran off.

What I didn't know was next morning she went to a police station and told an officer on duty, "I know where there's a dead body, and I know who killed him. A girl named Sandy Shaw."

The police were naturally skeptical, but they put her in a squad car, and she directed them out to Racel Street. Right to Cotton's decomposing body. She told police, "Sandy Shaw told me she shot him between the eyes, slit his throat and blew up his car with dynamite. And I know right where she lives." Then she told them Troy Kell and Billy Merritt were involved.

I later learned Dave Fletcher had taken kids out there to see Cotton's body on three different nights. One of them was Stacy, and Dave foolishly shared the details with her, figuring she and I were all buddy-buddy close, and she'd be tight-lipped. But the truth was, I had known Stacy for maybe a month, and she was the one who put the wheels of this murder into motion in the first place, selling my phone number to Cotton Kelly.

Mom had met her only briefly when I brought her home one day. That night, Mom said, "I were you, Sandy, I'd keep my distance from that girl. Nothing I can put my finger on—but there just something about her I don't trust."

Oh, I wish I'd listen to my mother.

The police had already found Cotton's car even before Stacy went to them and told them where they could find the body and that I was the murderer. The people at the nursing home where Troy and Billy ditched the car reported it, and the police ran the Alberta license plate. Canadian authorities traced it to Cotton's father and connected it with Cotton because he had been living in

Vegas about a year. Looking back, there was a lot I wished I'd known about Cotton and his family.

After they arrested me, the police transported me from the precinct to the Clark County Jail where I was formally booked for murder. At the jail, they took my mug shot, fingerprinted me, and at two-thirty in the morning, stuck me in a holding cell for the night. Nobody was allowed to be in the cell with me because I was a minor. On the outside of every holding cell, the jailers would put mug shots of those being held; they listed their ages and the crime they'd been booked in on. Cops and trustees and janitors who would walk by my holding cell would look at my picture and my age, and their eyes would pop out. A fifteen-year-old girl held for murder.

They were shocked.

And so was I.

37

Clark County Jail

The prison was nasty, smelly, and loud. It would be kind to call the Clark County Jail a piss-hole. Inmates yelled, screamed, and cussed most all night. I'd sometimes cover my ears with my pillow to try to make it stop, but it didn't. The air stunk with body odor and with cigarette smoke thick as fog off a bay.

I would be locked up there over four months before my trial, and seven months total before being railroaded into prison.

The day after they booked me, they moved me to a cell on the all-female ninth floor. Because I was a minor, I was in a single cell and not allowed to mix with the general population. Adult women got let out most of the day, but I got out only one hour a day to exercise when they were locked down.

It wasn't a traditional jail cell with bars; it was a small room with a dense, steel-reinforced wooden door. I had a bed, a sink, a toilet, and a thick, rectangular window that was just a slate of glass. The door had a slot in the middle to slide food trays through and a slit where I could see out.

My view was of the men's recreation area, and sometimes I could see Troy and Billy down there in their orange jumpsuits. From my ninth-floor room, I could sometimes talk to Troy, who was on the seventh floor. We had to empty the water out of our toilets and talk through the pipes. I was still really angry at him because if it hadn't been for him, I wouldn't be there. But I knew if I hadn't asked him to fight Cotton, he wouldn't be there either. I think I was exhibiting my ancestral Catholic guilt.

Troy said Billy ratted us all out, that he'd caved the moment they got him into the interrogation room. Later, after they transferred me to the second floor, Billy was in 2C, which was all juvenile males, and I was able to confront him. I called him a "rat-ass motherfucker" and he went off on me for getting him involved, though I *never* asked him to come along. I'd never met or heard of him before that night. Bringing him was Troy's bad idea.

I was too young to commingle with other inmates, but the jailors didn't care and illegally sold me cigarettes in my commissary. Soon, I developed a routine: because it was so loud at night, I read books and wrote letters most all night and went to sleep at daybreak. I would wake at two in the afternoon, be let out of my cell from 2:30 p.m. to 3:30 p.m. to shower, then go through the same routine, day after day after day.

I still didn't understand why they had jailed me, since I didn't kill anyone. Looking back, I should have been more scared than I was, but there was the emotional numbing and my teenage naiveté.

They held me on four charges: murder with the use of a deadly weapon, robbery with the use of a deadly weapon, conspiracy to commit murder, and conspiracy to commit armed robbery.

I was in only a few days when they took Billy and me to juvenile court—and we didn't speak to each other in court. I tried not to look at him. The judge certified Billy as an adult and dropped three charges against me: conspiracy to commit murder, conspiracy to commit robbery, and the robbery charge. I was still charged as a juvenile on the murder with the use of a deadly weapon and robbery with the use of a deadly weapon, even though, to this day, I've never even had a gun in my hands. And even though I heard the gunshots, I never even saw Troy with a gun the night of the killing. The first time I saw the gun was in evidence used against me.

In Nevada, at the time, anyone charged with murder did not have to be certified as an adult; you were automatically charged as one. So, prosecutor Dan Seaton charged me as an adult and tried me for the conspiracy and robbery charges.

At my bail hearing, the judge set my bond at three million dollars. I said to him, "Who do you think I am? Some female version of Charlie Manson?" He scolded me and warned me to watch my mouth.

Mom visited me twice a week, sometimes with Shane and Mike along. This crime was the talk of Las Vegas, especially in high school hallway gossip. Las

Vegas was more innocent then. The mob ran the casinos, and the casinos ran everything else. People weren't used to violent crimes because mobsters kept murders on the QT, so the FBI wouldn't come poking around and kill their Golden Goose. If the mob found a body, even if they weren't responsible, they often stuffed it in a car trunk and dumped it across the Arizona state line.

So, residents thought the town was safer than it was—and to read about three teenagers killing a man in what the newspapers claimed was a botched robbery must have shocked them out of their shoes.

Mom brought me newspapers, and Cotton's murder was tabloid fodder for months leading up to our trials. A *Review-Journal* story claimed we'd set Cotton up to rob him after finding out he'd won a lot of money gambling—not a thing about him stalking me. One story labeled me a "teenage temptress." Mom called the news desk at the *Review-Journal* and found out the source of all that false news was none other than Clark County Deputy District Attorney Dan Seaton, assigned to prosecute our cases.

Seaton spun a yarn that I took kids out to see the body on several occasions and bragged about my part in the murder. He had to know it was Dave Fletcher who did all that. Some clever headline writer called it "the Show-and-Tell Murder" and the public ate it up. Seaton was capitalizing on the popularity of a recent movie, "River's Edge." In the film, a teenager murders his girlfriend and dumps her body on the shore of a river, then brings friends out to gawk at the body.

Seaton also put in an order at the jail that I couldn't call anyone but Mom, my family, or his office on jail phones where other inmates could talk to whoever they pleased.

Mom came up with a clever idea to get Seaton to incriminate himself on a recording. So, I called her from the jail, and she used three-way calling to phone Seaton's office. She kept quiet, and since there was no caller ID, Seaton thought I called him from jail.

I asked him, "What would you do if somebody did that to your kids, lied in the newspapers and called them cold-blooded murderers?"

He didn't answer.

Then I asked, "Why are you saying those awful things about me when you know it's not true? I didn't kill nobody, but you're telling everyone I was the mastermind."

Seaton's answer: "Sandy, I know you didn't kill anybody. In fact, I'm sure if I let you out of that cell right now, you wouldn't commit a crime the *rest* of your life. . . . But this is my job—and I plan to make an *example* out of you." I also got him to admit I didn't take any kids out to see the body.

But he would tell the jury and the press otherwise.

Mom got all that on tape, but for whatever reason, my lawyer didn't get it into evidence for the jury to hear.

I was getting a ton of letters from people I didn't know—foolish teenagers, mostly, who thought I was some cool cult hero because I was in jail and my name was in the papers. I tried calling my dad, then wrote to him. I got a letter back from his wife, Cindy, who said, "We're not going to tiptoe around the subject of murder. We want to know what part you really played in it." That wasn't the supportive letter I'd hoped for.

Mom didn't have money to hire a high-powered lawyer, but the state appointed a public defender, Mike Miller. He was considered an up-and-comer and had won a lot of cases.

Then, shortly before my trial, Miller recused himself because an attorney named Willie Watters worked for the DA's office and had just been transferred to the public defender's office. Watters, who would be later disbarred and tied to cocaine use, had been Cotton Kelly's roommate.

Losing Mike Miller was an absolute disaster. As my February 9th trial date neared, I was without counsel. Mom asked my trial judge for a continuance to find a lawyer, but he denied her. Just sixteen days before my trial, we were still looking for a lawyer.

Somebody told her Ralph Rohay had never lost a case. So she scraped up a retainer and he agreed to defend me. What Mom didn't know, Ralph had never tried a criminal case in his entire life. All his wins were civil cases and real estate stuff.

I didn't realize it until the trial started, but having him as my attorney put me in a world of shit.

38

Five-Day Circus

Monday, February 9, 1986, broke sunny and chilly. Mom brought me a tasteful blue and white dress to wear to court so I wouldn't have to wear a cheap, tacky jail-issue dress. She would bring a different dress to the jail for each of the five days of my trial.

Billy Merritt had been certified to be tried as an adult, though he had now cut a deal to testify against Troy. They never certified me to be tried as an adult, which is illegal, but Seaton got away with it. How, I do not know.

Ralph Rohay met with me a total of only one hour before we went to court—the day before my trial. So, he wasn't at all prepared. Yet, I had faith in the justice system. I had faith in him. I was a kid and thought it would all be okay. Like Superman, I had faith in truth, justice, and the American way.

Mom was on the witness list, so she was not allowed to attend my trial. Tears in her eyes, she gave me a big hug on my way into the courtroom and went home. After the trial ended, she was allowed to attend the day of the verdict and the night of the sentencing.

I was doomed the moment Mom hired Rohay. For starters—in this was huge—on the way into court the day the trial started, he took me and Mom into a side room and told us the DA's office had offered me a deal: If I would plead to second degree murder, my sentence would be twenty years.

I felt like I'd just been slapped because twenty years seemed like an eternity to a fifteen-year-old kid. But here's the rub: Had Rohay known anything about criminal law, he would have told me, me being a first offender and a minor, I could petition the parole board after just four years. At the very worst, I would have been paroled in no more than twelve, but likely earlier. I would have been in my early to late twenties, still had my youth, still had time to maybe settle down and raise a family.

But Rohay didn't know any of that.

In fact, Billy Merritt's deal was ten years on the murder charge, five years on the weapons charge, both served concurrently. He went to the parole board after two years, got a two-year dump, then was paroled and out on the street after four years. That could have been my deal if Rohay would have pressed it. But he committed a defense attorney's mortal sin; he advised me to turn down the plea deal. Having dealt with a lot of defense attorneys since, really good ones like Bill Terry and Chris Oram, I realize any able defense attorney never advises a client to turn down a plea deal. The attorney should *always* leave it up to the defendant.

But I was a kid, and what the hell did I know about the law? Nothing. I trusted him because he was a grown-up with a law degree. He stood there in that room and pointed at me. "You're fifteen. You didn't kill anybody. You didn't want anybody dead. The jury will *never* convict you." Then he looked deep into my eyes and said, "Let's go to trial!"

"Well, okay then," I said. Mom agreed.

Had we only known.

I will say, Ralph was a nice man, a good man, a well-meaning man. He filed an appeal for me a year after I was in prison and didn't charge for it. But he was swimming in deep water, way over his head, and he should have known that from the get-go. He sealed my fate when he told me to turn down that deal. Years later, he acknowledged it publicly and apologized for it in newspaper stories.

But shame on him. He gambled with my life. And he lost.

Day One

The courtroom was packed with folks caught up in the wild wave of news stories. While Rohay was poorly prepared, Seaton was armed and ready. Seaton may have been a lot of things, but dumb and inexperienced weren't among them. He knew to put me on trial first because, with Troy pleading not guilty and facing the death penalty and Billy turning "state's," we would not be able to call either of them as witnesses. They could have refuted the tales Seaton would feed the jury, like the ridiculous story about a robbery plan. Billy's account would have verified my version that it was all about roughing up a stalker to scare him off.

Seaton was short, always well-groomed, and dapper in court. As the three-ring circus was about to launch, my Grandpa Bill and Grandma Marie were seated within earshot of the prosecutor's table. Grandma had great hearing. Many times over the years, my grandpa would mumble something about her from the other room, and she'd say, "Bill, I heard that!" That day, she clearly heard Rohay make a gesture of professional courtesy by turning to Seaton and saying, "Good luck, Dan."

She said Seaton grinned and fired back, "Ralph, it isn't about luck; it's about who can lie the best." He may have made it sound like he was joking, but I'm sure he was serious.

In his opening remarks, Seaton shot a volley across our bow: "Ladies and gentlemen of the jury," he pointed at me as he spoke, "do not be misguided by her angelic looks. The girl who Sandy Shaw appears to be today is *not* the girl she really is. She is a cold-blooded murderer."

He painted Cotton to be an upstanding fellow who would have never stalked an underage child for sex. He came up with a preposterous story that I used to dress up and go gambling, and that is how I met him.

When gambling? With what, I wanted to scream, since I barely had money for minimart snacks. He claimed I had met Cotton when I was shooting dice at Circus-Circus and noticed him win a lot of money. He said I then coaxed him into a date and recruited Troy and Billy to rob him of fourteen hundred dollars. Then when the robbery supposedly went south, and we murdered him.

Billy was Seaton's star witness against Troy, and Seaton knew from Billy the gambling story and robbery motive were nonsense. Billy's version of events was *exactly* the same as mine, that neither he nor I had touched the gun that night or knew Troy had brought one. And when he tried Troy, Seaton vouched for Billy's version—my version.

That tale about me shooting dice in Circus-Circus was ridiculous. If a casino can just keep its doors open, they prosper. But if they let underage kids gamble, they'll lose their license and get shut down. Security guards at Circus-Circus would have ushered me out the door before I could have even popped my bubblegum. Plus, when I was fifteen, I looked even younger. But somehow, Seaton put that jury under enough ether to sell them that story.

Establishing the robbery motive allowed Seaton to dispute my stalking story and strengthen his conspiracy charge. He told the jury I dreamed up the stalking story in the police station the day of my arrest.

I don't think Dan Seaton could have convicted me with the truth.

That first day, he began parading hearsay witnesses to the stand, mostly teenagers looking for notoriety or being paid to testify. I didn't know any one of them, including this guy in his early twenties, Christopher Cousins, who said he had been at Troy's apartment and heard Troy say he planned to murder Cotton.

To Rohay's credit, he had a rebuttal witness against Cousins, a girl named Lisa, who I also didn't know. She said she was at Troy's with Cousins that day and all Troy said was he might have to rough up some Canadian guy who wouldn't stop bothering a young girl he knew. She testified Cousins was so drunk, he almost passed out on the couch and wouldn't have remembered where he was, let alone who said what.

Seaton called another guy to the stand I had never met, who swore I told him I'd planned it all and set up Cotton to be robbed. Then a girl I didn't know from Adam who said I had told her exactly how I had killed Cotton.

Jesus! It was like a Ringling Brothers Circus, and I was in the center ring.

Seaton saved his big guns for days two, three, and four, and Rohay planned to put me on the stand on day five, which turned out to be a horrible idea. But I told him I really wanted to testify because I figured anybody innocent shouldn't worry about swearing on a Bible and speaking the truth.

Anticipating I'd testify, Seaton harassed me every day during every recess. He'd follow me around and say stuff like, "You're going to die in prison," or "They'll carry you out a wrinkled old woman in a pine box."

He bothered me so relentlessly that one guard, who'd had enough, stepped between me and Seaton and said, "What's the matter with you, fella. Why don't you stop bothering that kid!"

Seaton was undeterred.

In the meantime, Ralph Rohay was as lost and bewildered in that courtroom as I was. He didn't object to things he should have, and when he did, many objections were either ill-timed or overruled by Judge Mendoza. But I foolishly kept thinking, *Be patient. He's a learned man. He's gonna get his footing and start strutting his stuff.* But he never did. Like my Dad in his last battle in Vietnam, we were badly outgunned.

Stacy on the Stand

The first major prosecution witness was none other than Stacy Buhman. I don't have enough expletives in my cuss bag to describe what I think about her. At my preliminary hearing, she had testified for the prosecution before Dave Fletcher testified for me. She took the stand with her hair all ratted and her eyeliner caked on, telling Seaton, "Sandy Shaw said she shot Cotton Kelly between the eyes, slit his throat and blew up his car with dynamite."

That was a big lie, and I was so angry I jumped up from my chair and yelled, "You lying ass bitch."

That didn't go over well with the judge. He tore into me and told me to sit down and shut up.

At my actual trial, Rohay asked Stacy on cross about our fight. She denied we even had one and said she turned me in "to do the right thing." Rohay asked if she knew Cotton had been shot in the side of the face and neck, not between the eyes, and she just shrugged. Right then, he should have introduced the coroner's report into evidence, proving Cotton was never shot between the eyes and his throat wasn't slit. He could have also called someone from the nursing home to prove Cotton's car was found intact. Rohay had a copy of the coroner's report, and I had seen it. It proved Troy had shot Cotton five times in the side of the face, and then the fatal shot was in the neck.

Stacy also claimed I told her how Troy, Billy, and I had set Cotton up because we needed money. And that I came up with the elaborate plan to lure him to the desert to rob him. Truth is, I never mentioned a thing about that shooting to her or to anybody but Dave Fletcher and my brother Shane. Dave had taken her out there, I think a day after the killing, and told her the details she told police—except for the throat slitting, the shot between the eyes, and the car dynamiting yarn.

As Stacy left the courtroom, she leered at me as if to say, "I got my revenge on you, bitch!"

She sure as hell had.

The bruises I put on her head were gone in a week, but my wounds from her perjured testimony would last decades.

Day Two

Dave Fletcher took the stand. I didn't think he was on my side any longer, even though three months earlier, he had testified for me at the prelim. He had refuted all the lies Stacy told about me, said I never bragged about the killing like she claimed, or said I'd taken part in it; only that I considered myself a witness and was conflicted about going to the cops. He then testified he had called Stacy the night before and she was crying because she lied about me in her testimony. He was in the middle of saying how he was on an extension line at my house when Billy called and threatened me.

At that point, Seaton had stood up and asked for a recess, and the judge granted it. When Dave never got back on the stand to finish his testimony at my prelim, I was sure something was fishy.

Then, when he was sworn in at my trial, Seaton said to him, "I understand you want to change your testimony from the preliminary hearing, Mr. Fletcher." Dave hung his head and said, "Yes." He wouldn't look at me.

His testimony ripped through the truth like a cyclone. He had been my friend, and he knew the truth. I had no idea why he had turned on me and lied on the stand.

He told the court I was laughing and joking about the murder, not at all remorseful like he'd said during my prelim. He said I actually bragged about firing one of the shots.

I put my head in my hands in disbelief. He had no bone to pick with me that I knew of, and we had had no beef. It made no sense for him to lie about me. I knew Seaton had got to him. I just didn't know how.

On cross, Rohay went at him hard and asked him which time he was lying—at my prelim or today? Dave stuck to what he'd just told the jury: "I wasn't telling the truth at the preliminary," he said. "I was just trying to protect Sandy. But now I realize that was wrong."

Dave's testimony was extremely damaging. When he left the courtroom and breezed past my table, he looked the other way. He wouldn't even glance at me.

It would take more than twenty years for him to finally tell me and the world why he lied to help convict me.

Every day of the trial, guards took me back and forth to the jail. In my cell that night after Dave testified, I realized things were going bad for me. But I was still naïve enough to believe in the justice system, that the jury would realize I hadn't killed anybody, that I was just trying to get a friend to scare off a pedophile. I had faith Rohay was a smart man and surely had some expert witnesses he was going to spring on the court to save me. I thought he would pull a rabbit out of his hat. Like Perry Mason in the TV shows.

I was that young, that foolish, that wrong.

Day Three

I almost fell out of my chair when I heard Seaton announce, "The State calls Jessica B. Mallin."

Jessica? Whoa. Hold on. Testifying for the prosecution? *Against* me? Why? What could she say to incriminate me? We had been best friends, like sisters. And I hadn't seen or even talked with her in over two years. What did she know about any of this?

Turns out, Seaton didn't want me to get a drop of sympathy from the jury about those murders at her house that night that ruined my life.

Seaton had Jessica recount how we became friends, how close we were, and how long the friendship lasted. He asked her facts about the murders at her home but didn't make her go into detail—just about who died and that she'd lost her mom.

Then he asked when and why our friendship ended, and Jessica said, "After that tragedy at my house that night, I saw her only one more time. She started running with a real tough crowd of lowlifes and I didn't want any part of that."

Seaton asked, "Have you been able to deal with that tragedy? For the most part, to get over even the kind of loss that you can never really completely get over?"

I'm sure he already knew the answer because he would have interviewed her before calling her as a witness. I'm also sure he wanted to send a message to the jury that if a girl who lost her mother could deal with it, why the hell couldn't I?

"Yes, I've dealt with it," she said. "It hasn't been easy, but I've dealt with it. I moved on because I had no other choice."

Maybe that night had got to me more than it got to her. Maybe, like my mom once said, I was overly sensitive. Or maybe Jessica dealt with it better because she had got the kind of counseling her father could afford and we couldn't.

Then came the real stunner. "Miss Mallon," Seaton said, leaning in close, "Having known the defendant as long as you have and as well as you have, considering the direction she went after that incident, do you think Sandy Shaw might be capable of murder."

Rohay jumped up. "Objection! Calls for speculation. That is an *improper* question."

Judge Mendoza: "Overruled."

Rohay: "Exception."

Mendoza: "Noted."

Then the judge told Jessica she could answer the question. Had her answer been an ice pick, it would have stuck six inches into my back.

Seaton repeated the question—did she think I was capable of murder?

Jessica nodded and after a pause said, "Yes, I do." Her answer exploded through the courtroom and yanked all the air from my lungs. I noticed one juror's jaw drop and another scowling at me.

Rohay tried to get her to recant that part of her statement in his cross, but at the same time, Seaton kept finding ways to object to things Rohay was asking and the judge kept overruling. Judge Mendoza was securely in Seaton's corner.

Jessica might just as well have climbed up on a tall building with a high-powered rifle and put a bullet in me. She would go on to earn a degree from Georgetown University, marry a wealthy man and have children. I suppose she was destined and bred for that. Twenty-one years after her testimony in court, she would try to help me by writing to the parole board and stating that the night at her house had probably ruined my life. And later, she would make a generous gesture after I got out. I appreciated her help; it warmed my heart, and I was able to forgive her for what she'd said on the stand at my trial. Nonetheless, the damage she did with that statement was irreparable.

With all this going on, I was having to sleep nights amid that jailhouse clamor and was suffering from anxiety. I didn't get one decent night's sleep that whole week.

On the nights Mom visited me after each trial day, she shared the local newspapers with me, and we talked about how much of a zoo this trial was. Her friends were saying what their kids were hearing in the hallways. It was like a kids' game of "Telephone": You start with a true story, and by the time it goes around the room, the story in no way resembles the original. I suppose there were fifty versions of it making the rounds in the high school hallways. And not one of them was true.

All over the city, people gabbed about this crime. Mom was in a grocery store and heard two biddies in the cereal aisle yakking. "Can you believe that little Shaw girl and those boys just *assassinated* that young man?"

"Right between the eyes," the other woman growled." What kind of family raises a goddam kid like her?"

Mom wanted to slap the shit out of both of them, but she just pushed her cart past as fast as she could to get out of there. Meantime, she was doing all she could to give me hope. "It'll be okay, honey. You'll see. Mr. Rohay is a good lawyer. He will figure it out. The jury will believe your story."

If I'd had a real estate case, Ralph Rohay would have no doubt figured it out, probably won it for me. His heart was in the right place and he was trying, but he wasn't about to jump the learning curve of a felony murder case anytime *ever*. He was dog-paddling in the deep end and I was the one drowning.

Day Four

Stacy Buhman was like my personal Freddie Kruger: She was everywhere among my troubles and just wouldn't go away. In fact, jailhouse snitch Thomas Varela, who falsely testified against me on day four, was someone I'd briefly met through Stacy. She had asked me to go to the county jail with her one day to visit some guy she was sweet on, and I went because I had a friend named Mike who was in there for some petty thing. And while talking to Mike, we met another friend of hers, Thomas Varela. He complained he had no money in his commissary for snacks and smokes. I felt sorry for him and got thirty bucks from Mom and gave it to his brother to put in his commissary. That was the last I saw of him until my trial.

I had known Thomas only by his rep from the streets but had never met him prior to 1986. He was twenty-one and in jail for several credit card fraud and theft charges. Because he had been on probation when he was arrested, he was being held without bail.

He evidently saw one of the newspaper stories about Cotton's murder, and since he had met me the one time, he decided to use me to get a reduced sentence.

While I was being held in County, news came to me over the gossip wire: Thomas planned to testify against me as a snitch, even though he had *nothing* to snitch about. It was easier for him to do that because we both had the same prosecutor.

When I heard the rumor, my fifteen-year-old self wrote him a nasty letter from my jail cell, calling him every foul, rotten, horrible name I could conjure up. I cussed him up one side and down the other, called him a miserable piece of dog shit, a motherfucker, and a cocksucker. Seaton would find a way to use that letter against me.

Thomas took the stand wearing a suit and tie, looking more like Lord Fauntleroy than the habitual criminal he was. He was medium height, medium build, with long black hair. He wasn't anyone I'd ever go out with, although both he and Seaton would claim differently. Thomas' initial lie, I'm sure at Seaton's urging, was that I had a crush on him. "She said she'd do anything for me," Thomas said, looking at the jury. "She said she'd even kill for me if it came to that."

The jury gasped at that one, and I did, too. It came way out of the left field bleachers, and I wanted to throw a shoe at the son of a bitch. Sweet on him? In the words of Moon Unit Zappa, "Gag me with a spoon."

Then came the truly damning part of his testimony.

"Yes," he told the court. "She came to see me the *very* night of that murder. Right after the murder. Gave me three hundred bucks. I asked her where she got that money."

Seaton turned slowly to look at the jury as he asked Thomas, "And where did she say she got that much money?"

Thomas claimed that, at the jail the night of the murder, I had pointed my finger like it was a pistol and clicked my thumb like I was firing it. He demonstrated that for the jury.

Then Seaton said, "Ladies and gentlemen of the jury. Sandy Shaw had told this witness she would do anything, even kill for him. That's the type of twisted person she is. Mr. Varela was trying to raise money to make bail and she found a way to help get it for him—by robbing and killing James Kelly."

Thomas' testimony was incriminating, but if my attorney had done his homework, he might have shredded him on cross. First, Thomas' story about me visiting him in jail the night of the murder couldn't have been true. It was closing in on 8:30 p.m. when Troy and Billy dropped me off at home. I had no car, no driver's license, and even if I'd had a car, I lived probably a thirty-minute car ride from the county jail.

It would have taken nearly an hour to get there by bus. The county jail back then—the same as today—closed its doors to visitors at 9:00 p.m. So, even if I had found a ride, the jail would've been closed by the time I could have got there.

And here's the kicker: minors are not now and were not then allowed to visit inmates in the county jail without an adult present. The one time I went to the jail with Stacy, we had a grown-up with us. They wouldn't have let me in to visit him, even if I had miraculously made it there before it closed.

Seaton suggested I had robbed Cotton to get money to help Thomas make bail. But Thomas was arrested on something like fifteen counts of theft and fraud. His bail was originally set at one hundred forty thousand dollars; so, it would have taken 10 percent cash money—which is fourteen thousand dollars—to bail him out. Three hundred bucks wouldn't have put a pimple of a dent in it.

But even if I had had fourteen thousand dollars, I couldn't have bailed him out, and Seaton knew that. Thomas was on probation when he got arrested. And because of that, his bond was immediately revoked. He was being held without bail. So it wouldn't have mattered if I'd robbed the US Mint and brought a truck full of gold. He wouldn't have been able to bond out.

And here is the smoking gun between Dan Seaton and Thomas Varela. Even though Thomas was being held without bail, two weeks before he testified against me, the very day he cut his deal with Seaton, he was out on the street, having been released on his own recognizance. What are the odds Seaton didn't have his hand in that?

Just before my 2007 parole hearing, a journalist friend tracked Thomas down by phone and interviewed him for more than an hour, asking him to come forward and sign an affidavit about his testimony at my trial. Thomas' first question was a telling, "What's the statute of limitations on perjury?"

Then he said he was scared Seaton would find a way to pin some crime on him if he told the truth in an affidavit. He would not sign an affidavit but promised to write a letter to the parole board on my behalf and tell the whole truth. He told my friend, "I knew she didn't kill anybody because in county jail, Troy told me the whole story. I knew she was a bystander. She had been at the jail with some girl, months before that murder happened and not long after I'd been arrested. She gave my brother a little bit of money for my commissary. That was all the money she ever gave me and it was the only time I ever saw her till I testified for Seaton at her murder trial."

I don't know one way or the other if Thomas ever wrote that letter to the parole board. He wasn't a man of sterling character, so my guess is no.

My trial would last one more day, and I would take the stand in my own defense, hoping the jury would see I wasn't the monster Seaton made me out to be.

Day Five

The final day of my trial, I was sure if the jury heard my side, from me, they would believe me. They would let me go home and have another chance at a decent life.

Mom brought me a really nice, conservative, dark blue dress for that last day. I wore no makeup. The weather outside was warm, and the courtroom felt stuffy and hot.

Rohay asked if I was ready to take the stand. I said yes, but was nervous and breathing fast, but I honestly wasn't scared. I had the truth on my side. I wanted to tell my story and was naïve enough to think truth always wins out.

In the witness chair, my throat quickly got dry, and I asked the judge for some water. A bailiff brought me a pitcher of water and a glass.

Rohay questioned me first and went over the timeline of my story, asked me how I'd met Cotton and when the stalking started, and so on. I testified how Mom had gone to the cops and they said they couldn't help us unless Cotton hurt me. Then I bared my soul about everything that happened that night of the murder and what occurred in the days after, up to the time I got arrested.

Rohay asked, "Did you ever take kids out to see the victim's body?"

"Only David Fletcher. Nobody else. I asked him for a ride out there because I thought maybe I dreamed it all."

He asked me why I thought I could dream such a thing and think it was real and I recounted my "daymares" resulting from the murders at Jessica's. I don't think the jury knew what I was talking about.

When he had me recount that night at Rancho Circle, I finally read a little sympathy on some jurors' faces, and my spirits rose.

Now it was Seaton's turn. He cleared his throat and moved toward the witness stand very deliberately. I noticed beads of sweat above his upper lip.

He suggested I first met Cotton while I was shooting craps in Circus-Circus.

I said, "That is a lie you made up."

Then he asked, "Did you conspire with Troy Michael Kell and William Charles Merritt to lure James Kelly into the desert where Kell and Merritt lay in wait to rob him, at which time the robbery went bad, and Troy Kell murdered him in cold blood."

"No!" I answered firmly. "That never happened. You know it didn't."

I had been trying to figure Seaton out every day of the trial. One day later it would hit me—he wanted to win a sensational case and see his name and face plastered all over the news. The bastard had an ego that could barely fit in that courtroom.

He finally brought up the letter I wrote to Thomas from jail.

"When you found out the man you had a crush on—"

"I didn't have a crush on that creep. I found out from Thomas' cellmate he planned to lie about me in court, so you'd cut him a deal. I *never* had a crush on him. I gave his brother thirty dollars to add into his commissary, and that was weeks before Cotton was killed. I never had any interactions with him before *or* after that day."

Seaton turned and walked slowly back to his prosecutor's table, grabbed a sheet of paper, and walked back to the witness stand. He looked at me, then to the jury. "I have that letter in my hand right now, the one you wrote to Thomas Varela." He held out that letter like he wanted me to take it, his Adam's apple pulsing. "I want you to read this aloud for the court, so they—"

"Objection, your honor." Rohay had a copy of the letter and interrupted. "That letter contains no evidence, no admission of guilt. It has absolutely *nothing* to do with this case."

Seaton turned toward the judge. "To the contrary, your honor. It speaks to the defendant's state of mind, her true character."

The judge pondered and said, "Objection overruled. You may have her read it, Mr. Seaton, if it has relevance."

"It has relevance," Seaton promised.

"I don't want to read that out loud," I protested.

Judge Mendoza said, "I'm ordering you to read it, Miss Shaw."

I wanted to say to Mendoza, "You're in cahoots with the fucking prosecutor."

But I went ahead and read it aloud. I had called Thomas every dirty name I could think of or had ever heard my mom, dad, uncles, grandpa, or anybody else ever say. I sat there trying to come off ladylike saying words like "motherfucker" and "dirty lying cocksucker." I could tell by the jury's faces that letter disgusted them.

After I read it, Seaton took it back from me, held it up, and waved it around in the direction of the jury box. "Ladies and gentlemen of the jury, this is a young woman filled with anger and rage. The kind of rage that led to murder."

I shouted, "You're trying to make people think I'm a monster."

Seaton smirked. He'd pushed the right button. He turned to the jury again. "Pay close attention to these outbursts. They come from a heartless, cold-blooded killer."

And so his cross ended. I was hoping Rohay, on redirect, would allow me to explain why I was so upset and how I didn't normally blow up like that. But he didn't.

It was clear now why Seaton had shadowed me and baited me during those recesses. He hoped I would explode on the stand and the jury would think I was a maniac. I'm sure I didn't disappoint him.

Seaton and Rohay rested their cases and got ready for their summations. Seaton's wind-up.

This was all old hat to Seaton, as he faced the jury and spoke, "Let's do a hypothetical here. Sandy Shaw and Troy Kell, and Billy Merritt. They decide that they want to get some money and Sandy tells them, 'I know where we can get some money. This guy Cotton has got some. He's in town once in a while. He's here now and he just told me he's got fourteen hundred dollars. The way we can get it is we'll take him out in the desert, we'll beat him up, and we'll rob him.'"

He paused and fixed the knot in his tie. "Let's further assume—I'm going to give Sandy Shaw the best of it right here—Sandy, at that moment, says, 'Now wait a minute. You guys listen, we'll do that but no killing. I forbid it.' . . . Everybody says, 'Okay.'"

Seaton wheeled around and glared at me, then turned back to the jury. "Troy sneaks the gun along. And they get out there, and she goes out to the bathroom so they can get him in a position where they're going to take his money. All of a sudden, out of the clear blue sky, without any acquiescence at all on the part of Billy or Sandy Shaw, Troy Kell pulls out the gun and shoots James Cotton Kelly and kills him. Sandy Shaw is guilty of first-degree murder under those circumstances. There is no other conceivable decision that you can come to under the set of facts I just gave you."

There, he had done it—called his hypothetical "facts."

He'd used a fictitious premise that we all needed money and conspired to rob Cotton. He must have known if we didn't conspire to rob Cotton, which there wasn't, his hypothetical that I was guilty of murder was in the drain.

He explained my charge of conspiracy as "an agreement to commit a dangerous felony," yet he knew from talking to Billy that none of us had agreed to commit a "dangerous felony."

But Seaton had cleverly romanced the jury into accepting his hypothetical as facts.

Illegal Jury Instructions

Rohay's summation leaned on facts, but he didn't counter punch Seaton's emotional tactics. After the summations, the judge gave the jury instructions, telling them to consider only the direct evidence and ordering them to the jury room to deliberate and reach a verdict. But just before they left the courtroom to discuss the case, Judge Mendoza told them, "People who are fifteen years of age at the time of the submission of the offense of murder are to be treated as adults. However, they may not be tried as adults for the offenses of robbery and conspiracy. Even though Sandy Marie Shaw has not been charged with the offenses of robbery and conspiracy, you can still consider her participation in those offenses."

Those jury instructions were illegal, but getting a Pardons Board to one-day review those instructions would prove to be a steep hill to climb.

The Verdict

Guards took me back to jail to wait for the verdict. My stomach was all knotted up, and I chain-smoked and drank one soda after another. I mumbled several prayers, but God had either quit paying attention to me or was asleep at the wheel.

At two-thirty in the morning, Friday, February thirteenth, guards came to my cell and said the jury had reached a verdict. My knees wobbled as they took me back to the courtroom. The jurors had deliberated barely two hours, and I didn't know if that was a good sign or a bad one. I asked Rohay, and he said, "It could be either."

I sat at the defense table, squirming until the judge ordered, "All rise." The jury filed back into the courtroom from a side door. Not one of them looked at me.

Mom was never called to testify, and now she was in the courtroom sitting with my grandparents. Grandma Marie had hold of Mom's hand as Judge Mendoza ordered me to stand. The jury foreperson was a scrawny, fiftyish lady wearing granny glasses. She removed her glasses as my heart pounded against my chest. Rohay rested his hand lightly on my shoulder.

"How do you find on count one, capital murder in the first degree?" asked Judge Mendoza.

"Guilty," she said. The word cut through my heart as Mom's ear-piercing scream engulfed the room and she yelled, "*No! No! No!*"

"How do you find as to count two, use of a deadly weapon, a felony, in the commission of a crime?" said the judge. My feet felt numb, like they weren't there anymore.

The moment she barked out, "Guilty," several reporters scrambled out of the courtroom to file their stories, nearly knocking each other down in their rush to get out of there.

I barely heard Rohay say in my ear, "Don't worry, We'll appeal. We have grounds for an appeal."

It was all so surreal.

The Sentencing

Judge Mendoza would sentence me illegally, but at the time, I didn't know the law, and if Rohay did, he didn't object. My life without parole sentences were illegal because I was fifteen at the time of the crime, and Nevada law said no one under the age sixteen at the time of the crime could be sentenced to life without parole. The State's reasoning is that someone that age can be rehabilitated.

When you are tried for first-degree murder and you are found guilty, the next step is a penalty phase where mitigating circumstances are introduced and each side argues why the sentence should be higher or lower. Once this happens, a sentencing hearing is scheduled forty-five days later. Also, it is mandatory that everyone convicted of a crime is to have a PSI report (pre-sentencing investigation) done. I never had one.

In the predawn hour, only a few people were in the courtroom—a handful of reporters, a couple of Cotton's relatives, my mom, my grandparents, Mike Flanery, Rohay, and Seaton. Judge Mendoza ordered me to stand. He told me the crime I had committed was heinous and read my sentences.

"As to count one, capital murder, I sentence you to life without the possibility of parole. As to count two, use of a deadly weapon in the commission of a crime, robbery, I sentence you to life without the possibility of parole." He looked at me dispassionately. "Both sentences are to be served consecutively, not concurrently."

Did I hear him correctly? The rest of my life? No parole?

I had to steady myself on the edge of the defense table. They cuffed me, put me in leg chains, and led me shuffling out of the courtroom to the hallway to the jail. I looked back one last time at my weeping mother.

Holy Christ, the rest of my life in a prison. I'd just had my sixteenth birthday three weeks before, and it seemed my life was over. I would just rot in prison.

After sentencing, Seaton told the press that Cotton met his fate on September 29th and it was only right that I met mine on Friday the thirteenth.

Figure 1 *Sandy Shaw, childhood.*

Figure 2 *Sandy dancing with her grandfather.*

Figure 3 *Sandy as a cheerleader.*

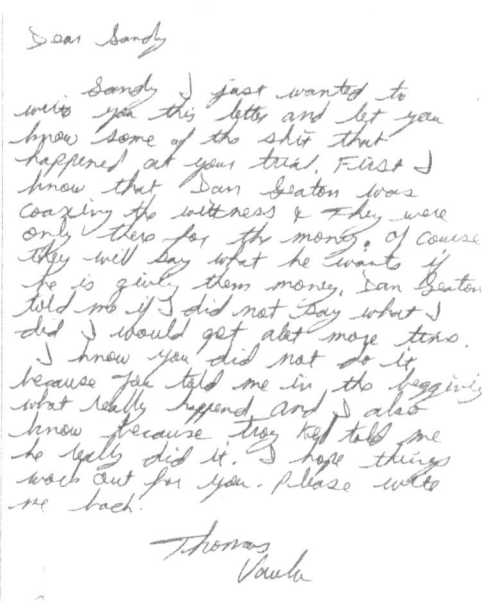

Figure 4 *Apology letter to Sandy from Thomas Varela, one of the witnesses that the prosecutor intimidated into lying about Sandy on the stand to get her convicted.*

Figure 5 *Sandy and Cindy.*

Figure 6 *Sandy c. 1987.*

Figure 7 *Sandy and Connie.*

Figure 8 *Sandy, Connie, and Marie.*

Figure 9 *Sandy, college graduation.*

Figure 10 *Sandy, Dad, and Mike, c. 1997.*

Figure 11 *Sandy, brother Shane, niece Oceania, in prison, c. 1998.*

AFFIDAVIT OF TROY MICHAEL KELL

I, Troy Michael Kell, having been first duly sworn upon my oath, do state the following to be true and correct:

1. Sandy Shaw and myself were convicted of the same homicide in Las Vegas Nevada.

2. Sandy Shaw had no prior knowledge of a weapon being in my possession nor did she have any prior knowledge that a gun was in the automobile or that a gun was to be used or displayed.

3. Sandy Shaw had no knowledge that I intended to kill the victim.

Dated this 26th day of May, 1998.

TROY MICHAEL KELL
Affiant

STATE OF UTAH)
:ss
County of Salt Lake)

SUBSCRIBED AND SWORN TO before me this 26th day of May, 1998.

NOTARY PUBLIC
Residing at: Salt Lake

My Commission Expires:

4-15-2001

NOTARY PUBLIC
STATE OF UTAH
My Commission Expires
April 15, 2001
RODGER WILLIAMS
14400 South Pony Express Rd
Draper, Utah 84020

EXHIBIT "10"

Figure 12 *Affidavit from Troy Kell, 1998, stating that Sandy never handled the gun he used to kill the victim and never knew he had it, let alone that he was going to use it that night.*

Las Vegas Metropolitan Police
Department
[address illegible]
Las Vegas, Nevada 89101
[phone illegible]

Atty. copy

JERRY
KELLER,
Sheriff

Nevada Board of Pardons
1445 Hot Springs Rd S# 108-B
Carson City Nv 89711

MAY 20 2002

Re: Sandy Marie Shaw NDOC# 24126

Dear Members,

This letter is in response to the attached notice requesting pardon or immediate release of this inmate.

Sandy Shaw was part of what the media referred to as the "Show and Tell Murder" and her involvement in this crime is exactly as she describes in her letter for clemency.

This agency has no interest in denying her commutation of sentence.

Respectfully Yours,

David F. Hatch

MAY 23 2002
PAROLE BOARD

Figure 13 *2002 letter to the Nevada Board of Pardons by David Hatch, Las Vegas PD homicide detective, who had custody of Sandy's case for many years, recommending Sandy's sentence be commuted.*

Figure 14 *Sandy with niece Oceania, c. 2004, Las Vegas women's prison.*

Figure 15 *Sandy on computers in prison.*

Figure 16 *Inmate Sandy Shaw and attorney Bill Terry, at a pardons hearing in Carson City, Nevada, c. 2004. Photo © 2004 by Nevada News Group. Reprinted with permission.*

Figure 17 *Day after parole, Flemming's, Las Vegas.*

Figure 18 *Pups on parole program.*

Figure 19 *Interviews on KLAS, May 5, 2008.*

Figure 20 *Sandy's half-brother Christopher, Sandy, Sandy's dad, Sandy's step-sister Candy, and Sandy's brother Shane (left to right).*

Figure 21 *Sandy's sisters Nicole and Leah with Sandy (left to right).*

39

On Hold

I feared prison for a lot of reasons. I'd heard stories about predators. I wondered, could I protect myself? Despite my concerns, I wanted out of that smelly, bug-infested jail. Prison food had to be better, and at least I'd have an exercise yard.

But I wouldn't be leaving anytime soon because Seaton arranged a hold on me. He hoped I'd testify against Troy and had the nerve to ask me. He sat across from me in the visitor's room, suddenly all buddy-buddy. This is a man who told the press he would have asked for the death penalty for me but was afraid the jury wouldn't go along because I was so young. Now the little prick wanted a favor.

When he asked me that, if my sneer had been a rope, he would have been dangling from a cottonwood tree. "You got to be the most egotistical turd I've ever met," I told him. "You lied in court to put me in prison the rest of my life. You branded me the Show and Tell Killer when you knew better, and you got witnesses to lie to convict me. And now you want a *favor*? File that one under fat chance." I pointed my finger in his face. "If there's a Hell, you're gonna fry in it."

But he was persistent and kept asking me. At one point he said, "Where are your morals?" I could not believe that man would bring up morals. "*My* morals! Where the hell are *your* morals? I'm not gonna do you any favors, you miserable little rat. Besides, I don't want to go to prison branded a snitch."

Still, he kept me on hold for two months, till Troy's trial ended with a conviction the same as mine, "life without."

To say most defense attorneys who had gone up against Seaton disliked him was an understatement. Two years earlier, Seaton prosecuted teenagers Dale Flanagan and Randy Moore for murdering Flanagan's grandparents for the inheritance. They got a death sentence.

The state Supreme Court overturned their convictions and ordered a new trial, mostly because of Seaton's misconduct. That included inflaming the jury by falsely telling them Flanagan and Moore were devil worshipers. This was something Seaton made up. He had lied to get a conviction.

Seaton had a wall weaving in his office made up of replicas of little electric chairs, one for each death penalty conviction he'd got, and he also had a hangman's noose displayed on his wall. Jesus H.—what kind of person does that?

After my verdict, I got moved from the ninth floor to the second floor, which housed solitary confinement (the "Hole"). Since those women were locked up all but one hour daily, I got to come out for eight hours daily. My window looked out onto the parking lot and the street, so I got to watch the bums hanging around out there. It was better than watching TV. One guy with a beard and a long, dirty white robe was out there every day, looking like Jesus, looking like he'd just climbed down off a crucifix.

I was there a couple days when Sheila Summers was moved to the room next to mine. At thirty-two, she was twice my age and had been on death row. She got convicted of a murder because of a bizarre deathbed suicide confession of a woman who was likely the real killer. Sheila won her appeal, and she was sent down to the county jail to either get a new trial or take a plea deal.

We chatted a lot through the vent and became cordial. She had grown up in Iowa and had two daughters by a biker she was still in love with. Sheila was the only human company I'd had in six months.

Every day, we would watch the bums and comment on their goings-on. We joked a lot; she was witty and I sure needed some laughs. She was interesting, college-educated, smart, and funny, and she gave me a short course about prison life.

She ended up taking the deal, pleading guilty, and was hoping to get a ten-year to life sentence so she could get a parole hearing. On appeal, the jury changed her sentence from death to life with the possibility of parole, but good ol' Judge Mendoza intervened and upgraded it to life without. Sheila was relieved that at least they couldn't kill her now. She would be out among the general population in the Carson City prison and told me to look her up once I got there. She would show me the ropes on how to not only stay safe in there, but sane.

Mom visited me regularly, still shook up about me going to prison. She promised to find an able lawyer for an appeal. Mom never gave up fighting for me, and same goes for my brother Shane. Their love and loyalty over the years helped sustain me.

After I'd been on the second floor a month, I started getting notes from a creepy woman named Cindi Smith. She had been convicted of felony DUI with a death involved and was about to go to prison for it. She'd got blotto and drove through the wall of a house. The mom was doing dishes, and the window faced the backyard. Her fourteen-year-old son was cleaning the pool, and Cindi's speeding car went right through the house, over the pool, killing the boy as the mom watched. She was sentenced to fourteen years in prison.

She started kiting me the notes—passing them along one inmate to another and finally under my door. They were sickening love notes, and I freaked. The first one said, "Whenever I see you, my heart skips a beat. I just must have you, darling." I let her know I wasn't into that stuff, that I was straight. I told her to leave me the fuck alone. But her notes kept coming.

I don't know how she pulled it off, but she got me moved to a cell right next to hers. Then she would gawk at me and talk to me through the connecting vent at all hours, day and night, every day. I pleaded to the jailers to move me, but they said it wasn't their problem. That predator hounded me, day and night.

Troy's trial ended in late March. Seaton wanted the death penalty, but the jury said no, mostly because he was just eighteen.

Up to the time of his trial, Troy was delusional, convinced he would beat the rap. In county jail, when we talked through the toilets, he said he planned to buy a motorcycle and, if I got convicted, he would ride up to every week to visit me in Carson City.

Billy was sent to the prison in southern Nevada and was beat up a few times because he had snitched on Troy. He told other cons up there it was me and Troy who had snitched on him, but those hard-skinned bad asses didn't buy it.

When April rolled around, I was convinced I wouldn't be in prison long; I was sure some crusading lawyer or judge in shining armor would rescue me.

I'd been better off believing the Tooth Fairy would get me out.

40

Welcome to the Rest of Your Life

April 9, 1987, 10:00 p.m.

I was on the phone with Mom when a jailer barked at me, "Get off the phone, Shaw. They're moving you now!"

He said to roll my stuff up. Everything that was considered mine now fit into a rolled-up blanket. Soon after, I was in an NDOC van headed for Carson City to the Nevada Women's Correctional Center to start serving my life sentence.

After a stop where we picked up more inmates, I was the only female inmate in the crowded van with a dozen males. All of them were going to the Nevada State Prison, adjacent to the women's prison. They were already incarcerated up there and had been in the county jail in Vegas for court hearings. I was afraid but buried my fear. I wasn't going to let anybody think they could mess with me or that I could be their bitch.

We were chained around our waists, wrists, and feet. We hadn't gone far before some greasy-haired jackass in the seat behind reached around and started groping me. I would slap his hands and push them away, and he would stop for a while, but every time I would lay my head back on the seat-rest and shut my eyes, he would start on me again. If the van driver and the armed guard heard the commotion, they didn't give a shit. It confounded me to be fastened to those chains and not be able to protect myself other than to block his hands like a boxer trapped in the corner.

Finally, he asked if the chains around my waist went through my belt loops.

By this time, an inmate named Jimmy, in the seat directly across the aisle from me, who'd been at the county jail with me, noticed what was going on. "Hey, what the hell you trying to do, *fella*?"

The inmate messing with me said, nonchalantly, "I was tryin' to get her chains loose so I could try to fuck her."

Jimmy scowled. "Listen, mother*fucker*. You lay another hand on the kid, when we get to the joint, I'll find you in the yard and kick your ass till your ears ring. Then I'll shank you from your belly button to your asshole. And *don't* think I won't."

Jimmy was a slim but tall, rough-looking dude with a patch over one eye and a deep baritone voice.

The groper knew Jimmy was serious and stopped and sat back like a little boy scolded by a gruff teacher.

"Thanks," I said, breathing relief.

"Think nothing of it, little sister. I don't tolerate fuckers like him or shit like that."

Jimmy was doing life without. Like Sheila Summers, he had been on death row but had got his sentence reduced. He had been in prison a really long time and got to telling me about it as we headed north on our long trip.

He related how he lost his eye, and it was crazy. He'd been in the middle of a prison riot with a lot of Blacks fighting outnumbered whites who were getting murdered. He figured somebody would get him, too, so to get to medical, he popped his own eyeball out of the socket with a damn *pencil*. Imagine doing that.

He'd asked me, "You look mighty young to be goin' into an adult prison. How old are you?"

"Just turned sixteen," I told him.

"Hell, you look younger. You're just a kid. What got ya in the slammer?"

"Murder and a weapons charge."

"Jesus. A little badass. What's the stretch?"

"Life without."

He winced. "Damn. At your age? That don't seem right"

"Yeah, but I don't think I'll be there long."

"Oh? And why's that?"

"Because I'm *innocent*."

He shook his head. "Aren't we all, little darlin', aren't we all. But just the same, you best gear up for the long run. Case the Lone Ranger's horse throws a shoe, and he don't get here in time."

The heater in the van was on the fritz, and it got colder as we went up in elevation from Las Vegas, at two-thousand feet, to Carson City, at the base of the Sierra Nevada Mountains, at forty-six-hundred feet. We didn't ride far till the headlights illuminated snow on the ground, several inches in some places just off the road, puffed up like ice cream cones. Lucky for us, there was a lot of body heat in that van.

Jimmy advised me how to take care of myself in prison. "Kid your age, those bull dikes are gonna be on you. Don't do no good to go tell the guards or the warden, 'cause they don't care what goes on in there. They care about keepin' order. They figure that's your world, not theirs. And then you'd be labeled a snitch."

"Yeah, well, then what can I do?"

"Fight. Can you handle yourself in a melee?"

"If they're my size, I can."

"Well, hell, some of 'em are gonna be bigger 'n' you, but you gotta fight 'em anyhow."

"Yeah, what if they gang up on me?"

"Make yourself a shank, for starters. It's easy to get razor blades in there. You just ask around. Then you melt one with a cigarette lighter into a toothbrush, on top of where the brush part is, and you file it down on the concrete. Maybe wrap the handle with a lot of duct tape."

"Jesus. That's some scary shit."

He shrugged. "It's a scary place. Another good weapon is a bar of soap in a pillowcase or a sock. You twist it up and tie a knot in it, see, and you got you one badass weapon, anybody fools with you. Better than a billy club."

I was amazed how much he knew about protecting himself, and I soaked it in like a sponge.

"Another thing, you bust you a hand mirror, get a shard of glass, make a handle for it, and you got a lethal knife."

"Well, I guess I'll keep all that in my head. I sure hope it never comes to that."

"I hope it don't, too. But you gotta always be ready. Keep your head on a swivel. Watch every fucker at all times."

The ride would take eight hours, and we all got one sack lunch with one sandwich wrapped in waxed paper, one apple, and one bottle of water.

The sun popped up over the Sierra Nevadas when we finally made it to Carson City. The van pulled up to this big, medieval-looking, scary-ass place with tons of razor wire and huge, concrete gun towers with guards packing high-powered rifles with scopes. They were all glaring down at us like assassins. My eyes bugged out. "*Hol*-y shit. Is this where I'm going?"

Jimmy laughed. "Naw, this is where *we're* goin'. You, you're goin' to that elementary school up the hill."

They let all the men out, and I thanked Jimmy for what he did for me and all his advice. I wished him luck.

He said, "Keep your head on that swivel, little sister. You're goin' into a jungle. Trust nobody."

Then they drove me a short way up the hill to the women's prison. It was by no means daunting, not as much high fence as the men's, no gun towers, and not nearly as much razor wire, but enough to slice you up really bad if you tried to climb over those fences.

It was really cold when I got out of the van and I slipped on a patch of ice. I fell hard and cut my ankle badly on the shackle. Blood ran down into my sock, and I thought, *Welcome to the rest of your life, Sandy.*

41

Lockdown in the Fish Tank

It really did resemble an elementary school. The main building was just a one-story sally port (controlled entrance to a prison complex). It was like walking into an ordinary place of business if you didn't know. Several inmates sat around waiting to go to Intake or had just come out. It all seemed benign till I heard one heavy hocked, frizzy-haired, butch-looking inmate say to another one, "I got dibs on that young one."

The hell you do, I thought. I shot her a hard eye and flipped her the finger.

I quickly got the lay of the land. The warden's office was off to the left, separated by two doors and iron bars, and a door on the right led to the Intake facility. Catty-corner to the right, separated by a glass window, was the laundry room, and behind it, two mess halls, and to the left, a guard control bubble right next to a day room. Behind the control bubble was a pay room and a beauty shop, then a hallway of offices with a door leading out to the recreation yard. Culinary, education, and medical were all in that same large building.

Three units housed prisoners. Units 1 and 2 were cell rooms on opposite sides of the recreation area (the "yard"), and Unit 3 was all trailers for minimum-security inmates.

They brought medical to me to patch up my bleeding ankle, which hurt like crazy, then they ushered me to a bus and drove me back down the hill to the men's prison for fingerprinting and mug shots. They issued me prison number 24126. I thought of the concentration camps. Even my mail was addressed to 24126.

They brought me back and locked me in a single cell with a small metal bed and a toilet, no window. They didn't tell me much, except this was Intake (better known as the Fish Tank) and would last for three weeks. I already missed Mom, missed talking to her, missed her support, missed her hugs. I was sixteen, bewildered, alone, and dejected. But I had no choice but get used to it, until such time as some legal mechanism would spring me. Even after everything that went on with my trial, I still believed in the justice system.

They brought me my stuff from the county jail. Going through it, I found a Christmas card Mom had given me in jail. I'd never opened it but wanted to look at it now. It was one of those electronic cards that played Christmas music:

> Away in a manger
> No crib for a bed
> The little Lord Jesus
> Lay down His sweet head
> The stars in the sky
> Look down where He lay
> The little Lord Jesus
> Asleep on the hay

I had barely cried in ages, except once in my cell right after my guilty verdict when I saw Mom and them out in the prison parking lot, going home. But that musical card dug into my heart. I wept till my teardrops soaked the bed. I must have cried an hour 'til I cried myself to sleep. But when I woke, my emotions were numb once more.

The Intake section had once housed the now-vacated women's death row unit. The rooms were dark, cold, depressing, and ratty-looking, each with a few single beds and some double bunk beds, a sink and one toilet, where women once waited unpleasantly to die.

The room I was in had small slats covered over with chicken wire that served as a fake window. I could look out into the dreary hallway or at the people in a room across the hall.

First day, they took me to the medical center for a complete physical. They did blood work, checked my blood pressure, heart rate, and just about everything else. Day two, I got assigned a case worker. Every inmate gets one.

They operated like social workers inside the prison. They developed training programs for inmates, evaluated their progress toward parole, recorded their behavioral history and serve as liaisons with the warden and other agencies.

In Intake, you were classified as minimal security, medium security, or closed custody. Since I was in for murder, so I was closed custody and was watched more carefully than others.

Time in prison went by very slowly, and time in the tank went even slower. Every hour felt like a day. It would be easy to fall into a routine, turn into a zombie, and go through the motions, day after day after day after day until you became one of the Walking Dead. I saw several of those types in the prison, dead but they didn't know it yet. I didn't want that, and I thought of ways to fight it. I decided to keep myself upbeat, always put on my makeup, wash my hair, and keep it brushed.

The only good thing about being in the Fish Tank, they let me leave an hour every other day to shower. Soon as I got my phone call list approved, I could make calls for an hour or so after my shower. I ordered writing materials, and they allowed me one book to read a week. It had to last, so I read slowly. I ordered hygiene stuff, like menstrual pads, but they, too, had to last a week. If they didn't last a week, too bad for you.

I'd been cautioned about the violence, and it found me even before I was out of Intake.

42

Breaking Point

A week into Intake process, I got my period. I would get really bad leg cramps when I did, like somebody was beating me on the legs with a ball bat. When I'd been in county jail, those cramps were so bad they called Mom to see if she knew what to do.

Another woman in the tank with me, name of Elaine, in her late twenties, was on the bottom bunk. I was on the top bunk. My legs hung off the side, and she kept poking them and bumping them with her shoulders, like she thought it was funny. It hurt like mad. Jimmy had warned me not to let anyone push me around, and she pushed me beyond my limits when I kept telling her to stop, that it hurt, and she just kept on doing it.

I was already PMSing something awful, then when I told her one last time to stop and she wouldn't, I lost it.

I didn't want to start out a troublemaker, but I knew I was on my own. So I jumped down from the bed and hit her so hard with a right cross I almost came out of my shoes. She fell backward onto her bunk, then jumped up and came at me. I grabbed a metal chair and started beating her with it. She was heavier than me and a few inches taller. But the chair was my equalizer, and I beat her all over that room. When I was done, she was wiping gobs of blood off her face with a towel, and her right eye was already swelling. That chair was demolished—two of the legs were on the floor and one side of the seat was hanging by a bolt.

Shortly, a male guard stuck his head in the door and snapped, "What's the goddam commotion in here?"

"Nothing," she said.

I piped up, "The chair broke when I was getting off the top bunk."

He shrugged and went and got us a new chair.

I was scared she might stab me with a shiv, so I slept uneasy. But she either didn't have a shiv or didn't have the inclination. Next day, after I came back from my shower, we had a third inmate; this one was younger and friendlier, a Latino and recovering druggie in for armed robbery of a convenience store. Not even with a gun but a poker from a fireplace, which was why it was likely a bad idea to rob a place when you're high.

I had no more trouble the rest of my time in Intake, and Elaine and I would later become cordial. But I had learned you can't talk your way through most situations in a prison, so when your philosophy fails, you better punch somebody. After Rancho Circle, I had wanted nothing to do with violence, but it had found me. And now I was in among the savages.

Maybe I was one of them now.

43

What to Do With Me

She was bald, had a bunch of earrings, at least ten nose rings and more tattoos than I'd ever seen on a woman. Her prison nickname was "Lizard."

Lizard's job had been bringing clean linens to Intake, and a few times she'd laced my bundle with candy and other items in my bundle, but I would put it all back out the slat. I didn't want her to think I owed her anything. She would say, "You're going to get me in trouble."

I always answered the same, "I don't care; I don't want anything from you."

Come to find out, my friend Sheila, the one I'd met in county jail, was sending the stuff to me through Lizard, who turned out to be Sheila's friend.

During Intake, word got around there was a new and very young girl about to officially enter the prison. When some inmates found out which window went into my cell, I started hearing catcalls. Then one time I heard someone holler, "Hey, Shaw. Sandy Shaw. That you in there?"

I said, "Yeah, I'm right here."

The voice called out, "You ready to come play with the big girls?"

I tried to sound rough and tough. "I'm ready but I'm not playing."

I was considered "fresh meat" before I was even released out there into the multitudes.

Then one day, some woman in the yard came up to my window and yelled, "Is there a girl up there named Sandy Shaw from Las Vegas?"

I said, "Yeah, that's me. Who wants to know?"

"Sandy, hey, it's Sheila Summers," the voice echoed back. It was the woman who had been my cell neighbor in county jail and there for court on her death penalty appeal. I called back, "Oh, hey, Sheila." So, now I had at least one friend in that prison to look out for me.

After several days, I was summoned to Captain Miles Long's office. At first, I thought, *uh-oh* and wondered if it was because I worked over that crazy bitch who came onto me in the Fish Tank. I was already in trouble, and I had just got there.

"Ms. Shaw," Captain Long wasn't an imposing man—5 feet 11 inches, average build, but he commanded respect among the inmates. "I called you here because, well, I don't know what the hell to do with you."   "Whatta ya mean?"

He shuffled papers, looked down at his desk and back at me. "First off, I got no idea why they sent a girl your age to an adult prison. Good lord, they should've sent you to a juvenile facility till you turned eighteen. I think was pretty stupid on their part, but I don't have any say-so in all that. Fact is, you're here now and I have to figure out what to do with you."

"Do with me, *how*?" I didn't know where this was heading.

"I really don't want to put you in general population, because, well, you're a kid and it could be dangerous. Most inmates get along with each other but there are some nasty eggs roaming around, and you will likely become somebody's prey."

I nodded. "Yeah, I'm already aware of that."

He paused, fussed with more papers, then rested his elbows on the table. "One option is we keep you in isolation for two more years till you're eighteen. You okay with that?"

I wasn't okay with it. For one thing, isolation meant being locked down most of the day. "Look, Captain, I appreciate your concern and all. But I just spent six months isolated in county jail and if you read my record, you might understand why I'm half-crazy from hiding my feelings and hiding from people since I was thirteen. So, you'd be doing me harm keeping me on ice two years. I couldn't take it. You'd have to stick me in a padded room."

I was trying to be polite, but in my head I'm saying, *Fuck off, you think I'm gonna be alone, locked down two years in this joint.*

He let the thought cook a minute. "Okay, okay, I'll put you out there, that's what you want. I'll move you to another cell with a roommate, someone close to your age, then in maybe a week I'll let you out among the hordes. You're gonna have to learn to say no to people. Like *really* say no."

"I'll be fine. I can take care of myself."

"So you think." He eyeballed me and rubbed his chin. "The way life is inside this prison you'll have to do *exactly* that. Take care of your own self. We have only so many guards and they can't watch everybody all the time. You get my drift?"

I nodded to let him know I understood.

As I was leaving with the guard, I glanced back and he was rubbing both temples with his fingertips, like I'd given him a headache. It wasn't the last headache I would give that man.

44

First Day in the Yard

It was May and the weather was glorious. The sun was high in the sky and the mountains still had a touch of snow on the peaks. It would have been much more glorious if the fences weren't there and I wasn't locked in prison.

It looked like a painting framed by razor wire on steel fences. I was in the yard, the first time I'd been outside since I was jailed in October, eight months ago. I was nervous because I didn't know what to expect, but that fresh air was energizing.

When I looked around, I was shocked to see what was going on out here. Inmates could wear their own clothes, and there was this huge gaggle of ex-hookers putting on a fashion show in the yard. And there were inmate judges for the contest. Women pranced around in ruby red high heel shoes and sequin dresses, every color of the rainbow. It was like being at the circus. One woman had about a dozen rings in her nose, four different earrings and more tattoos than a sailor.

I wasn't outside long till Sheila Summers found me. I felt secure having a friend out there, especially the way the manlier women were gawking at me.

Sheila was about 5 feet 8 inches, maybe a 140 pounds, dyed blonde hair, nice enough looking but rough around the edges. Inside her shell, she was an artist, a philosopher, a poet. I tried giving her a little harmless hug when I first spotted her, but she backed off and told me that's against the rules. "You gotta realize you can't do anything humane in here, kid. You can't even give somebody a little hug if they've had a bad day. They'll write you up, take your privileges, maybe even stick you in The Hole."

As I observed cliques and groups out there, Sheila explained prison families.

"Men's prisons got gangs. We got no gangs, see, but we got families. Some are gay, some are just 'gay for the stay' and will go back to their boyfriends once they get out. Some are just social, or maybe they join for protection. Tell you what though, that family shit is *not* for Sheila Summers."

"Not gonna be for me either," I said.

After Sheila had left her native Iowa, she moved to Las Vegas on her own as a teenager. She finished high school and got a college degree in psychology. Sounds like a pretty good start, so how she ended up on death row is a bizarre story she would tell me later.

Being my first day, I was told to go in at a certain time, earlier than everyone else, but I stuck around and watched the hooker parade because it was such a hoot. On my way back inside, a guard intercepted me and said the sergeant wanted to see me. I thought, oh, shit, and I wondered what I'd done. But when I got there, he was holding a bouquet of flowers.

"Someone sent you flowers, Shaw," he said.

What the—? I knew they weren't from Mom or she would have told me. Maybe one of my aunts, but why?

"Who from, sir?"

"A Mrs. Smith?"

"Smith? I don't know any Smiths."

"Everybody knows a Smith," he joked. "That's what the card says. Mrs. Smith." He handed me the flowers, then the card.

It read, "These are on behalf of my daughter, Cindi Smith."

I took a step back. Shit! Cindi Smith. That woman who was after me in the county jail. She was still down there and got her mom to send me flowers. I'd made it clear I wasn't interested. This shit had gone too far. I didn't feel like explaining anything to the sergeant, so I smiled politely, took the flowers, went back to my cell, and tossed them in the trash.

I then wrote her mother and said thank you for the flowers, but I asked her to please tell her daughter to stop. "I'm not attracted to women," I wrote. "I made that clear to your daughter. Please tell her don't pester me. No cards, no flowers, no nothing."

I hoped I'd seen the last of Cindi Smith.

No such luck.

45

Monica

Warden Brenda Burns, whom I met after Intake, was a large woman, tall and on the burly side, but not butch looking. She had dark hair and a kind face and was in her late thirties. I was told she was straight and that was a relief because the last thing I needed was the warden hitting on me.

Warden Burns moved me into a double room with bunk beds and a roommate name of Monica. She was seventeen, pretty, with long, reddish-brown, curly hair. We were about the same size. I called dibs on the top bunk because I didn't like people climbing above my head.

Monica didn't come off as the type who would be in prison for conspiring with a boyfriend to kill her ex over a custody battle for their kid. She seemed nice and mild-mannered. The boyfriend had lain in wait in a closet, and when the ex came to visit, he charged out of there firing a pistol. But it jammed. When the ex ran for the door, the boyfriend grabbed a kitchen knife and chased him down. He stabbed him in the back, but the blade broke off. Luckily for the two of them, the guy lived. And even luckier for Monica, she got off with three years and would get out in just eighteen months.

She and I got along good and I was glad to have somebody my age to talk to after six months of isolation. She evidently went through boyfriends at a high clip and had snared a new one just before she went to prison. He was coming to visit her in a few days, and she wanted to impress him, but she couldn't find anything attractive to wear.

She took a beige outfit of mine out of the closet and held it up. "This would fit me perfect. Can I wear this when my beau comes to visit?" She put on a pouty face. "It would mean so much to me."

"Sure. Do it." I never had a problem sharing my stuff with people.

So, on visitor's day, she got all dolled up, did her hair and looked really smart in that outfit.

A few days later, I saw my outfit back in my closet. But damned if there wasn't a hole right in the crotch of the slacks. I held the slacks up. "What the *hell*. Monica?"

She was reading a magazine on her bunk. "What?"

"There's a hole in the crotch."

She sighed. "I'm so sorry, Sandy. He's a passionate guy and, well, I cut a hole in the pants so we could screw."

I couldn't believe it. I was more stunned than mad. I asked how they got away doing the nasty in that crowded visitor's room.

She looked up from her magazine. "I sat on his lap."

When I stopped laughing, I said, "You need to find a sewing kit." Then I said, "On second thought, keep the outfit. I don't want to wear something somebody else wore when they did the deed."

She smiled. "That's really nice of you. Now I got me a prison fuck outfit."

She had her mom buy me a new outfit and send it to me, so it was all good. Mainly, I admired her ingenuity to steal a few moments of affection in a place that totally forbade it.

46

Wall of Noise, Den of Violence

The Carson City prison was far cleaner than the Clark County Jail, but far noisier and much more dangerous. It was loudest at night when the animals were caged. I lay awake sometimes for hours because I could hear screaming, cussing, and yelling. One night it finally got quiet enough for me to drop off to sleep when a screaming voice woke me from my slumber: "Bitch, I will fry your ass like Sunday's bacon."

It would keep Monica up, too, so we'd talk through it, shoot the breeze, and tell jokes. We'd then find time to take naps in the daytime, which isn't a safe time because your cell doors are unlocked. If somebody is gunning for you, you are an easy mark.

We both marveled at how many fights there were. Unless somebody got hurt really bad, the guards stayed out of it. Some of the more serious fights would be out of view of the security cameras. Inmates called that "catching a corner."

Convicts fight over stealing each other's lovers or stealing each other's stuff; they fight over drugs; they fight over using the telephone; they beat up snitches, they beat up pedophiles, and they beat up people just for looking at them funny. But the majority of fights are over relationships and drugs.

Many inmates are just plain mean and cruel and would do things to sabotage each other for no good reason. I kept my bar of soap in a sock handy and under my mattress. I showed Monica how to make one, and we both stayed vigilant because you never knew when somebody would jump you because they had a bad day or just didn't have anything better to do.

47

Facing a Predator

Except for the woman who came onto me in Intake, I had avoided arguments and fights and kept my head on a swivel in the yard. I went out there daily, soon as it was open, to grab all the clean air I could in that foul-smelling place.

I had just the one cellmate because I was in for murder. Some inmates doing softer time lived eight to ten to a big room. One girl not much older than me was in a room with ten women. She and I were chatting in the yard, and she told me two women in her room had sex right in front of everyone else. She shook her head in disgust. "Every day, and they don't even *care*." She shook her head. "One of my cellmates soiled her underpants and the whole room smells like urine, day and night."

Now that I was in the general population, I had to take showers when others did, and some of those big bulls would stand there and gawk at me the whole time I showered. It was creepy, but I couldn't do anything about it.

Soon, a big, rough-looking woman started coming onto me in the yard. I kept blowing her off, but she was persistent. She was up around 6 feet, in her forties, and had a wispy mustache that made her look even more manly. She was hefty but had enough muscle definition to send the message it wouldn't be wise to mess with her. Her crew of four toadies followed her around like she was Moses going to lead them out of the wilderness.

Sheila said they were a queer prison family. The big woman called herself "Dolly." After looking me over for several days, she sashayed up to me, hands on her hips. "You're the little Shaw girl."

I knew what she was up to. "Yeah, I'm aware of that. So? What's it to you?"

"Ohhhhh," she said, turning to one of her sidekicks. "A spicy one. I like 'em spicy. I wouldn't want a horse didn't buck a little." Two of them in her entourage giggled.

Dolly looked at me. "You need a mom in here, young lady. To keep you safe."

I sucked up some attitude. "Not a chance. I got a mother at home. I don't need one in here."

"Well, we'll see about that." Then she turned and sauntered off, her crew trailing her.

Sheila heard the exchange and warned me. "You steer clear of that big bitch. She's notorious. Do *not* mess with her."

"I get the picture," I said. "I've been trying to avoid her."

But Dolly had her heart set on me and would troll me most every day.

Then one day in the yard, I ran into the girl who'd been in Intake with me, the one who tried to rob the convenience store with a fireplace poker. Her name was Angela, a tall, slim, black-haired Latino in her early twenties and doing five-to-ten. She was pretty, despite some pockmarks on her cheeks. I told her about Dolly bothering me every day. Angela was from the mean streets of Reno, and she didn't hesitate. "You gotta fight her, kid."

"You nuts? She's twice my size."

"Don't matter." Angela lit two cigarettes and handed me one. "You either fight her or you'll be her little bitch. Your choice. She won't stop. She and her posse, they'll jump you in the shower one day and rape you, and it'll be curtains."

I said, "If I fought her, she'd kick my ass from one end of this yard to the other."

"Not if you do it right."

"Do it right? Whattaya mean?"

Angela plopped down on a wooden bench, and I sat next to her. "She's a bully, Shaw. I know bullies. Grew up around 'em. You hurt a bully, they quit. You got to hit her first, though. Sucker punch her."

"Easy to say, not so easy to do."

"Shit. Nothin's easy in here," Angela cracked her knuckles "But I'll show you some tricks."

I shrugged. It was a dumb idea, but I was willing to listen because Dolly wasn't likely to stop hounding me anytime ever.

"My big brother was one hell of a street fighter," Angela explained. She then showed me how to protrude my middle finger's knuckle when I made a fist. "You hit her like that, in the solar plexus, with that knuckle, and *wham*, you'll knock the wind clean out of her. She'll go down when the air goes out, and that's when you start throwin' punches. I guarantee, she'll quit. And that'll be the end of it."

"Ya really think so?"

"I know so. I been there, Shaw."

For the next several days, Angela trained me on the proper delivery of that knuckle punch to the solar plexus until I knew I could hit the target blindfolded. Nonetheless, I still hoped Dolly would just forget me and find somebody else to stalk.

I lay in my cell one night and considered every reason why I shouldn't start anything with her. But the "why I had to" outweighed the "why I shouldn't." Jimmy had told me, "Be ready to fight. Cons start thinking you're easy pickings, you're cooked."

Next morning, I told Angela, okay, let's do this. We were in the rec yard on a breezy, overcast day. It wasn't long till Dolly and her gang came lumbering in our direction. "Remember," Angela said. "Sneak attack, like the Japanese at Nagasaki."

"Pearl Harbor," I said.

She shrugged. "Same difference."

Dolly closed in on me and started making her pitch again to be my prison mommy. I took a deep breath of courage and watched for my chance. She held her arms wide open and outstretched as she looked away and said something to one of her crew. When she took her eyes off me, I saw my chance and took it. I moved fast and threw that knuckle punch like an uppercut.

Bullseye, a direct hit in her solar plexus.

Her eyes almost popped out of the sockets as she gasped for air, but there was no air. The instant she doubled over, I stood over her and started punching her face, over and over, one after another. I was small, but I had fast hands. I worked on her nose to bloody it and landed a hard, short right on the point of her chin. Her eyes rolled back in her head, and down she went.

Now flat on her ass, she struggled to prop herself up with one hand but went back down. I knew she was done for. She wiped blood off her face with the back of her hand and examined it, then looked up at me, bewildered. I saw fear in those eyes. Her gang didn't make a move, just stood there as I stared them down. Angela had stepped up next to me as if to let them know there were two of us if they wanted more.

Just then, applause and cheers broke out from inmates in the yard who must have had scores to settle with Dolly.

Two of Dolly's crew helped her up.

I said, "Don't bother me no more, lady. Keep your goddam distance."

Dolly looked pained and beaten as she limped away, her shoulders sagging, her crew trailing behind her, suddenly no longer rec yard hotshots. Angela was right about bullies. I had taken a huge risk. If I'd missed with that punch, she might have beat my cracker ass all over that yard and hurt me really bad.

A few women patted me on the back and said stuff like, "Way to go, kid." I knew one guard saw everything, but he didn't say a word to me. Just kept twirling his nightstick like nothing happened.

As we left the yard, Angela was grinning. She patted me on the shoulder. "You got street cred now, kid."

"Not what I wanted. Just wanted her to leave me be."

"Well, ya got it anyway. All the he/shes will think twice about messing with ya."

Dolly and her crew took the long way around me in the yard or in the mess hall after that. I realized if I hadn't fought her, it would not have ended well for me. I also knew if you get in a prison fight, you never know how crazy some revenge-seeking bitch might be. So, I always kept an eye on her out there, just in case. Then, some six months later, Dolly made parole and was off my radar forever.

But maniacs always encircle you in there, like the woman doing twenty for pouring battery acid in her own baby's vagina. Good God! Once in prison, she fell madly in love with a male guard. When she realized he was only toying with her, she slit both her wrists and wrote him a poem on the wall in her blood. Was just another day in the jungle.

I suppose there were as many problems in there as there were people. But because I had stood up for myself in the yard, a bunch of nasty-ass predators wouldn't be one of mine anymore.

48

Ordeal in the Prison Kitchen

Right out of Intake, they classified me for work. I wanted to go to school, get my GED, then take college classes, but they wouldn't let me because they didn't likely care about me bettering myself. I was just a commodity in a warehouse. Instead, they put me to work in the kitchen. I hated it and was determined they would regret their decision.

Prison jobs paid a whopping ten cents an hour—eighty cents for an eight-hour day, four bucks for a forty-hour week. And out of that, we had to pay the prison 20 percent for room and board. In Nevada, men got the decent jobs; they made license plates, got welding jobs, and outdoor jobs I envied—like caring for horses. We women got domestic jobs—cleaning toilets, scrubbing floors, doing laundry, or working in the kitchen like I did. The prison system has always used convict labor to make profits for the prison; it remains a huge profit center.

I was so pissed they wouldn't let me get educated and thereby become a better person by taking college classes, I totally rebelled.

My first job was serving carts of food to people in Intake and in The Hole. This big, fat, scary-looking black woman named Cocoa, who had a deep knife scar that ran four inches across her face, ordered me to deliver meals on a cart. She didn't run the kitchen, but you'd never know it by the way she bossed people around. "You get that food out there pronto, ya hear me, little bit?" she told me.

"Yeah, yeah, blah blah," I shot back. I went out the door on my way to Intake then said screw it and took a hard left. I rolled the cart to the outside door, opened the door, and dumped all that food down a hill. I did the same thing with the next cart she gave me and the one after that.

After the third time, word got back to the kitchen that women in The Hole were complaining they weren't getting their meals. I got back to the kitchen, and Cocoa was staring at me, her fists doubled up. She picked up a butcher knife and came at me. I thought, *Oh, shit*, and I ran. I was too fast for her and ran her around the long prep table in circles till she was so worn out she was gasping for air.

Next day, they moved me into the dish room, which had a big window right by the back door. I climbed out and left the kitchen through the back door and wandered around the prison all day, sightseeing and piddling. Cocoa found out, and the next day she came after me with that butcher knife again. I knew she couldn't catch me, so I taunted her and made faces. As she plopped down on the floor, exhausted, she said, "I'm gonna kill you, ya little bitch. Just you wait."

The prison administration just kept sending me back to the kitchen. One day, I just couldn't take it anymore, and I exploded. A guard said something smart-alecky to me, and I threw a coffee mug at him and barely missed his head. I was yelling and cussing at him when another guard walked in. I sailed a plate at him like a Frisbee; it went just over his head, smashed against a wall, and shattered. A female guard heard the commotion and came in and tried to stop me. I threw an iron skillet at her, but she ducked. Then Cocoa made a move toward me, and I zinged a fry pan at her as she took cover under a cutting table.

"You *fuckers*," I yelled. "I am *not* a slave. I got sentenced to life without, not life with hard labor." I flung another fry pan at somebody, then a rolling pin and a big steel spoon. I held the guards off for about a half-hour, and when they finally got to me, Warden Burns gave me thirty days in The Hole. But The Hole in Carson wasn't so bad. Like a regular cell room with a small cot, a toilet and sink, no windows. But at least I had privacy, and at least I wasn't working in that goddamn kitchen. They even let me read books. So, in that sense, I figured I'd won.

But when I got out of The Hole, they put me back to work in the kitchen and I did the same stuff I'd done before. Then back in The Hole I went. Back in the hole, I discovered I could open my window and talk to others doing time in solitary with me. To make life more fun for all of us, I organized a game of Truth or Dare. Those who got a dare would come out of their cell to get their food tray from a guard, and they might have to start singing and grab a mop and dance with it.

When I came out, Warden Burns brought me to her office and asked why I hated kitchen work so much.

"Warden Burns, it's not that I hate kitchen work so much."

"Then what is it?"

"Truth is, ma'am, I'm a sixteen-year-old who's boiling over with rage for getting railroaded into this prison."

She seemed shocked by my blunt answer and stared at me a long moment, perhaps gathering her thoughts. "Actually, I read the background stuff on you. Could be you're right about getting a raw deal. I sympathize but there's nothing I can do about that. Just wish you luck on your appeals and keep doing my job."

49

Just a Bar of Soap

I had some reason to be optimistic about the appeal Ralph Rohay was working on. Family visits boosted my spirits but were emotionally hard. When I got visits, even from family, I was only allowed to hug them twice—once upon their arrival and again when they were leaving. Beyond that, all touching was forbidden. It was a lonesome existence but I tried to make the best of it till I could change it and go home. Even Mom was optimistic that I'd be coming home soon. Every time she visited me, she would cry, and so would I.

I was allowed to visit Troy Kell in the men's prison down the hill because we had the same case and were permitted to discuss appeal strategies. We would visit in the visitor's room, him on one side of the table, me on the other. Unless he was in The Hole, which he sometimes was, then I would talk to him through Plexiglas.

His attitude when I visited him was usually macho or joking about the whole ordeal. I didn't get that. I saw nothing funny about prison. I wasn't as mad at him anymore, but it was always there—if he hadn't brought that gun, I wouldn't be in here. Troy was considering filing an appeal based on ineffective counsel, the most common first appeal in any case. We didn't talk much about the case or appeals. We mostly just chatted about old times and better times.

I was curious and asked him once if Cotton said something that night, which might have provoked Troy to shoot him. He wouldn't tell me, and to this day, he never has.

Being eighteen when he went in, seen by older inmates as "fresh meat," Troy was just as concerned about sexual predators as I was. His first year in, he saw some black kid about his age get badly used and abused by sexual predators, and the guy never fought back enough to get them to stop abusing him. It got so awful for that kid, he ended his sentence by hanging himself in his cell one day. Troy had a tough exterior, but what happened to that kid affected him deeply. That first visit with him, Troy looked in my eyes. "Sandy, I came in here a man and as God is my witness, I will *leave* here a man." To keep from being the mouse in the prison cat and mouse game, Troy joined the Aryan Brotherhood. They were racists, but I knew Troy had no good choice—prey on people as part of a gang or be the prey.

That decision eventually would lead him to the death house.

Coincidentally, to my utter surprise, Bill Lynch was doing time in Carson City. I got an invitation to visit him and took him up on it. He had landed there after doing time in California. I didn't have any urge to say much to him. I only agreed to see him so I could get away from the women's prison for a while.

Last I'd seen him, I was hanging onto his hair when he was trying to run off with Nicole. I went to see him only once, and we chatted a little bit, and I told him Nicole was doing fine, and I never went to visit him ever again.

I hung out only with a few carefully chosen friends. I lived mostly in my thoughts and imagination and in the books I read. I was a solitary person, which wasn't how I used to be; at one time, I leaned toward extrovert and was always the most gregarious person in the room.

One day, four women approached me in the mess hall to try to get me to join their religious group. "Have you found Jesus?" one asked.

"Gosh, I didn't know he was lost. I can't go looking for him right now, but maybe after I get off my work shift." I was trying to be funny, not mean. I just didn't appreciate being bothered by anybody, religious or otherwise. "Look, I talk to God in my own way," I explained. "It's between me and Him, and He's been busy with other stuff for a while. So, thanks, but no thanks." Three of them smiled, but one shot me a little up-from-under sneer.

At some point, most convicts find Jesus, Mohammed, or Buddha, or some religion. Some are sincere, but a lot of them just figure the God stuff looks good at their parole hearings. Once they get outside that big gate, they tell Jesus, "So long, best of luck, maybe I'll see ya around." Christianity says there are three persons in one God—God the Father, God the Son, and God the

Holy Spirit—but in prison, there's a fourth one, the most popular of all—God the Fire Escape.

Maybe God had been distracted, maybe at the circus eating cotton candy when my life went down the drainpipe. Or maybe He had bigger fish to fry. Maybe I just wasn't high enough up on the totem pole. So right now, I was clinging to my family for hope and support.

I reached out with a letter to my grandma Clara Shaw and when she wrote back, she said, "I do want to hear from you, Sandy. But I need you to send your letters to another address because I don't want the mailman to know I'm getting letters from a convict in prison." That was it. I thought, if she's that ashamed of me, I'm not going to go through all that rigmarole to send her letters, and I never wrote to her or heard from her again.

All my time in prison, all twenty-one years, I never truly accepted prison as my real life. I did everything possible to have everything I wanted and needed to be as comfortable as I could be, and for the most part, I was. I had a few good friends, I minded my own business, didn't take shit from anyone, and never got into the drama of prison politics.

Many female inmates who needed support joined those prison "families." There were butch girls; there were lesbians who were girly girls, playing those roles to get somebody to take care of them and protect them. There were people like Dolly, who wanted to act like your mother or father, or a lover to the people who sorely missed a significant other on the outside. It didn't take me long to figure all that out. All those relationships were taboo, but they went on anyway.... *Went on?* Hell, they ran rampant.

Then there were the guards to deal with. I quickly learned which to trust and which not to trust. Some were humane, others lowlifes and sadists, and you had to quickly learn which was which. Several inmates I knew of got pregnant by guards. Some guards actually brought drugs into the prison and sold them to inmates. But inmates manipulated guards, too, in exchange for sex, the only bargaining chip they had. One inmate quipped to me one day, "I got a nice ass and it's gonna pay off like a slot machine."

Those guards might write you up for the littlest things. I lost privileges for a whole month early on because I gave a bar of soap to some poor girl who had just come to prison and didn't have one thin dime in her commissary. One lousy bar of soap, and a write-up that went on my record as "contraband," the same to a parole board as if it had been heroin.

Those guards didn't give a pea in a pod whether you were guilty or not. It meant nothing to them. They actually got paid bonuses on the number of inmates they had to oversee in the prison, and the prison got money from the state based on the number of inmates. That's one reason why once you are in prison, it's so hard to get out, even on a good appeal, even if you're innocent as a little baby lamb. Once you get put in the system, the free world abandons you; you are out of their hair and off their radar.

Prisons are run like big businesses because that's what they are. So far, I had seen no efforts to rehabilitate, and most of my years in prison, I didn't see any. Prison was just a place to warehouse lawbreakers, the dregs of society.

Once I got access to the library, I did research and read that about 7 percent of the prison population is innocent, though I don't know how they came up with those numbers. While 7 percent sounds like a trifle, when you figure there are some two million people imprisoned in the United States, that's 140,000 innocent people rotting their lives away in those joints.

There were a lot of rules, and the inmates who were more savvy and experienced than me found ways to get around them. I began learning their techniques and even picked up a little local prison code talk. It was a weird kind of lingo, not actually Pig Latin, but something like it; not actually ghetto talk, but a little like it. Inmates used it so guards wouldn't understand them. In Carson, it had been introduced by a gang of pickpockets out of Chicago and New York who traveled from city to city and worked crowds. Of course, working the Strip and the malls in Vegas was a great way to find people with fat wallets. Then their luck ran out in Vegas, and they got busted and sent to Carson.

As for the guards, I realized the best policy is don't get cozy with them. They may take advantage of you, and even if they don't, if you get too buddy-buddy, cons think you're snitching and you got a target on your back. You could get beat up, even stabbed if you are suspected of being a snitch.

The worst incident with guards during my entire incarceration, I was in about three months, and these two sadistic guards stuck a red-hot curling iron up a girl's vagina. Jesus H. I have no idea what she had done, but nobody deserves that. They fired the guards but didn't prosecute them. They should've gone to jail for assault and battery and torture, but inmates don't get that kind of respect or that kind of justice.

There were, of course, some good people working as guards, but most of them, to me, were simply the Gestapo. Best I could, I steered clear of them.

50

Return of My Jailhouse Stalker

Trying to escape a stalker is what landed me in this prison. Now I was about to be confronted by another one.

Maybe three months into my sentence, I woke to the cold light of dawn with a female guard telling me I'd been issued a bed change. "A bed change?" I didn't believe it. "I didn't put in for no bed change. Me and Monica here, we get along fine."

"Yeah, we do," Monica said, rubbing her eyes and waking up. "What gives?"

The guard shrugged. She was a short, stocky thirtyish woman with glasses thick as Coke bottle bottoms. "All I know, I got the order. Better grab your shit and come on."

"I'm not gonna get my stuff," I huffed. "I'll go with you but this is bullshit." I looked at Monica. "Somethin's not right about this."

I followed the guard over to Unit 1, on the other side of the yard. The guard showed me to a room with bunk beds and said, "This is where you live now."

I walked in and who do I see smiling at me on the bottom bunk but Cindi Smith, my stalker from the Clark County Jail.

I took a step back. "Uh-uhh, no, no, no, no. No way! What the fuck are *you* doin' here?"

"Good morning, my little darling," she said, as the guard turned on her heel and left.

"I'm not your darling. I'm not your fucking anything. Figure it out fast, 'cause. I don't want any damn thing to do with you. How the hell did you—?"

I wondered who might she have known to arrange this bed change? She had to have some pull or maybe her mother paid somebody. Whatever it was, no way I was going to move into that room.

"If you only knew how I've dreamed about you," she cooed. She stood up from the bunk bed. "We'll get to know each other now, honey. I know you'll learn to care about me." She stood there with a silly grin on her mug.

Reasoning wasn't going to work. So, I strolled over to her and busted her in the mouth with those keys sticking out between my fingers. She stumbled back and fell on her ass. Those keys cut her mouth and the blood was gushing. She looked up from the floor surprised, but I can't for the life of me understand why.

I turned and walked out of that open door. The guard, standing in the hall, escorted me to a new cell on the other side of the yard but said I couldn't go back to my old room. My new roommate was a good egg, thank God. No guard or nobody in admin said anything about me punching out Cindi Smith. Cindi gave me a wide birth whenever she'd see me in the yard or anywhere else in the prison. I don't know who ended up being her cellmate, but I pity the poor woman.

I hoped I was done having fights. I was getting good at it, but I can promise you, I didn't enjoy it. I always felt sort of sick to my stomach afterward.

51

Sheila's Ordeal

I'd been in a few months when Sheila finally told me about her case. It was what my Grandpa Bill would call "a six-beer story." We had commandeered a wooden bench, and I was listening while eating jellybeans.

She had been living in Vegas with her biker sweetheart when it went down. Joan Mack, a woman Sheila barely knew, was going on a vacation to Florida and called Sheila sometime after midnight and asked her to house-sit her trailer. Sheila was awake, smoking a joint, and said okay, what the hell. She left a note for her boyfriend where she was going.

"Well, I got to her trailer at like two-thirty in the morning and there was Joan standing there, two goddam revolvers in her hands and some woman I didn't know on the floor, covered with a bloody sheet and moaning like a motherfucker. I lifted the sheet and saw she was bleeding really bad from her abdomen. Joan had shot her in the goddam liver." Sheila recognized the woman to be Joy Spinney, who she'd met once before.

She asked Joan what happened, and Joan said she'd shot Joy when they got into a tiff because Joy was going to interfere in her relationship with her boyfriend, Charlie, which she'd done once before. Joan appeared to be hammered. "Her breath was hard as gasoline. I told her to call an ambulance but Joan stuck one of the guns in my face and ordered me to drag Spinney's dying body to Spinney's car. Said if I didn't, she'd kill me and hurt my kids. So I did as I was told. Put her in the back seat and Joan made me drive."

This was getting intense, so I put my jellybeans down and lit a smoke. Sheila took my cigarette from my fingers, took a long drag, and handed it back to me. "I tried to drive the woman to Southern Methodist Hospital, but Joan wasn't having it. She says, 'No ya don't' and stuck the gun barrel in my head and made me drive to some deserted spot outside town. She dragged Joy's body out of the car, shot her right in the head and killed her."

Sheila went quiet a few moments, reflecting. "When Joan was out of the car, after she shot Joy, I thought about driving off, but what she said about hurting my kids made me think twice. Bitch knew where I lived."

Joan then made Sheila drive back to the trailer, got in her own car and drove off for Florida.

"I was doing a hell of a lot of drugs back then and needed money. Joan had left the guns in the car and I took them out and buried them. Next day, I called a drug addict I knew by the name of Autry and said I'd sell him both revolvers for a hundred a piece and told him some of what happened. So he goes to the cops, and they have him wear a wire and go with me. I told him the story, but I was so damn high, when I said Joan told me, 'So what else you gonna do with a horse with a broken leg but shoot it in the brain?' It came out garbled, like *I* had said it and I had shot her. The cops arrested me."

A big, dusty wind gust came up and blew her hair all over, and she paused to push it back and hold it with a couple bobby pins. "They nabbed Joan down in Florida 'bout a week later. The drug addict, this guy Autry, he testified at my trial, said I called him from the jail and told him I wasn't worried because Joan Mack was going to take the rap. I never said that. I said I wasn't worried because Mack did the killing and she held a gun on me the whole time. He'd evidently made some sweet deal with the law."

She shook a cigarette from her pack and lit it, took a long drag, and kept talking. "Joan Mack's cellmate in Clark County Jail turned snitch on her and testified at my trial that Joan told her she'd fired both shots but planned to blame me for the murder."

She tried to blow a smoke ring, but the wind sucked it up in a gust and scattered it. "This is where this story gets really fucking weird," Sheila said.

Before her own trial, Joan Mack committed suicide, but she left a note. "It said, 'I finally found a way not to ever be harassed again in my life—just to die. I'm too old and sick to go through a trial that is unnecessary at my State of Nevada's cost. I am not guilty of anyone's death. Sheila killed my best friend, Joy Spinney. Please, dear Lord, make Sheila serve the time and die the death penalty.' I was beyond stunned. I don't know why she wrote such a note. Maybe she hated me for some reason I never knew, or just wanted the world to always think she was innocent. But that was a pure evil thing she did. It was that note that did me in."

The jury found Sheila guilty of first-degree murder with the use of a deadly weapon and with depravity of mind. They sentenced her to death.

I flipped my cigarette away and went back to the jellybeans. "Jesus, that's the most bizarre story I ever heard. So how did you win your appeal?"

"My trial judge should've never admitted that suicide note into testimony because there was no way my attorney could cross examine a dead woman. I just can't believe they didn't cut my sentence to time served. Then that asshole Judge Mendoza upped me from life *with* to life *without*." She sighed and shook her head. "Hey, believe me. I might be a lot of things, kid, but I'm no killer."

I said, "That makes two of us . . . but the State of Nevada disagrees."

Sheila sucked in a deep breath and let it out slowly. "Yeah, well, there's that."

All the time I was in prison, except when I got transferred a few times, until she got her sentence reduced on appeal and got paroled out, Sheila Summers was my best friend, the smartest person I knew, and the only inmate I truly ever trusted.

52

First Appeal and Varela's Contrition

I spent most of that first year rebelling, but I began settling down some and even following orders once they let me start using the library. I could get totally lost in books and escape from prison without ever going over the wall.

Before the year was out, Ralph Rohay was working on my appeal. I still had hope. The appeal was based on the felony murder rule and that I didn't have any of the underlying felonies charged to me when I went to trial. The juvenile courts had dismissed those charges, and they were never legally reinstated. So, I was convicted on crimes I had not even been formally charged with. That issue was so strong I was more confident than ever I'd be back home and free within the year.

I pinned my hopes and dreams to that appeal. Rohay had been lousy in court, but he was a studious fellow who was known to write good briefs, and with a law book in front of him and pen in hand, I figured he could fashion me a winner.

I had been in prison nearly a year when I marked my seventeenth birthday eating overcooked chicken in the mess hall with Monica and Sheila. I'd called Mom and talked to her, to Mike, Shane, and Nicole. Baby Leah was now three years old. After dinner, I went to my cell to read my mail. I had a letter and birthday card from Mom, a letter from Nicole, and a card from one of Mom's sisters.

Then, as fate arranged it, I saw a letter postmarked from a men's prison in southern Nevada, return address of one Thomas Varela. I thought, *What the? . . . why is that lying jackass sending me mail?*

Turns out he wanted me to punch his ticket for his guilty conscience, but there was more to it. The letter was handwritten because most inmates didn't get access to word processors or typewriters.

I kicked my shoes off, lay back on my bed, and tried to wash down the taste of that dinner with a juicy orange. I would later get my case worker to make three copies of Thomas' letter: one of which I sent to Mom, one to Ralph Rohay, and an extra copy for me, for safekeeping.

This is word for word what Thomas wrote:

Dear Sandy,

Sandy, I just wanted to write you this letter and let you know some of the shit that happened at your trial. First I know that Dan Seaton was coaxing some of the witnesses & they were only there for the money. Of course, they will say what he wants if he is giving them money. Dan Seaton told me if I did not say what I did I would get a lot more time.

I know you did not do it because Troy told me all of it in the beginning and said he really did it. I hope things work out for you. Please write me back.

—THOMAS VARELA

Many years later, when my journalist friend found Thomas and interviewed him about his testimony, the first thing Thomas said was, "What's the statute of limitations on perjury?"

I sat up on the edge of my bed and stared at that letter a long while. When Thomas was on the stand, Seaton asked him if he had promised Thomas any favors, and Thomas looked toward the jury box as innocently as the baby Jesus and answered, "No." He claimed he just wanted to tell the truth. Which was, of course, a pile of steaming shit. If he had had the character to tell the truth on the stand, maybe I would've been acquitted, and the same goes if Fletcher and Buhman had not lied. Their perjured testimony was the main reasons I was sitting on a hard bed inside a prison and not back home getting invited to the junior-senior prom or eating birthday cake with my family.

Thomas had been facing fifteen to twenty years for all those felonies as a repeat offender and got sentenced to only one year. That could have only been the handiwork of the prosecutor.

If I had been smart and not so immature, I would have written Thomas back. I would've asked him details of exactly how Seaton had coached him to lie about me in front of a jury, and to say I had a crush on him. and that hogwash that I'd come to visit him the night of the murder and gave him three hundred dollars. I would have got it all in writing. But I was so angry with him, I thought, the hell with him, and never answered his letter.

But his declaration of perjury gave me a morsel of hope. Also, during that year, Dave Fletcher had contacted the prison several times trying to get on my visitors' list. I ignored his messages but shouldn't have. Maybe he would've gone to a judge and fessed up, and I would've found out what Seaton did to change his testimony, while there was still time to do something about it.

But I was teenage mad at Dave, so pissed I didn't want to see him or hear from him ever again. He actually might've written me a few letters over the years, I don't recall, but if he did, I didn't read them. That's what a dumbass I was. It would be twenty more years before I found out exactly what happened with Dave in that courtroom, and why.

I tucked that letter from Varela safely away and enjoyed the rest of that orange, then sang the happy birthday song to myself. I avoided any self-pity because what would that do but lay me low? I had to stay strong and clear-minded to survive and fight my way out of there. I had to look ahead and not back. The reason they make the windshield way bigger than the rearview mirror is because the road in front of you is more important than what's behind you.

53

Changing My Tune

I grabbed onto the wheel of maturity and started turning the corner when I was still sixteen. I never totally quit rebelling, but I softened up. My thought process began changing, and a dark fog that had followed me for three years, ever since the murders at Rancho Circle, began lifting when I plunged into books and continued my education.

Sometimes I wonder, did prison actually save my life? I say that because I was doing drugs when I was an adolescent and there was all the violence going on around me. I became a magnet for murder after Rancho Circle. But that doesn't mean I needed to be locked up for two decades to get over it. A couple years would have straightened me out and got me on a different path with different friends if they had let me out.

I started changing my attitude one day when I was walking along toward the rec room. By a fluke, I happened onto the associate warden as he gave a tour to at-risk youth. He stopped me and said, "Shaw. Tell these kids how old you are."

"I'm sixteen."

"And tell them what your sentence is."

"Life without the possibility of parole."

He shook his finger at the kids. "She's likely never going to get out of here, all because of one mistake, one bad moment, one bad choice."

I saw a couple kids' eyes widen. "Holy shit," one boy mumbled.

"So, talk to them, Shaw," the associate warden said.

I told the kids my story, how one bad decision cost a life and cost me mine. Some of the kids cried when I told my story. I almost cried too.

Afterwards, the associate warden called me to his office and asked me if I'd like to give tours on the "Scared Straight" program. "Sure, why not?" If nothing else, it cut into the boredom of prison life, where every minute seems like an hour and every hour seems like a day. Beyond that, I saw a sense of purpose trying to creep into my life. No matter where you are, if you don't have a purpose, you'll be miserably lost.

Every time at-risk kids would tour the prison, I would talk to them, counsel them, listen to their stories, tell them mine, and try to give them advice. One day, this cocky girl, maybe fourteen, chunky, with long hair down her back, was popping her gum and looking like she was way too good for the market. She was staring off to the side, paying no attention. I stopped talking, walked up to her, and got my face close to hers. "So, why are you here?"

She frowned. "'Cuz they *made* me come here."

"No, I mean what did you *do*? What trouble got you here?"

She grunted. "Ain't none a your beeswax."

I got even closer to her face. "Don't sass me, brat. Lip off in here, you could get your ass kicked into the middle of next week. Is that what you want?"

Her arrogant look disappeared like a gnat in a windstorm. "Um, I, uh." She paused and finally coughed up the words. ". . . I *shoplifted* stuff."

"You do that a lot? Shoplift?"

She looked down at her feet and nodded, "Yeah."

I backed off and gave her space. "You keep that up, one day a judge will send you to prison. You could end up here. This is a dangerous place, not a happy place, take my word. There are mean women in here who might stab you if you smart off, beat you up just because they can, maybe even rape you and make you their bitch."

She bit on her lip and rolled her head a little. I noticed sweat on her forehead.

"Next time you stick something in your pocket and don't pay for it, you think about all that. I hope I don't see you in this place again, because if I do, you'll be coming here to do time and I wasted my energy talking to you."

She paused a moment, and said, "Yes, ma'am." She told me "thank you" when she left. Convict or not, I felt like I'd done something important.

It wasn't long before the associate warden had me speaking regularly to groups. He even took me to the Chamber of Commerce to give them ideas on how to keep juveniles from going wrong. But the best thing, I was finding purpose in my life. I needed it for a multitude of reasons—mostly to keep my attitude positive and keep fighting to get the hell out of there.

54

Appeal Denied!

May Day, 1988.

I had been cast-iron certain I would be going home soon. The Nevada Supreme Court was about to hear my appeal. That night I dreamed Lady Justice rode up to the prison gates on a fiery horse and said to me, "Hop on, motherfucker. You're going home." Her exact words.

How naïve I was to even dream such a thing.

Rohay had sent me a copy of the appeal and I read it over. Inmates have a year from their conviction to file an appeal, or they are what's called "time barred"; that is to say, screwed. So he had started on it right after my trial. And it was powerfully written. The strongest point was how when I was first charged with the underlying felonies of murder and robbery, the juvenile court dismissed them. I was never even legally charged as an adult with those crimes.

The Nevada Supreme Court heard my appeal on May 2. Next day, my hopes went down in flames when Rohay gave me the bad news. The High Court unanimously voted to uphold my murder conviction and reject my appeal. They dismissed each one of our arguments, point by point. In fact, they claimed being charged with the underlying felonies was "a harmless error." Harmless? To whom? To them maybe, but not to me. They were going home to their families. I was locked in prison. I saw nothing harmless about it.

The second part of the appeal centered on when police detectives took me from my house and grilled me six hours without Mom there. I kept asking for her. "I want my mom here. . . . I don't want to talk to you unless she's here." They ignored me and kept pressing.

Rohay's appeal stated that according to the law, statements I gave leading to my arrest were involuntary and should have been suppressed. He cited how the government is "the legal protector of citizens unable to protect themselves"; because I was a minor, I was legally incapable of protecting myself. He noted, while police can legally lie when they question suspects, they can't mislead a minor to get a confession. So, their interrogation violated the law.

The Nevada Supreme Court dismissed that part, too.

Here was the rub: A couple years later, that exact same Nevada Supreme Court ruled on a similar case where the defendant wasn't formally charged with the underlying felonies—the exact error as in my case. They reversed that conviction but decided it wasn't important to be "retroactive" with that ruling. Not in my case, anyway. That made no sense to me and still doesn't. If it is wrong now, why wasn't it wrong then?

Mom sent me a copy of the news story about my appeal in the Las Vegas *Review-Journal* the day after it was denied, and they described me like I was a homicidal maniac. The *Review-Journal* had reported my case subjectively from the start. During my trial, for instance, they ran a news item showing my picture and a headline reading: "Shaw Admits to Planning to Rob Victim." I never admitted that, and I never will because it never happened. I was tried in the press before I was ever tried in a courtroom. The *Review-Journal* was a major daily newspaper that reported the news like a tabloid.

The *Review-Journal* also reprinted Seaton's courtroom tall tale that I had met Cotton while I was shooting dice at Circus-Circus and that Seaton had produced a letter in court I had written, saying how I "would kill to get bail money for a jailed boyfriend," meaning Varela. No such letter ever existed, but it was now a part of the "Show and Tell" murder legend.

If the newspaper reporter had fact-checked, he could have dug up the truth. But to the *Review-Journal, I wasn't a person; I was just a ten-inch, two-column story on page three. I crumpled the news article into a ball and flung it in the garba*ge.

55

Bitter Winter and off to Reno

Early January of 1988.

I woke one morning shivering and squinting at ice cycles on the inside of our cell window. I was freezing, and the cold wind outside howled like a witch.

Winter had roared into Carson City, and by some glitch, our cell didn't have heat. Administration couldn't figure it out but didn't have any place to move us immediately because the Carson City prison was already overcrowded.

I piled clothes on top of my blankets and shivered at night, and my cellmate Sheila did likewise. Even when she was freezing to death, Sheila could always keep my mood up. She was smart as a whip and as witty as she was smart. We worked on complicated jigsaw puzzles, and she taught me how to paint. She was inventive, philosophical, and wise, and like me, doing life without parole. Now she began educating me on hypothermia, and I kept asking her to change the subject.

Winters got cold as Jesus up in Carson, at forty-seven hundred feet, where the wind howled down from the mountains like wolves. Winter nighttime temperatures could drop way below freezing, and the wind chill was often lethal. Without heat in our room, I thought I'd catch pneumonia.

Our room was at the end of a hallway, and while we could get out of there in the daytime, we were locked in at night. We managed to each get an extra blanket, but they were so thin they weren't much help. Even with clothes piled on me, my teeth chattered.

A few days into this, I woke to see the always resourceful Sheila sitting on her bed, a blanket wrapped around her. She snapped her fingers as an idea popped into her head. "Hey, by God, I got it!"

"Got *what*?" I put a Levi jacket on and wrapped myself in a blanket. The window was glazed over with frost.

"A space heater. That one in the education center."

I didn't recall any space heater in there. But soon as our door was unlocked, she jumped up and dashed out. In maybe ten minutes, she strolled back in carrying a three-foot by three-foot space heater and grinning like a cat that swallowed a canary. But I looked behind her and two angry inmates were closing in. A Black woman who looked as tough as she was big ran in and tried to grab the heater from Sheila and said, "Bitch, I had dibs on that." It took both of us to wrestle her out of our room, and when we gave her a last little shove; she fell down on her ass just outside our door.

Sheila set the heater down and we both grabbed our soap in a sock. She reminded the woman, "Possession is 90 percent of the law. I got to it first."

"That's 'cause I got a sore ankle and had to limp to it," she said.

"Wasn't a handicap race," Sheila shot back.

"Yeah, but I got to the room first, and you ran past me."

Sheila sat down on the heater. "You faded down the stretch."

The woman got up, brushed herself off, and gave up on stealing the heater we had stolen that *she* had planned to steal. As she limped off, I heard her say, "No good, murderin'-ass, peckerwood bitches."

Before it finally thawed and warmed up in the spring, I got transferred a half-hour down the road to a shut-down, decaying old county jail in Reno, now officially serving as a women's prison. To ease the overcrowding in Carson, they took mostly long-termers and segregation inmates. They kept Sheila in Carson. I was pissed about the transfer because it was a dump, and they told me I would have to start all over with the paperwork for college classes.

Reno was a modular jail with one long hallway and six pod units on each side. Each pod housed fifteen inmates with five-person and two-person cells. Most everything we needed was in the pods, including metal tables serving as everything from dining tables to places to play chess, checkers, and cards. The phones and shower stalls were also there in your pod.

I did like the rec yard. It was a big, fenced square area right in the middle of town. I could look out from the yard to the Truckee River and the state mental hospital. The river was surrounded by clumps of trees and shrubbery, and I would often watch townies walk along the river with their families to picnic in the little park. I would often envision me out there and them in here.

A lot of guards in Reno enjoyed making our lives even worse. One day, I had been trying to call Mom by connecting on the three-way from the control bubble. But just as it began to ring, the officer in the bubble hung up on me. I knew he did it on purpose because he did it to other girls a lot. So, I picked up a broom and smashed their spy camera into the Plexiglas and called him a lot of foul names. Then I calmly sat down and waited for somebody to come give me a write-up and stick me in The Hole.

I spent lots of time in The Hole in Reno, but it wasn't any sweatbox chain gang hellhole. It was just another cell in one of the pods, and if you were in there for more than fifteen days, you even got TV privileges. So, I got a lot of time to read, improve my mind, and stay out of everyone else's drama.

One book I ordered was *All His Father's Sins*, written by a journalist and a police detective about a serial killer couple who kidnapped and made sex slaves out of mostly teenage girls before murdering them. It turned my stomach. Gerald Gallego and his wife Charlene Williams were the evil bastards who did all that killing—in California, Oregon, and Nevada. They got caught in Nevada, and Gerald got the death penalty, but Charlene turned states on him and cut a deal for eighteen years.

Okay, so one day I walk out of my cell and I have that book with me. And who do I see walking out of the cell right next to mine: Charlene Fucking Williams, the murdering bitch. I recognized her from the photos in the book. She was with some woman who turned out to be her girlfriend.

I got right up in Charlene's face and held that book up. I said, "This is *you*, bitch. You tortured all those teenage girls. I ought to beat the shit out of you." I called her a lowlife twat, and her girlfriend stepped between us and said, "Mind your own business, bitch."

I said, "I just made it my business, and you call me bitch again, I'll beat your ass right after I beat hers."

Charlene didn't say a word, just stood there looking creepy, a half smile on her mug. Then they went around me. I kept an eye out for Charlene in the yard. I really did want to beat her up, to get a least a little bit of justice for all those girls my age she and her husband tortured and murdered, who weren't going to get justice otherwise. But before the opportunity arose, I got transferred back to Carson City.

It also pissed me off she got only eighteen years, and I was doing life without. When she got released after doing her time, she held a press conference and claimed she was Gerald's victim, too. But from people I knew that knew her, that was a load of crap. As for Gerald, that son of a bitch cheated the poison needle by dying of cancer.

I also found out, when Charlene had been in Carson City, her girlfriend had been none other than Cocoa, the woman who chased me around the kitchen with that damn butcher knife.

It was a small world, but as my grandpa Bill used to say, I wouldn't want to have to paint it.

56

Troy's Troubled Life

All the time I was in prison, I was linked one way or another to Troy Kell, and I likely will be for the rest of my days. He'd get in trouble and make the news, and my name would get hauled through the dirt in the papers.

Not long after he'd gone to prison, he got written up for threatening to slash a female guard's throat. Then he tossed scalding hot soup through a food slot at a guard and gave him first-degree burns. He then threatened to kill a guard for searching his cell. And after joining the Aryans, he and another Aryan brother beat a black inmate senseless.

Then in 1990, he wooed a female guard, Tracy Cortez, who fell in love with him. She smuggled him in a handcuff key and fifty-two bullets for a homemade wooden gun he'd fashioned. His plan was to take some guards hostage and take over his cellblock, then somehow escape. But before he could try it, guards found the bullets and handcuff key in his cell during a routine shakedown.

Cortez was fired and got six years in prison. That incident made the Vegas papers and TV news, and my name came up as a co-conspirator and fellow murderer when they mentioned in his first offense. The next year they transferred him to Utah in a swap, and that would seal his fate.

57

The Annabelle Hall Situation

In January 1991, like the old Merle Haggard bleeder says, I turned twenty-one in prison doing life without parole. But on the upside, I almost never got psychotic intrusions anymore.

It wasn't long after, I got transferred back to Carson City from that eyesore in Reno. Sheila's cellmate had just made parole, so we were roomies again. I signed up for college classes at Western Nevada Community College and then buried my head in books to keep my mind off my hard reality.

I researched library law books and was well aware only inmates on death row got free legal representation. Everybody else had to pay a lawyer. If they couldn't afford a lawyer or luck out with pro bono, they had to write their own appeal and file it with the court. Mom could not afford a lawyer for my first appeal, but Rohay did it gratis, figuring he owed me.

I learned that by 1991, I was procedurally time-barred from even making another appeal, since it had been more than two years since the last one. Once you file an appeal and they adjudicate it, you have two years to file the next one throughout your time in prison. I hadn't known that because nobody gives you a manual when you go to prison, and you don't get notices in the mail saying you're about to be time-barred.

I was bummed about that till one day I read in a law book there are exceptions to the rule if a case is worthy enough. I figured mine was plenty worthy. I planned to write my own appeal and file it with the judge. Since all inmates have their original trial judge and the same courtroom for all their appeals, I thanked God the old hanging judge, "Maximum John" Mendoza, had retired from the bench. His replacement was Jeffrey Sobel, reputedly fair, ethical, and reasonable.

But as I started writing my appeal, Mom managed to scrape, borrow, beg, and save enough money for an appellate lawyer. A federal district court judge in Arizona recommended attorney Annabelle Hall from Reno. I looked her up, and she'd been a member of the bar since 1979. That's all I knew.

She drove from Reno and met with me a few times, and we talked some on the phone. She was short and skinny, and while not an imposing physical appearance in the courtroom, she sure knew how to write a brief.

She jumped right in and started researching my case through trial transcripts, and within a few months, produced a fantastic brief for post-conviction relief. It was so good it should be framed and hung on a courthouse wall. Her brief was based on a whole laundry list of issues—ineffective assistance of counsel, illegal sentencing (Nevada law mandates nobody under age sixteen at the time of a crime can be sentenced to life without parole), and illegal jury instructions from Mendoza, for starters. I also hadn't gotten the mandatory presentence investigation report or the penalty phase investigation required in every murder trial in every state in the Union.

That brief was loaded with enough prosecutorial bungling, I should have walked out the door the moment the judge saw Hall's brief. Had it been dynamite, it would have blown the Clark County Courthouse to smithereens.

But the facts had to be presented in an evidentiary hearing in court. As the judge set the date for the hearing, Hall got to work strengthening our case in other ways. One strategy, she hired John P. Wilson, out of Cleveland, a leading expert on mental illnesses caused by trauma, to interview me for a week. Wilson, a college psychology professor and president of the Society for Traumatic Stress Studies, was the nation's leading expert on PTSD. He had interviewed and treated hundreds of suffering combat veterans. I knew only a little more about PTSD than I knew about South American lizards, except how Dad had been diagnosed with it from his hell in combat.

After a week interviewing me, Dr. Wilson took his notes and questionnaires back to Cleveland and determined I suffered from massive PTSD. Also from other emotional disorders that all had their conception on the murder night at Jessica Mallin's home.

Those sessions gave my lawyer more fodder, but they also made me face—for the first time—why I had shut down my emotions and failed to deal with them. He made me confront my fractured childhood, and it started me on a path to healing that would change my life.

The judge scheduled my hearing for early July, but about a week out, as I was prepping for it, I got a notice it was postponed.

When Annabelle called me, I asked what went wrong.

"Nothing's wrong. The Clark County prosecutor's office did that. They have that right."

"But why would they?"

"Maybe they weren't prepared."

"How could they prepare; they got nothing?"

"Exactly," she said. "They are running scared because they don't have squat."

She said all the prosecutor's office would accomplish by postponing was give us more time to better prepare.

The hearing was quickly rescheduled for late October. Relying on Hall's comment that the other side "didn't have squat," I waited patiently to expose all the backstabbing and dirty dealing the prosecutor's office pulled to get me convicted.

I began sleeping soundly and dreaming about home.

But as October neared, I got another notice from the court that my hearing was again postponed.

"What the hell?" I asked Hall over the phone.

She said, "This was some snafu on the judge's court calendar. We'll get it scheduled again. I'll do that this week."

Christmas came and then New Year's 1992, and my March hearing got canceled again. That was three now. Hall explained it was the prosecutor's office. David Roger, not Seaton, was the lead prosecutor now, but Seaton was still trying cases, and I figured he was still pulling some strings. Mom had sent me news articles from time to time about how the state Supreme Court and the Nevada State Bar Association had come down hard on Seaton for misconduct in several murder trials. A defense lawyer I had talked to called Seaton "a pimple on the ass of justice."

That same year, my wonderful, loving grandpa, Bill Fosteson, died of pneumonia. He was only sixty-two, and I was so sad.

My hearing got rescheduled—then postponed again, and in 1993, it was postponed three more times. That made *seven times* in three years.

My confidence in Annabelle Hall had eroded. Mom had scraped all that money together to hire an attorney who couldn't seem to even get me to court. I was twenty-four now. If I'd taken the plea deal in 1987, I probably would have been home three years by now.

Then, miracle of miracles, in the fall of 1994, nearing my twenty-fifth birthday, Hall called and promised this next one was going to come off. She was positive. She went so far as to guarantee it.

It was set for November 4, 1994, and I was to be transported back to Clark County the night before. Excited, I called Mom and told her the news.

58

Sold Down the River

Thursday, November 3, 1994.

I was among eight convicts in an NDOC prison van early that morning, bound from Carson to Vegas. All of us had court hearings.

About four hours into our eight-hour ride, we witnessed a total solar eclipse as the Moon passed between the Earth and the Sun. I chose to take it as a sign from above that everything was going to turn out well. As we rolled along the hills and through the valleys, I was nervous but eager, anxious but hopeful.

Mid-afternoon, we made the turn off the freeway onto Casino Drive, and the Clark County Jail jumped up and said Boo. After getting checked in, they locked me in a holding cell in the women's section. It had two long benches, a concrete floor, no beds, and was freezing cold. Later that night, they started bringing street hookers into that cell, and the more crowded it became, the more disgusting it got. But at least the room warmed up from the body heat.

Around 7:00 p.m., a male guard said my attorney was ready to meet with me. Adrenaline surged on the elevator ride down to a visitor's room, where the guard removed my cuffs and waited with me till Annabelle Hall made her entrance. When she came in, he went outside and waited because he couldn't be privy to attorney-client privileged conversations.

I was beaming with hope. She took a seat across the large round table and put the papers in front of her. My smile was genuine; hers seemed forced.

"How was your ride down?" she said.

I rubbed my wrists; they were sore from being cuffed on the trip. "Long as hell. But I saw that eclipse."

She nodded. "Yeah, that was something. I caught a few seconds of it out my office window." She stared down at the papers in front of her, not at me, and she shuffled them.

I was bursting with enthusiasm. "I'm ready to do this!"

She slowly raised her eyes from the papers until they met mine. I sensed something was off.

She drew in a breath and let it go. "Sandy . . . I made a deal with the prosecutor's office."

"Uhmm, okay . . . "

She cleared her throat. "Listen, they're going to resentence you to two life sentences *with* the possibility of parole and dismiss our hearing. If you go through the hearing, and lose, you will spend the rest of your life in prison."

"That's what I'm already doing." My head was spinning. None of this made sense. I couldn't believe what I heard. "That's *it*? Two lifes . . . with a *chance* for parole?" I pushed back my chair and scooted away from the table.

She leaned toward me across the table. "But if you lose—"

I felt like the top of my head might blow off. "Jesus *Christ*, Annabelle. That judge was gonna *have* to *re*sentence me since the sentence I've been serving the last eight years was *illegal*. What's the matter with you?"

"Sandy, you don't seem to understand how—"

"Oh, yes, I do. You just threw me under a *bus*. All those issues I had, I could've *walked*."

She paused and took another breath. "Look, I have great connections to the pardons board and—"

I pointed at her. "You took my family's money, you let the prosecutor postpone my hearings seven times then you sold me out. Without a *fight*."

I wanted to scream.

She claimed David Roger was willing to negotiate but Seaton was behind the scenes saying no.

I said screw Seaton and it didn't matter what the prosecutor did. The judge could rule on all that evidence and they had no say-so. I knew I was right.

When she kept insisting she did what was best for me, I was sure she had made a deal with the devil to sell me down the river.

She held up her hand. "Like I told you, I have great connections and I intend to walk you through to the pardons board. We'll get your sentences to run concurrently." She held up the papers she had signed with the prosecutor. "This makes you parole eligible."

"I'm not signing *shit*."

She let me know she signed as my legal representative and that made it a done deal. I would have to attend the hearing the next morning, but it would be a formality. There was nothing more I could say or do about it, so I asked the guard to come get me and take me back to the holding cell.

By now, that holding cell was so crowded with street hookers, it smelled like dime-store perfume. I had on jeans and a denim shirt I had picked out for court, and my hair was done up in curls. But now I was in a foul mood. A skinny, half-drunk woman with breath like kerosene stared at me and said, "Where are you coming from looking like a Barbie doll that just left the beauty shop?"

I squinted. "I'm down from prison, fuck head, and I'm in a sour mood. You'd be wise to keep your distance and shit-can your smart remarks."

Soon, they were all trying to find places to lay down and sleep—on the benches and the freezing floor, using each other's bodies as pillows. I kept pushing them off me and trying to get a few hours of decent sleep before the hearing.

By 10:00 a.m. in the morning, most of the hookers had been bailed out when the guard came for me.

Annabelle Hall was already sitting in the front pew of the courtroom. Prosecutor David Roger was on a bench on the opposite aisle. I plopped down on the other end of the bench where Annabelle sat. Soon, Judge Sobel came out of his chambers in his black robe, a court reporter and a bailiff tailing him. It went down like she had said. Just a formality because I was a formality.

She explained to the judge in the matter of *Sandy Shaw v. Nevada*, her client Sandy Marie Shaw had reached an agreement with the prosecution to withdraw all other requests in exchange for a resentencing of both charges from life without to life with.

That meant I could apply for parole on both the murder and the gun charge after ten years in. But the catch was my sentences were being served consecutively, and I'd have to do ten years on the murder then another ten on the gun charge to win my release. Unless I could get to the Pardons Board and get both sentences to run concurrently.

The judge barely glanced at me. Hall and Roger submitted their documents; he looked them over and signed, then he dismissed each one of my issues, one by one. And my hearing was over.

To this day, I don't know why Annabelle Hall cut that deal. It didn't make sense then, and it doesn't now. In light of what I learned about the Thiede family and their drug activities, I wondered if they got to her and paid her off, but that's just conjecture; I have no proof. I also thought maybe that is just how she did business: took on more cases than she could possibly try in court, collected the retainers, and cut last-minute deals; or that Seaton or Roger traded her a favor with one of her other cases. I got no proof of any of that, either. It will likely remain a mystery.

Annabelle Hall would never keep her promise to "walk me through" to the Pardons Board; I would have to get there on my own.

Then one day, my mom called the prosecutor's office and asked David Roger why he postponed my hearing seven times in three years. He went quiet for a few moments and said, "Mrs. Shaw, this office never postponed your daughter's evidentiary hearing. That was her attorney Annabelle Hall who did that—all seven times."

When Mom told me that, I was beyond flabbergasted. I was angry as a badger. Years later, someone from the prosecutor's office told me my issues with that evidentiary hearing were so strong, if Hall had pressed it, they were ready to let me walk.

Some six months after Hall stabbed me in the back, I was watching TV news in the rec room, and a reporter said a disgruntled former client of Reno attorney Annabelle Hall had barged into her office and tried to strangle her.

Another inmate turned to me. "Holy shit. That is *totally* shocking."

I shrugged. "Not to me, it isn't."

59

Our Escape Plan

A year earlier, in 1993, Sheila and I contracted with an outside company for a prison job installing circuit boards. For TVs, radios, jet airplanes; you name it, we did it. We worked outside in the yard when the weather allowed, and we got really damn good at our jobs.

My first five years in prison, I was positive I'd get out. The next five years, I thought I never would. I was deep down in the dumps about that evidentiary hearing that never got heard. So, one day, on impulse, I stole a pair of our wire cutters and buried them in the yard. Just in case it came down to having to break out to get out. I was determined not to die an old woman in prison. I used my heel to kick and kick and kick till I had a hole deep enough to hide them. I marked the exact spot by pacing it off from the start of the fence line so I would know where they were.

After I buried the cutters, me and Sheila talked half-serious about escaping. She had life without, and I'd already spent seven and a half years locked up. Even with my parole eligibility, I would have to endure twelve and a half more years of this before I'd have a shot at getting out. And there is no guarantee a parole board will approve you on the first try. Matter of fact, they may not approve you till you're old and feeble.

After cutting that deal with the prosecutor's office, Hall had said she saw a light at the end of my tunnel. I saw that same light, but when it got close, I realized it was a freight train coming at me.

I sat on the side of my bed just before lockdown one night, my spirits low, and Sheila picked up on it. She was looking in the mirror, removing her makeup. Without turning around, she said, "Maybe we should just bust out of this goddam place."

I thought she was talking just to talk. But then she turned around and looked at me. "A couple snips on that fence over by the trailers, we'd be gone before the guards got the egg out their beards."

"Yeah, sure but to *where*? We got no place to go, Sheila. We'd be running around the woods till we either starve or they find us. So what's the use?"

"My biker buddies in California. That's where. My guy is still real sweet on me and he swore if I ever wanted to make a run for it he'd help me."

"You for real?"

"I'm for *real*. He has connections that could get us out of the country. The Mexican cartels. They're pretty buddy-buddy, all that drug shit."

I thought about it for what seemed like forever, then I said, "Screw it. Let's do it."

It was on!

We talked continually about it the next week, mostly in quiet whispers, out of the range of guards and snitches.

Sheila's biker friends had a word code if some undercover cop eavesdropped or the FBI tapped their phones, since their income came mostly from lawbreaking. Sheila was fluent in their code—symbols and word associations, sort of like Navajo code talkers but not as sophisticated: "Coyote" meant policeman, "rabbit" meant a fugitive, and "jackrabbit" meant somebody that planned to break out of a jail.

She wrote a coded letter to her biker boyfriend and within a week the two of them were talking on the phone and using the code since all our calls got recorded.

The wheels were turning and, after a whole lot of intricate planning, we set the escape date for the night of January 30, 1995. The almanac in the library said it would be a new moon and it would be pitch black outside.

Tower guards walking the catwalk at the men's prison were at eye level with our prison and could put eyes on our main fence. But they rarely paid any attention to stuff going on over here. We weren't dangerous like the men, and that's who they were paid to guard. But the problem was those were double fences with razor wire on the top and bottom, and would take way more time to cut through. And the tower guards might spot us.

We decided the only feasible way out was on the other side, near the minimum-security trailers. It was so far away, tower guards couldn't see us. That area had just a single fence with razor wire only at the top, not the bottom. It might take five minutes, tops, to cut a hole big enough to step through.

Because it got dark early in the winters, they would bring us all in from the rec yard before 6:00 p.m. daily. But we could then go to the rec room, mess hall, or anywhere else in the building till they did the head count at ten o'clock for lockdown. That gave us a solid three-and-a-half hours' head start before they realized we'd flown the coop.

Coming in from the yard, it would be easy-peasy to duck unseen between A Hall and B Hall buildings. Inmates would slip in there all the time to talk in private, do drugs, or have sex.

We planned to dress in all black for that dangerous dash through the open field to the road after we cut through the fence. That was probably the biggest risk because tower guards might see us. Once to the road, we would lay flat in the long grass till her biker friends pulled up in their van, hopefully in fewer than five minutes. It had to be a quick pick-up; if a car stopped and lingered on that road, guards on the towers would see it and call the cops.

Sheila's boyfriend's van had an undetectable false bottom for moving drugs. That's where we'd snuggle up and hide. It was only a half-hour drive down Highway 50 to the California line, then twenty more minutes along the Pioneer Trail into the dense Eldorado National Forest. Sheila's boyfriend had secured a small cabin tucked way back into the piney woods and stocked it with provisions.

We were sure the police wouldn't search anywhere that far from the prison because they'd figure one of two things: we were on foot or we had hitched a ride. If we were on foot, we wouldn't have gotten more than three or four miles from the prison after they started looking. They would know if we hitched a ride, we were long gone and far away.

The really ingenious part would come after we would lay low in that cabin several days till the heat died down. A group of maybe thirty bikers would ride into South Lake Tahoe, on the California side, for a night of partying. Nothing unusual about bikers raising a little healthy hell.

Before sunup, two of them would come to get us at the cabin, bringing helmets to hide our faces, leather biker chick jackets, and fake IDs. Then, as the big group would ride south out of Tahoe on Highway 50, we would be on the back of two of those choppers and just slide right into the formation and ride all the way to an LA safe house.

From there, Sheila's boyfriend and another guy would take us to San Diego, where we would board a thirty-six-foot fishing boat all the way down Baja California to Puerto Vallarta. Armed with fake passports, we would meet up with a "friendly"—some cartel guy her boyfriend knew. He would take us to San Miguel de Allende, a mountain town of some seventy thousand people, four hours north of Mexico City.

It was the only escape plan I'd ever heard that seemed worth the risk.

San Miguel de Allende had a large American expatriate population—artists, writers, retirees, that sort. A couple gringo chicks who didn't speak much Spanish would barely be noticed. And through the biker group's connections with the Mexican cartel, they would make sure we got jobs. There we would stay and live out our days, and the State of Nevada Department of Corrections could go piss up a rope. I wouldn't be home and free, but I wouldn't be rotting in some nasty prison anymore, and in my current state of mind, that was all the motivation I needed.

In the prison library, I found a *National Geographic* book about Mexico and read up on San Miguel de Allende. It was a beautiful old Spanish Colonial town. Its big square was decorated with nicely landscaped shrubbery in view of an ancient pink-stone neo-gothic church with a gigantic steeple. It all looked so welcoming.

I put myself there in my mind, free to stroll their cobblestone streets and hike up to the hot springs and the Jesuit sanctuary. As I thought about it, my cares and woes and the realities of prison faded. I was no longer inmate 24126, but a woman living far away and free.

When Mom came up for Christmas, it hit me I would not be able to contact my family once I made a run for it. Maybe not ever. Their phones would be tapped, and it would be risky to even get word to them where I was or even that I was okay. We would be on the lam as two escaped murderers, and the FBI would never stop looking. Ever.

A few nights after Christmas, Sheila and I were watching TV in the rec room. "America's Most Wanted" was on, and John Walsh narrated how thousands of tips from his popular program had caught eight fugitives in the past month alone. One of them was even a former biker, of all people, hiding out in Mexico, of all places. I started getting cold feet.

Next night, back in our room, I told Sheila, "I've had a change of heart?"

I saw the disappointment swimming around in her eyes. "*Shit*, Sandy. You mean a change of heart about leaving this hole? You don't want to *go*?"

I couldn't look her in the eyes. I looked down at my shoes. She had called in so many favors, and her friends had already done all that intricate planning. I felt like shit. And with her still having life without, escape seemed to be the only way she could ever get out of there.

"Sheila, here's the thing. I got no doubt we can bust out, probably make it to Mexico. But the law has time on their side. They won't stop looking, never ever. It'll be just a matter of time *when* they find us, not *if* they find us. We'll be looking over our shoulders our whole lives. Might be a couple months, maybe a couple years, but they'll get us. Then they'll haul us back here and tack ten more years onto our sentences. And we'll likely do two years in the hole, to boot."

She went quiet for a long time. She paced around the room, her thumb against her chin, lost in thoughts. After about ten minutes, she said, teary-eyed, "No doubt that's what they'd do. They'll get us."

I said, "And if you got an escape on your record, odds of you getting your sentence reduced to life *with* is slim to none."

"Yeah," she sighed. "Slim and none—and Slim just left town."

"Then, if we ever *do* get out of here, we'd either be really fucking old or really fucking dead."

Her body sagged with disappointment. She had less to lose than I did, because of life without, but I was disappointed, too. I so wanted out of that miserable existence. But after she thought about it a while, she agreed with me. They'd get us sooner if not later and we would be far worse off.

"Look, you can still go," I said. "Hell, I'll spot for you at the fence, you want me to. I'll cut the hole."

She shook her head. "Naw, shit, Sandy. How would you get back inside for a head count? You do that, you may as well go with me. I'm not going to go to no damn Mexico by myself. Like you say, I could get there. But one day they'll drag my tail back here."

"Yeah, all those TV tip shows like 'America's Most Wanted'. They eventually find everybody."

She lay back on her bed and looked up at the ceiling. "My lawyer's working on an appeal that looks promising, based on that suicide death bed shit. It shouldn't have been admitted at trial because unless you can hold a séance, you can't cross examine a corpse. So, I reckon I'll just hang tight and lean on that. Get out of here the legal route. If I lose the appeal, I'll call the bikers back. Already got a damn good plan and I can say *Adios, Carson Fucking City*."

I thought about it. "Your friends are gonna be pissed, all that work they did. You owe 'em a debt but you can put it all on me. Say it was a two-person operation and I backed out, 'cause I just did."

She managed a smile and waved her hand like she was swatting at a fly. "Naw, hell, those guys, they'll just shrug it off. They'll charge it to the dust and let the rain settle it, and if I ever decide to do it again, they'll be right there and ready." She made a "tisk-tisk" sound. "Was sure fun plannin' that son of a bitch, wasn't it?"

I smiled. She was right. It gave us some great hope while it lasted. "Yeah, like we were writing a movie script but decided not to make the damn movie. If and when I ever do get out of here, I'm going to visit San Miguel de Allende. It looked like a wonderful little city."

There would be no busting out for me. I'd have to do it the legal way. And the way things were going, that was becoming a tall order.

60

What Happened in Between

While I was dealing with my emotional stuff with counseling and working to get an evidentiary hearing, Troy committed another murder. I was flabbergasted and saddened to hear about it. He stabbed fellow inmate Lonnie Blackmon sixty-seven times with a homemade shank on July 6, 1994, in the Utah state prison at Gunnison. Attacked him while they were being transported to medical. It was all caught on prison video. I was sad for Lonnie Blackmon but also for Troy, who was being called a monster but was actually a product of a racist, violent environment in that Utah prison. In his defense, Troy said the day before, Blackmon threatened to get him and he took "get him" to mean "kill him" in prison lingo. Like Jimmy had said, it was a jungle.

I had no idea what was true, but one thing I did know was those men's prisons up in Utah were breeding grounds for white supremacy and racial hate on both sides. Prison officials actually claimed the attack had nothing to do with racism. But the prison videos had Troy on tape yelling, "White Power" when prison guards were putting on their riot gear to go in and get him.

It was a dangerous, maximum-security prison and likely if Troy hadn't gotten Blackmon, Blackmon would have got Troy. That's the world they lived in and that prison allowed it. It was a death penalty trial, and Troy had his lawyer subpoena me and my mom to testify as character witnesses.

When the Vegas press reported the murder, as always they rehashed Troy's original conviction and dragged me through the mud with him. Troy killed

Blackmon two months after my failed evidentiary hearing. But in spite of that major disappointment, I had got one good thing out of dealing with Annabelle Hall. She hired Dr. John P. Wilson to do the interviews with me. His interviews were the spark that eventually changed my life for the better.

Dr. Wilson, in his mid-forties then, had already treated hundreds of combat veterans by the time he came and saw me. But what impressed me most about him, his interview style; it was cautious and comforting—a smart approach because I didn't trust opening up to anybody back then. He was the first person in my whole life I had shared some of those feelings with.

He helped me face my worst memories, starting with seeing Dad beat up Mom when I was three and getting kidnapped back and forth between the two of them like it was ping-pong. He got me talking about the turmoil that had kept me from feeling anchored in my home life when I was growing up. He even helped me get eyeball to eyeball with memories of Alex Egyed and come to grips with why, though I had been able to show regret, I hadn't been able to feel sadness or empathy when Troy killed Cotton.

After he went home and looked over all the results of our interviews, he classified me with a major case of PTSD. He also diagnosed me with a Conduct Disorder and the highest level of stress on his chart. He said he was surprised I could even function day-to-day.

In layman's terms, I was all fucked up.

Those sessions paved the way for seven years of prison counseling that brought on a radical change.

Here is how that happened. One day, not long after those interviews, a clinical psychologist who kept an office in the prison and counseled inmates around the state stopped me in the hallway. He had been trying to talk me into sessions since I first got to Carson City, but I always blew him off. But that day, he informed me Warden Burns had a new program where if inmates joined self-help programs, they got extra privileges. He dangled a carrot: if I signed up for two half-hour sessions, he would credit me for two hours counseling. That was too good to pass up, so I scheduled two one-on-one sessions.

Both those first two one-on-ones, we just gabbed about the weather. But the third time, I began sharing some awful things about my past. I soon got comfortable enough with him to pour out my soul. He knew when to listen and when to talk, and I found myself wishing I'd had that kind of counseling after the Rancho Circle massacre. Maybe my life would have turned out different and I wouldn't be in prison.

This man got me to examine every traumatic incident in my life, one by one. Then, I'd deal with each trauma as a separate case, all linked in a long chain of trauma. It took a long time to experience really dramatic changes. But as I continued the counseling over seven years, starting when I was nineteen, I eventually realized numbing my feelings had been a desperate act of self-preservation.

Even after only months of counseling, inmates and guards I knew couldn't understand how I walked around smiling every day inside a prison. Don't get me wrong, I still felt like I was in a concentration camp, but I stopped dwelling on it every damn minute of every damn day.

I eventually discovered to catch joy in little moments: a funny joke, watching a sunset or a sunrise in the yard, reading a good book, shooting the breeze with friends, or laughing out loud at a comedy show on television. One day I sat with Sheila in our cell, enjoying sweet treats from the vending machine, and I said something I would never have said in my early days in prison: "Tell me, Sheila. Who you know has it any better than we do right this minute?"

She grinned. "Nobody!"

I had also been addicted to cigarettes since I was fourteen, and I kicked the habit forever.

I figured out the best way to get my mind off my own troubles was to put it on somebody else's. It worked wonders. Like when a sixteen-year-old girl named Crystal came to prison in Carson City for bank robbery. That was when I was twenty-four. I took her under my wing mainly because she was the same age I was when they locked me up. Her life was just as much of a mess as mine had been, maybe more. She'd robbed a bank with her ne'er-do-well boyfriend—went along with him to try to fit in so he'd accept her—and now she was doing five to ten. And she came to prison very pregnant.

For starters, she needed to deal with her selfishness. A girl was being put in The Hole for thirty days and trusted Crystal with a hundred dollars' cash to keep for her till she got out of solitary. Crystal decided to spend that girl's money on herself. She bought stuff from the commissary with it, and this and that, until the money was gone.

I found out about it and confronted her. She didn't seem to think she'd done anything wrong. I went off on her and told her how even in prison, people better have ethics and a moral code. "You can't pull shit like that on people," I said. "I don't know how or where you're going to get the money to pay her back, but you better start figuring it out. Your reputation means everything in a place like this. And if you don't pay her, I'm done helping you."

She got the money from her mother, and a week later, she gave it to the girl the day that girl got out of The Hole. That was a big turning point in Crystal's young life.

I would give her advice from time to time and find her decent maternity clothes. I taught her the Do's and Don'ts of prison conduct, how to stay out of trouble with the guards and other inmates, and how to spot the violent ones.

I didn't hang out with her all that much, but I kept an eye on her and talked to her when she needed to talk. She did a complete three-sixty with her attitude in the following months and became a responsible, ethical young woman. She had never had those qualities on the outside. When her baby was born, she asked me to name it and be the baby's godmother. I was humbled and honored, and I named the baby Savanah. Crystal's mother raised Savanah until Crystal got out of prison after six years.

I stayed in touch with her, and she eventually married a nice man and they bought a nice home, raised Savanah right, and are now raising a son to honorable manhood. That boy is also my godson.

Since the day she left prison, Crystal has been there to support me at every turn and at every hearing I've ever had. On the positive side of my ledger, I consider Crystal one of the better projects in my life.

But I couldn't have helped her if I hadn't started reconnecting with my emotions in those counseling sessions. I could now be a positive force for others and for myself. And I could do what I never could do after Rancho Circle—simple things like telling family members how much I loved and appreciated them, or giving a friend a supportive hug. As I got inside my own head and my own heart, I began to leave behind that confused, frightened, fifteen-year-old who had first come to prison.

I continued my formal education and spent many hours every day with my nose in a textbook. In 1993, I earned an Associate degree and then, two years later, a second Associate—this one in General Studies, both from Western Nevada Community College. When both degrees were conferred, I got to attend graduation ceremonies. My family attended those ceremonies, too—Mom, all three siblings, and my grandmother, Marie.

With my second degree, I had the highest grades in the entire class—not just among inmates, but the entire college throughout the state of Nevada. I was selected as class valedictorian. What an honor that was. My family members were so proud. I was slated to give the valedictorian's speech, but I always was and remain today terrified to speak in front of large audiences. So I talked the salutatorian into giving the speech, and she was awesome.

After I got those degrees, I completed my high school diploma from Carson City High School just for my own satisfaction.

No matter my accomplishments or the fleeting highs that lifted my spirits, reality was always there—whispering in my ear, tapping at my shoulder, reminding me I was still behind bars, with no hint of when or if I would ever be free.

61

Shakopee Prison and Troy Kell's Fate

In late 1995, the State of Nevada started transferring inmates out of Carson again because they were building a new women's prison in Vegas. They would phase out the Carson women's prison and make it an expansion of the men's prison. I beat them to the punch after researching Shakopee women's prison in Minnesota. I put in for a transfer and got it.

A handful of us left two days after Christmas in a prison-contracted van, on a tedious five-day drive with intervals of twelve hours on the road and twelve-hour rest periods. We got checked into local jails during the rest periods. The contracted van driver was sweet on me, kept leaving treats on my seat every morning, and one day suggested if I wanted to escape with him, he could arrange it. I said no.

We got to Shakopee on New Year's Eve of 1996. The prison, which looked more like a college campus, was in a residential area in a small town southwest of Minneapolis. Surrounded by trees and shrubbery and blanketed with snow, it looked like a scene right off a Hallmark card. When the spring thaw came, every morning you could taste the pine riding the breeze.

The prison had no fences and no razor wire, just a vast, wide-open wildlife refuge that discouraged any escape. There were no traditional prison cells; we had nicely appointed single cottage rooms that locked from the inside, not the outside. I was astonished when they first handed me my own room key and said as long as I logged thirty hours a week of either work or school, I would never have to lock my door at night. I could come and go as I pleased.

Guards wore uniforms, each of them identifying them by their names, not badges like in Carson and Reno. We were allowed to wear civilian clothes; the guards and staff called us by our first names, and we called them by theirs. That even included "Warden Connie."

The staff never dehumanized inmates. It was the only prison I was ever in whose purpose was to rehabilitate, not just warehouse offenders. They trained the inmates rather than punished them, hoping to release them free of the very issues that put them there. It might have been a model for every prison in America: their recidivism rate was only 6 percent, compared to nearly 25 percent in Nevada.

I quickly got a job as a telemarketer and was good at it because I made conversation easily. I filled any free time reading, doing daily workouts in the gym, and then, when spring came, playing center field on a prison softball team. The downside, I was a long way from Mom and missed her visits, but I reconnected with Dad. He was a three-hour drive away and drove down twice with my half-brother Chris, the son he had with Cindy. Dad was pushing fifty now. We chatted small talk about all sorts of stuff, but we avoided talking about the bad stuff, him and mom kidnapping us back and forth or how he used to beat her up. Dad was supportive, and it was all I needed from him.

I only spent six months in Shakopee. I left reluctantly in early July, subpoenaed to testify at the penalty phase of Troy's Utah murder trial. He'd been found guilty the month prior. At the same time, Nevada was calling back all female inmates who had transferred out of state to ready us to relocate to that new prison soon to open in Vegas. But the biggest reason I needed to go back to Carson, I would be going to the parole board and writing an appeal to get to the Pardons Board for the first time. If my hearings were in absentia, I'd have no voice and little chance of a favorable outcome. I had to keep fighting because the alternative was to quit and morph into one of those institutionalized zombies.

The Utah Department of Corrections arrange my flight from Minneapolis to Salt Lake City, wearing handcuffs with a jacket draped over them so the passengers wouldn't get the heebie-jeebies. I was put in the back row, sandwiched between two hefty Utah police detectives. Then it was a two-hour drive south to Gunnison, pretty much a one-stoplight town. The prison and the town were out in the middle of a lot of unappealing, mountainous nothing.

I really didn't want to be there, but I was sure it would be the last time I would ever see Troy, and I wanted to remember him as the pleasant little boy who was my childhood friend. Not the grown up man who had lived a dangerous, violent existence in a men's prison.

The upside was Mom had also been subpoenaed as a character witness, and I'd get to visit with her. They stuck me in a cell near the front of the men's prison, a little scary considering it was a maximum security penitentiary, but they kept guards nearby my cell. The trial was in a makeshift courtroom in the prison rather than the town courthouse because they considered Troy a security risk.

Next morning, they fed me breakfast inside my cell, then two guards took me to the prison courtroom. I saw Mom in a chair in the first row, looking regal in her Sunday best. She winked and waved and I smiled back. Then I spotted Troy at the defendant's table, looking somber, but he managed to flash a smile when he saw me.

Troy's prosecutor was brief with me, asking only about the night Troy killed Cotton Kelly and to establish he had been the shooter. Troy's lawyer then had me recall sentimental things, when we were kids living the innocent days of our youth. I recollected how Troy always looked out after me and Shane and how close he was to my mom, and to that day still sent her flowers every Mother's Day. I mentioned how strict his parents had been, and that was about it.

The same two police detectives took me to the Gunnison County Jail for what would be a dreary thirty-day stay. Nevada was never in a hurry to get someone back when they were secured somewhere else. Maybe one less mouth to feed?

Mom came to the jail before she went back home, and we had a nice, two-hour visit. "I feel sad for Troy," she said. "They're probably gonna kill him, you know. I don't believe in that eye for an eye shit." But she didn't dwell on it and was pleased I would be transferred fairly soon to the new prison in Las Vegas, and we could visit more often.

Two days before those same Utah detectives drove me back to Carson, the judge sentenced Troy to death by firing squad. It saddened me so to hear that. He had written me at Shakopee before his trial, promising to kill himself if he got the death sentence. I didn't respond at the time because I wasn't sure what to say. But when I got back to Carson, I wrote him and said: "I understand why you might do that—end your own life before they can end it for you. But consider this: You lived the way you lived, and you did the things you did, and you have put your family through enough. Now you say you're going to kill yourself and lay that on them, too. Don't!"

62

Fighting for a Parole

In 1996, still in Carson City, I went to the parole board on the murder charge. I had served the required ten and was eligible, though the court said I still had ten more to serve before I could try for parole on the weapons charge.

The hearing was inside the prison in a visiting room, and I was nervous yet confident they would approve me. After all, the law was clear: anyone convicted as a juvenile who had completed their education and didn't have any major infractions like assault or escape attempts was to be automatically approved, no exceptions.

When I entered the room, there were only three of them seated—a commissioner and three board members—and some guy in a tacky red-orange double-knit sport coat leaning against the back wall.

I wasn't sure who he was, and I didn't know what to expect, since parole board members aren't jurists. None of them are steeped in legal knowledge, just everyday Joes and Janes the governor appoints for four-year terms. Likely, they were personal friends of the governor's or people he owed favors to, who wanted a side job as judge, jury, and executioner for the parole-eligible.

For an hour, they questioned me about all sorts of stuff, from specifics about the crime to all the minor infractions I'd had in recent years, to how remorseful I was for my crime. When they finished, they turned the floor over to the fellow in the red-orange sport coat leaning against the wall.

He glared at me, and as the saying goes, *if looks could kill.*

He said he was George Thiede, Cotton's brother. I figured half-brother because of the different last names. He said he knew for a fact I was the ringleader, solely responsible for his brother's murder. He asked the board, on behalf of his family, to turn me down and let me rot.

I went back to my cell when it was over because a parole board never gives an immediate answer. I had to wait maybe three weeks to find out they not only denied me but gave me a three-year dump, meaning I couldn't try again until 1999.

By then, I had given up all hope of Annabelle Hall ever getting me to the Pardons Board. I had tried to call her many times over the past two years, and she wouldn't even return my calls. So I read over her original brief and wrote a letter to the Pardons Board, and to my surprise, they accepted me. I got scheduled for late July 1997. I was excited because I thought I had a good chance.

At the time, Christopher Oram, a really sharp defense attorney from Las Vegas, was putting together a writ of habeas corpus for me on some strong issues and working pro bono. Among the evidence, he discovered Dan Seaton had arranged for Billy Merritt to take a polygraph test prior to my trial. Seaton wanted the polygraph so he could go to a judge and get Billy's plea deal approved.

In his polygraph exam, Billy said there was no robbery planned, that he and Troy were supposed to beat up a guy stalking his friend, which was me. He said neither he nor I had handled the gun or knew that Troy had a gun or planned to use it. In his request to get the judge to okay Billy's plea deal, Seaton told him Billy had passed the polygraph "with some of the highest scores I have ever seen."

Oram had discovered Seaton's written report about the lie detector test, proving that when Seaton tried me, he knew his allegations in court about a conspiracy and a robbery motive, and the facts of how I had met Cotton were all false. Oram considered it proof of very serious prosecutorial misconduct.

But I asked Chris not to file it because I discovered the Pardons Board wouldn't hear any case that had an appeal pending. Soon after that, I was time-barred from that habeas corpus appeal. Oram wanted to then appeal to federal courts, but I knew those appeals took forever, and so he dropped it. I decided to roll the dice with the Pardons Board instead.

The Nevada Supreme Court has headquarters both in Carson City and Las Vegas. My hearing was set for Carson City.

The Board consisted of Governor Bob Miller, state attorney general Frankie Sue Del Papa, and the seven Justices. I was petitioning to reduce my sentences to run concurrently, instead of consecutively, so I would be parole eligible on both charges. I figured I had a good chance because I outlined all the illegalities in my original trial that had been strong enough for Judge Sobel to grant my evidentiary hearing in 1991.

I no sooner was seated than Annabelle Hall walked in and plopped down at the same table. I had asked the court for a public defender, but she was still my attorney of record, and they forced her to show up and represent me. She said hello, and I just nodded and said nothing.

Soon after the Justices started grilling me, I noticed Governor Miller was reading something very intently. I was close enough to him and at an angle where I could see the letterhead on the paper, which read: *Office of the District Attorney.*

After I answered a few more questions, maybe a half-hour into the hearing, Governor Miller suddenly spoke up. "I want to inform this Board there is no reason to proceed with this hearing, because I have made up my mind to vote no."

My jaw dropped open, and my heart sank.

The governor continued, "This applicant, Sandy Marie Shaw, has too many infractions on her record, for one thing, and other matters of such consequence that I do not believe she is a good risk for release."

The governor had to vote yes as part of a majority yes vote for me to win my petition. It still had to be five to four but the governor's vote had that kind of weight. The hearing I worked so hard to get ended abruptly on that note.

Annabelle Hall said, "Governor Miller, and your honors, all those infractions happened when she was first incarcerated. She was just a sixteen-year-old kid."

Governor Miller reached for a sheet of paper. "Well, then how do you explain all these infractions?" He started reeling off some more recent write-ups from a list compiled after I was sixteen. None of them were for anything major and nothing violent, but it didn't matter. Hall shouldn't have spoken up about what she didn't know. I was humiliated when the governor started reading from the list of infractions. It didn't seem like he or the Justices gave a damn about the illegalities at my trial, or whether I had even *had* a fair trial. This hearing was over, and I was screwed.

As I gathered my papers before the guard took me back to prison, I noticed Governor Miller reading from that letter with the Clark County Prosecutor letterhead. Suddenly, he stopped reading and stared at me with what I interpreted to be disdain. I then wondered what that asshole meant by "other matters of such consequence."

As I walked out of that courtroom, I was kicking myself for telling Chris Oram not to file that writ. I had taken a risk and lost.

Two months later, in September of 1997, all inmates from the existing women's prisons—Carson City and Indian Springs—got moved to the new prison in Vegas. It was designed to hold five hundred inmates, about double the capacity of Carson City. It was tiered, and there were nine pods. I found it ironic, almost comical, that the street address was "Smiley Road." Our happy place, indeed.

It was the first and only privately owned prison in Nevada and was contracted with Corrections Corporation of America (CCA). Warehousing criminals was fast becoming big business in America. CCA owned and operated a wide assortment of private prisons and detention centers all over the country. Their stock was traded on the New York Stock Exchange, and inmates were their product.

We weren't in Vegas long before convict Cathy Woods used a cigarette lighter and hairspray to set herself on fire. Guards managed to put the fire out in time to save her, but she was badly burned. This sad woman, who later had tried to cut her tits off, had been the product of mental hospitals in Louisiana before unofficially confessing to a Nevada murder and getting life. As a result of setting herself on fire, the prison overreacted and made a rule none of us could have cigarette lighters or hairspray. Not long after, two lifers planned an escape using an outside guy. They were busted before they could make their break, but from then on, the prison decided we needed to be easily identifiable and could no longer wear our own fashionable clothes. We could wear only denim, blue and white, or navy blue. It was another blow to individuality.

Then CCA declared makeup, hair dye, bras, and panties contraband. The cheap bastards also furnished us with two really low-grade rolls of toilet paper, which were supposed to last the whole week, and eight cut-rate Maxi pads—but if you had money, you could at least buy your own tampons. That's one way CCA could assure they made a profit for their investors. Spend as little as possible on the human beings they housed.

Soon after arriving, I got hired for the usual ten cents an hour as a prison janitor. One perk of the job was when Mom came to visit, she hid makeup, hair coloring, and other contraband in the waste cans in the visitors' restroom. Then, when I would clean the restrooms at night, I'd fetch the contraband and hide various items in the back of my radio and in my pillow. I had cut the pillow open to hide the stuff in between the stuffing inside the pillow and sewed it back up.

As for Cathy Woods, real name Anita Carter, while she had been a patient in a Louisiana mental hospital in 1980, she told staff members she murdered a University of Nevada-Reno nursing student four years prior. Woods had worked as a bartender in Reno at the time of the killing and had a long history of schizophrenia (first hospitalized when she was eleven years old). She made a lot of false statements to police, but they decided she knew enough about the crime that she was the killer, even though everything she told them had been in the Reno papers. She was tried, convicted, and sentenced to life.

I would see her around the prison now and then and felt so sorry for her because she was so pathetic and didn't belong in a prison; she needed to be treated in a mental hospital. Woods/Carter would do thirty-three years in Nevada prisons before DNA on a cigarette butt proved the killer was one Tony Lima. After all those years doing the Thorazine shuffle, Woods/Carter was exonerated, then sued the state of Nevada and pocketed three million dollars. I thought, good for her. I hope she enjoyed the hell out of that money before she died in 2021. When asked why she had first made the false, incriminating statements to the mental hospital staff in Shreveport, she said she hoped to get a nicer room in the hospital.

Go figure.

In 1999, in the new prison in Las Vegas, now thirteen years in, I went back to the parole board on the murder charge. I was always really nervous and scared before those hearings and would lose my appetite for weeks and have to cut another notch in my belt. I was about to sit down and face people who had my life in their hands. Just before I walked into my 1999 hearing, my caseworker, Mr. Clark, said, "Oh, by the way, that cheap-looking pimp of a brother of his is here." He meant George Thiede.

While Commissioner Dennison was questioning me, Thiede interrupted and started on about how I was a problem inmate who shouldn't get paroled. Dennison pointed at him and snapped, "Don't interrupt me again and don't you ever tell me how to do my job."

The Board immediately paroled me on the murder charge, which automatically paroled me to the weapons charge so I could keep right on serving time—time that kept crawling by.

63

The Mob Cop and 2002 Pardons Hearing

In early 2002, an inmate and good friend of mine talked her dad into loaning me money to hire the best criminal lawyer in Las Vegas, Bill Terry. Terry was known as hard-driving tough in the courtroom but also as a very honorable man. It wasn't long after I hired him he came through and got me a Pardons Board hearing to try to get my sentences to run concurrently. That would make me immediately eligible for parole on the weapons charge and, hopefully, out the door I'd soon go. I was thirty-one now and had been locked up sixteen years; I'd spent more than half my life in there.

It was about that time I had some really strange run-ins with prison security officer/retired NYPD police detective Stephen Caracappa. He was lanky, gaunt, 6'2", around sixty years old. When he locked eyes on you, he looked straight through you. A killer's eyes, I thought. Like Alex's that night. I didn't trust him.

I never gave Caracappa a good reason to write me up. I was being extra careful not to have infractions for my next trip to the Pardons Board. But one day, Caracappa just started giving me write-ups, for no good reason, or so it seemed, and he didn't stop. Sometimes it was for contraband—having too much jewelry or some piece of clothing that he said was not within the dress code. Or sometimes just on hearsay. But by the end of that month, he'd hit me with a dozen infractions, and I was mystified.

Then one day, I heard he was leaving for another job, and I approached him. "Look, Officer Caracappa. How come you gave me all those write-ups, and for no reason. What the hell did I ever do to you?"

He looked around to make sure nobody was in earshot. "Maybe there are people higher up out there who don't want you to ever get out of this place. Maybe I was doing a favor for some people I might know."

"Bullshit. Favor for who?" As he walked away, I called out, "I don't even know any fucking people."

It was maybe a month or so after Caracappa left his prison job, a guard came got me in my cell. Two FBI men wanted to talk to me. "FBI?" I was speechless and a good bit nervous. "What the hell for?"

"I dunno," the guard said. "They got a room set up. I was told to come fetch you."

The guard took me into the room, closed the door behind me, and went outside. The two men definitely had the G-man look—well-groomed, wearing black suits, like a couple actors from central casting. Even their ties matched. One was up around 6′3″, the other maybe 5′7″. I thought of Mutt and Jeff from the Sunday funnies. Mutt showed me his FBI credentials in their black folding case, and Jeff did the same.

"Please have a seat, Miss Shaw," Mutt asked.

I sat down, and Jeff offered me a cigarette and I waved him off. "Am I in some trouble here?"

"No, no, not at all," said Jeff. "Just want to ask you about some things."

"Ask away," I said. "I got nowhere better to be."

"You know a Stephen Caracappa?" Mutt said.

"Yeah, he used to work here. Pardon my lingo, but he was a real prick."

Jeff leaned back slightly in his chair and braced his foot against a table leg. "We are curious why he gave you so many write-ups and didn't give other inmates any. Almost never. Did ya have a rift with the guy?"

"No, sir. No rift. I never did anything to him. I swear. He just suddenly took a disliking to me. Or so I thought—till he said something to me before he quit his job."

Jeff finally lit his dangling cigarette and took a long drag. "Oh, yeah? What was that?"

"I asked him why he had it in for me and he said nothing personal. Told me some people he knew didn't want me to ever get out of prison. Claimed he was doing a favor for somebody, but I didn't buy it."

Jeff straightened his tie. "Anybody you could think of he might be doing the favor for?"

"Not really. I mean, nobody he'd likely be connected with, being an ex–New York cop and all."

Mutt offered me a stick of chewing gum, and I took it.

"Well," Jeff said, "we think it likely *was* somebody he was connected with."

The two looked at one another and nodded.

Then Mutt tipped his head. "That's all we needed to know, Miss Shaw. You can go now. Thank you and good luck to you."

It was a weird meeting, and I was confused why they even wanted to talk to me about that bony-faced jerk.

A few weeks later, I had my pardon hearing at the Las Vegas Supreme Court Regional Justice Center. Sure as hell, Chief Justice Young brought up those twelve-infractions I got from Caracappa and wondered why I couldn't keep the rules in prison. Terry explained it as well as it could be explained, but saying Caracappa had it in for me didn't fly.

Governor Kenny Guinn sided with me, but we lost the petition, five to four. Governor Guinn said, "This is one of those cases where you start wondering how much time is too much time." I had now spent more time in prison than women who committed premeditated murders, poisoned their husbands, and even murdered their own kids.

Chief Justice Young told me he wanted me to do closer to twenty years. I turned to Terry and whispered, "He wants me to do twenty, he thinks I killed the man."

Terry agreed. "They evidently think you were a shooter, but where'd they get that idea?" Terry had entered a sworn affidavit from Troy Kell saying I never handled the gun, had no idea a gun was in the car that night, or that he planned to kill Cotton. But the Board didn't seem to consider it.

Even though we lost, Terry said the hearing was encouraging and promised to start pushing for another right away. "We'll win the damn thing next time, I guarantee." I had confidence in him and left that hearing reassured.

Then, several months later, I was watching TV in the rec room, and a news story came on that totally knocked me off my gait. I couldn't believe what I was hearing. The reporter said: "Two former Las Vegas residents and retired NYPD homicide detectives, Louis Eppolito and Stephen Caracappa, have been arrested by the FBI and indicted for multiple counts of murder. According to the indictment, while serving as New York homicide detectives, the two were on the payroll of the Lucchese and Gambino crime families. They performed hits for the mob, according to the indictment, and were paid up to one-hundred-thousand dollars per killing."

The indictment claimed Caracappa and Eppolito used their police resources to find people the mob wanted murdered, then they arrested the victims, took them somewhere secluded and killed them.

A newspaper story next day said Eppolito's father had been a Gambino family mobster, and after retiring as an NYPD cop, Eppolito got small parts in movies, including "Goodfellas." Eppolito got sentenced to life without, and Caracappa got life plus one hundred years. When I heard that news, I hoped every time that son of a bitch Caracappa lay his bony butt down on that hard-ass prison bed, he would see my face.

Both of them would die in prison. I was beginning to wonder if that would be my fate.

Then something really fantastic happened, something bizarre. A few months after that failed 2002 pardons hearing, in my prison mail I got an anonymous packet in a big Manilla envelope. It contained proof of illegal and unethical actions that both got me convicted and had kept me in prison.

64

The Mystery Packet

When I got that packet in my mail, I was suspicious at first because it had no return address. I made sure I was alone in my cell room when I opened it. The evidence inside was an eye-opener, a shocker, and I couldn't wait to get all this stuff to Bill Terry.

Someone had spent a lot of time preparing the information. At the very top of the batch was a letter LVPD homicide detective Dave Hatch had written in my favor to the parole board and simultaneously to the Pardons Board for my 2002 hearing. I knew nothing about detective Hatch, other than in researching my appeals, I had come across his name as having custody of my case for years after McGuckin and the other detective who arrested me retired. I had been around the system long enough to know that if a police detective wrote to a parole or Pardons Board concerning a convict, it was always to assure that convict stayed behind bars.

Yet Hatch had petitioned the Board on my behalf, saying, "{Sandy Shaw's} involvement in this crime is exactly as she describes it in her letter for clemency," and "this agency has no interest in denying her commutation of sentence." Stapled to his letter was a handwritten note Hatch had initialed, addressed to someone else in the homicide division. It said, "I'm going to catch a lot of hell for writing this letter, but I don't care. This is the first and only time I have ever written to a parole or pardons board in favor of an inmate. I am totally convinced this girl got a raw deal."

Beneath that letter were copies of selected pages of my trial transcript, with certain passages of testimony circled. Then came a jolt when I saw a copy of the original police report about Cotton's murder—before we were even arrested. It included a fax from the Edmonton, Alberta, Investigative Unit that the plates on the recovered vehicle indicated that James Cotton Kelly was actually "James Thiede"; and further, he and both his parents and an uncle were under investigation at the time by the Royal Canadian Mounted Police for drug smuggling and money laundering. All of them had been using the same alias, "Kelly." This was the *first* time I knew his real name wasn't Kelly.

Lead prosecutor Seaton would have seen that police report within days of my arrest and would know Cotton was a suspected drug smuggler. Don't get me wrong, he didn't deserve to die for smuggling drugs, but this report was exculpatory evidence Seaton should have shared with Rohay. It countered Seaton's assertion in court that Cotton was a Canadian version of the "All American Boy" who never would stalk a minor child for sex. That police report was a smoking gun.

Also included was a copy of a 1991 news article in the Edmonton, Alberta *Journal* about the arrest and indictment of a "Justin Ross Kelly," alias Thomas Alfred Thiede, for possession of high-grade cocaine for the purpose of trafficking. Thomas Alfred Thiede was Cotton's father and had been living in Las Vegas at the time he was arrested in a Toronto hotel room, and the RCMP seized 837 grams of high-grade cocaine.

Paper-clipped to that news item was information about the arrest of a woman and another man, both using the Kelly alias, also for possession of cocaine with intent to traffic; they turned out to be Thomas Thiede's wife and brother—Cotton's mother and uncle.

I concluded that Cotton had moved from Canada to Las Vegas in 1986 to help run the family drug business. While Rohay should not have put the victim on trial, the information about the RCMP's investigation would have shot a big hole in Seaton's claim that such a good boy as Cotton Kelly (James Thiede) would have never stalked me for sex or trolled a teenage arcade to pick up fourteen-year-old Tina Wilson.

So, if the jury didn't buy Seaton's fictional account of Cotton's sterling character, they also wouldn't have bought into Seaton's ridiculous yarn about a robbery motive. And without the robbery motive, his "teenage temptress" fabrication would have gone down the drain, and I most likely would have been acquitted.

Next was a Xerox copy of a note from Seaton to Deputy District Attorney David Roger asking him not to negotiate with me in my 1994 evidentiary hearing.

But maybe the biggest bombshell was a copy of a letter from the Office of the District Attorney, dated June 27, 1997, addressed to the Nevada Board of Pardons, and stamped "Received" on July 1, 1997, just before my first Pardons Board hearing. It was a two-page letter regarding my pardon application. The DA's office objected to the commutation of my sentence and included a section "Statement of Facts" that was pure fiction. It was bogus information.

The letter claimed what Stacy Buhman told detectives were "facts," including that after Troy Kell shot Cotton once and when he was on the ground moaning, I shot him between the eyes and finished him off.

That letter maintained I told these things to Stacy when I took her out to view the body, which I never did—Dave took her out there. The letter went on to say, "Ms. Shaw killed a man so she could get a portion of sixteen hundred dollars."

Even Dan Seaton, in court, trying his damnedest to convict me of murder, finally acknowledged I didn't pull the trigger. The author of that letter, Chief Deputy District Attorney Christopher Laurent, had only to check the coroner's report to learn Troy not only fired all six shots, but none of those shots were "between the eyes." Five were into the side of his face, and the fatal shot was in his neck.

Laurent was an educated man with a doctorate in law, but his math skills seemed lacking. He stated I had "killed a man to get a portion of sixteen hundred dollars." But in the previous paragraph, he said the amount was "fourteen hundred dollars," and then he said further down I received "six hundred dollars and the two guys each got two hundred." That adds up to a thousand dollars, and I would have asked him if Billy gave the rest of the money to a passing coyote to buy chickens. If you're going to make up lies, at least be consistent.

Laurent manufactured that false report to keep me in prison, to further damage my life by costing me another ten years. I realized that every time I had gone to a parole hearing or a pardons hearing from 1997 on, Laurent's letter, or one just like it, got into the hands of board members and prejudiced them against me.

Laurent's letter looked curiously similar to the one I saw Governor Bob Miller reading at my 1997 Pardons hearing, regarding his statement about "other matters of such consequence," when he ended the hearing by saying he would vote "no." The ink would have still been fresh on his letter. I think "other matters of such consequences" was Laurent's letter full of lies.

I noticed his letter had been addressed to the "Honorable" board members and wondered how a man like Laurent would be allowed to use a word like "honorable."

Since 2002, I have tried without success to find out who delivered that packet to me. My best guess is the late David Eugene Hatch, a twenty-seven-year veteran of the Las Vegas homicide squad, who had written the compassionate letter on my behalf to the Pardons Board earlier that year.

Dave Hatch, ex-Marine, twice wounded in combat in Vietnam, a man for whom the term "honorable" was just lying there waiting for him to be born.

65

Big Win at the Pardons Board

When I was twenty-six, in 1997, I earned a business certificate, and three years later started working as a teacher's aide in the Las Vegas prison's education department. I trained inmates on computers so they would have skills to help them get jobs once they were released. It was a good feeling to help inmates going out into society again. But I kept praying I'd get released too, before I was old and gray and had to limp out the gate.

Right about that time, there was great news for my long-time friend Sheila Summers. She had gone to the Pardons Board and got her sentence reduced from life without to life "with," then got paroled out in 2003. She went back to her hometown of Sioux City, Iowa, and found work driving a taxi cab. According to her daughter April, she loved that job. For an outgoing person like her, it was perfect work. She had been railroaded into prison as well, convicted by a suicide note from a mentally unstable woman. I was so happy for her that she wasn't going to die old and lonely in a prison.

I'd always liked life better when I had a sense of purpose. I found one when I got involved with a prison program called "Pups On Parole." We inmates got dogs and cats from local shelters and trained and cared for them in our cells and in the rec yard. When they were trained and ready, the shelters adopted them out to families and the community. It was a wonderful program that gave us some little critters to love and to love us back. It was just hard to get so attached to them and see them leave. I took to one particular dog I trained and named "Bossy." She was a mid-size mix who was very loving, timid, and terrified of men.

That same year, Bill Terry got me scheduled at the Pardons Board. This time we had to go up to Carson City in January, where they housed me at the county jail. It was freezing in that jail and some inmate needed a blanket. For some reason, my cell had several extras and I passed one out of my cell and it got passed along, inmate-to-inmate, to the girl who needed it.

But shortly after, guards inspected her cell and found a prescription pill in that blanket. Because the blanket originated with me, they wrote me up for it. I knew nothing of the pill, and anybody in that conga line could have stuck that in there. Bill Terry immediately canceled the hearing because he knew I would be rejected for the infraction. He would need time to properly explain it to the Board in another hearing. So he got me rescheduled ten months later, for November 2004, and this time we won the damn thing.

Hallelujah!

My sentences were now running concurrently, and I was immediately eligible to be paroled out.

I got to the parole board on December 17, 2004, but they denied me and gave me another three-year dump. I'd been so full of hope, and now I was deflated.

The parole board members change every four years. George Thiede was at that hearing and spoke passionately about keeping me locked up till I died. This was the first time the new board had seen me or heard from him. So, I was sure he impacted their decision. I am also convinced they got the same letter that Laurent had sent to the 1997 Pardons Board, about me shooting Cotton between the eyes.

66

2007 Parole Hearing

Maybe it was paranoia, but I was beginning to fear the parole boards were going to keep giving me three-year dumps till I was an old lady. But I was also more confident with this one. Knowing the prosecutor's office was going to likely send the board that same lie about me being the shooter, I sent them a letter with a copy of the coroner's report showing the victim was not shot in the head or between the eyes. I included a copy of Troy's affidavit that I had neither handled the gun nor knew he had one.

A friend helped generate a big letter-writing campaign to the parole board for several months, with letters from people all over the nation, including defense attorneys and former prosecutors, a former parole officer, and even a former US Congressman.

As always, I was absolutely terrified before the hearing, and I lost my appetite the entire week before. It was set for Monday, August 27. The night before, to get to sleep, I used a deep breathing relaxation countdown a friend had shown me, and I did it again the next day before the hearing.

This one was set up with cameras for closed-circuit TV, with the board members all in Carson City and me in the prison visitor's room in Las Vegas. I sat at a table facing the screen and cameras. Seated behind me was my family—my mom, both sisters, my brother, my grandmother Fosteson, and my friend Crystal—the former inmate who would attend every hearing I would ever have.

George Thiede was in Carson City attending the hearing.

We got started just after lunch. I answered their questions as calmly and thoroughly as I could, one right after another. I purposely spoke slowly so I wouldn't sound anxious and make a lot of flubs.

One of the female members commented, "Judging by all the letters we received on your behalf, Ms. Shaw, you have a lot of people in your corner." I was glad to know they had actually read those letters.

At one point, George Thiede interrupted, "I don't know how you expect this *convict* to keep the rules on the outside if she can't keep them on the *inside*—all her infractions."

The parole commissioner replied, "Actually, Ms. Shaw has kept the rules quite well. She hasn't had even one single infraction in the past three years."

Thiede looked confused, like he'd been ambushed. I had behaved myself, and there was no Stephen Caracappa to help him out this time.

The hearing lasted just over an hour, and I thought it had gone well. But I knew I would have to wait—as long as three weeks—for their decision. I busied myself as best I could every day following the hearing. And I did a shitload of praying.

Then on Monday, September 10, my case worker asked me to come to the warden's office; the parole board had made its decision. When I walked in, both the warden and my case worker looked somber. Nobody said anything at first, and I thought, *Oh, shit*. Finally, the warden smiled wide and said to my case worker, "Aw, stop fooling around and tell her the damn news."

He smiled wide. "You made parole, Sandy." I looked up at the ceiling and said, "Oh my God!" I asked the warden, "Can I call Mom and tell her?"

The warden made the call for me. "Mrs. Shaw," the warden deadpanned, "it's about your daughter, Sandy. She wants to speak to you."

I could hear Mom on the line say, "What the hell has she done this time?"

The warden handed me the phone. My voice was cracking so bad with emotion I could barely choke out the words. ". . . Mom . . . I'm coming home."

67

On Parole Forever

With all the paperwork and red tape, they didn't release me until Monday, December 17, just in time to celebrate Christmas as a free woman after twenty-one long, tedious, stressful, often depressing years. But I learned there would be no end date to my parole. I was getting out on the rare condition of "a lifetime parole."

Being released after all those years was like strolling out into the Land of Oz. But I had kept up on life outside the prison walls and adapted quickly. I got a driver's license within a couple days and was comfortably driving a black Mustang convertible a dear friend had gotten for me. I settled back into society easily because I had never let myself get institutionalized and totally out of touch with the real world.

Parole is a tough go and very restrictive. I would have to be constantly on my toes to avoid any violation that would land me back in prison. It had taken me twenty-one years to get out, and I didn't intend to screw up and go back. I read every line of the fine print of the terms of my parole. Jesus, I couldn't even have a glass of wine at a holiday dinner. I also wasn't to contact any inmate I knew from prison, and I couldn't travel out of state without a travel pass. I had to report monthly and had to pay the Board a thirty-dollar monthly fee for the privilege of being on parole; if I missed a payment or was late with one, they could toss me back in the joint.

Parolees are set up to fail for one reason—money. Whenever someone in Nevada goes to prison, the state gives the prison system twenty-five thousand dollars, and they get that much every year that the inmate is in prison, and that includes parole violators. Many, if not most, parolees have no families to go to and take care of them while they look for work. They are on their own out in the hard, cold, free world and unable to make a decent living or get a decent job, what with the stigma of "ex-con" on their resume, all too often they turn back to lives of crime as armed robbers, burglars, or drug dealers. When they break parole and go back to prison—cha-ching—that's another quick twenty-five grand of taxpayer money into the prison coffers.

When they opened the gates on December 17, a prison van took me to a parole office to register. My family met me there and took me to Mom's house. Regarding the "lifetime" terms of my parole: I had belonged to them since I was sixteen, and they wanted me to be theirs till the day I died. But after another ten years, I could petition to be removed from parole.

The day I got out, I stopped on the way home and paid a two-hundred-fifty-dollar adoption fee and brought my sweet dog Bossy home. "We've both been sprung," I told her, and she jumped all around. I think she sensed she had a new home.

That first night home, everybody was there—Mom, Leah, Shane, Nicole, and her four kids. And Mike Flanery stopped by. I was bursting with happiness, and we all chatted on about this, that, and the other. Then about ten o'clock, one by one, everyone but me started going to bed. I was soon sitting in the living room all alone—so much for my big homecoming. Even Bossy had gone to sleep, though Shane's sweet pit bull Gauge came and lay by my feet.

The next night, a friend who'd helped me get out treated me to a fabulous dinner at Fleming's Steakhouse. First time I had had steak and a baked potato since I was fifteen. I felt out of place in that fancy joint at first, but I settled into it. My friend's friends had chipped in for a thousand-dollar gift card for me to buy clothes and another thousand-dollar Visa card to tide me over till I found work. A few days later, Jessica Mallin and her husband surprised the hell out of me with an eighteen-hundred-dollar bank draft. I felt blessed, but with expenses being what they were, the money would go fast.

I had an advantage over most ex-cons because I had friends and family helping me.

I wasted no time looking for work, but the door was slammed shut at every stop. "What about this twenty-one-year gap in your resume?" they would ask. When I said prison and I had felony convictions, they would usually say something like, "We'll think about it and call you."

None of them ever called.

Lucky for me, a local writer sympathetic to my case, Jack Sheehan, and his wife hired me to do Girl Friday stuff for them. I also did a two-part interview with George Knapp of Channel 8 News. An attorney contacted Knapp after it aired and said he would like to help me by giving me a job. I got hired and soon moved out of Mom's because I didn't want to be a 37-year-old dependent child.

But that job was short-lived because he didn't have enough business to justify keeping me full-time. Yet, lo and behold, help came from a very unexpected source: David Fletcher.

A writer friend tracked Dave down after all those years to find out why he had turned on me during my trial. Turns out, Dave had been shouldering that heavy burden for all these years and finally revealed why he lied to help Seaton put me in prison.

Dave had recently moved back to Vegas after living in South Carolina for years. When my friend located him, at first, he hesitated but finally agreed to come clean. He decided to fess up, he said, because he had a daughter now the same age I was when I got arrested.

Here is how it had all gone down.

He was on the stand at my prelim, testifying on my behalf about how he took me out there that morning after the murder because I thought I'd actually dreamed it. He was about to tell the court he was the one who took kids out to see Cotton's body, not me, thus my infamous "show and tell" nickname in the press. I'm convinced the Show and Tell moniker kept me in prison for another ten years.

Dave had taken Stacy to see the body on one of his three trips and foolishly told her the details about who was involved. That was how she knew to tell the cops after she and I got in that fight. Dave was about to tell the court he had called Stacy the previous night and she was crying. Crying over lying about me on the stand. He had tried to convince her to come back to court and tell the truth, but she was scared of perjury charges.

Seeing exactly where Dave's testimony was headed, Seaton abruptly asked for a short recess, and the judge granted it. Dave's account of what happened next: "Seaton ushered me into a side room and there stood two uniformed police officers. Seaton told me those cops were there to arrest me for larceny, or maybe something related to grave robbing, I can't quite recall. One night, I had taken my stepbrother out to the murder sight and he stole Cotton's watch off his wrist and his ring off his body. Next day, I hocked them at a pawn shop. The cops somehow found out and took me in and questioned me. I admitted what happened, but they didn't arrest me. But when Seaton interviewed me when I was summoned as a witness at Sandy's prelim, Seaton knew about it and asked me, so I admitted it to him."

Dave said he stood there looking at two cops in that side room, and Seaton got up in his face, looked him in the eyes, and said, "Davy boy, you go back on that stand and if I don't hear exactly what I want to hear, you're going to *prison*."

"I was seventeen," Dave explained. "I wasn't going to go to prison for *nobody*."

To the casual eye, Dave's exchange with Seaton appears to be his word against Seaton's, but what tips the scales in Dave's favor is his mother and girlfriend—today his wife of twenty years and mother of his kids—who were waiting just outside the door of that side room. They heard every word and have verified the conversation exactly as Dave relates it.

Dave didn't finish his testimony after that recess at my prelim, so I knew something was screwy. Then Seaton called him to testify for the prosecution at my trial, and he perjured himself so he wouldn't get arrested, and he helped Seaton convict me.

The day after confessing to my friend, Dave went to my lawyer Bill Terry's office and dictated an affidavit about how it all went down, then swore to it under oath, and signed it. A few days after Dave came clean, Jack Sheehan arranged for feature writer Jeff German to write a story in the *Las Vegas Sun*. The headline read: "A little late, witness in 'show and tell' figure's trial recants his testimony."

Accordingly, Las Vegas Channel 8 news anchor George Knapp, who for years had been in my corner, set up a two-part interview with me. When it ran, Seaton came crawling out of his hole and called Channel 8 News. He claimed none of what Dave said was true and alleged that Dave was "just trying to help his friend." Well, if that were true and Dave just wanted to help me, why the hell didn't he come forward when I was still in prison and it might have exonerated me? I didn't need his help now; I was out of prison. It was between him and his conscience, his act of contrition, and it took a hell of a lot of courage to come forward. He had nothing to gain by doing so. In fact, it surely embarrassed him to publicly admit he'd lied to get an innocent girl sent to prison for twenty-one years.

Dave phoned me after he signed the affidavit and begged my forgiveness. I forgave him and told him what he had just done was brave. Then he mentioned—oh, by the way—that the plumbing, heating, and air conditioning company he worked for as a tech was looking for a dispatcher.

Next day, I called the company and dropped his name and got an interview with the owner. I admitted up front I'd been convicted of a felony, but that I was fifteen when it happened. He hired me full-time as a dispatcher. I promised myself I would grow into that job and make a career of it. And seventeen years later, I'm still working there as head dispatcher, having gone from an hourly employee to salaried with benefits.

After Dave helped me get that job, my mom said to me, "Was real nice of Dave Fletcher to help you get that job, but what he did to you back then, he's still got a long ride before he hits the break-even point."

68

Last Visits With Dad

The Board periodically switched my parole officers, and that was normal. I didn't go out anywhere but a movie now and then or to dinner occasionally with my sisters and brother, where I was always the designated driver. Four years went by fast, and on January 18, 2011, I looked in the mirror and realized I was forty years old.

One year later, my half-brother Chris called me and said Dad had stage-four cancer. The terms of my parole required me to get a travel pass from the parole board, but I would have had to wait five days to get it approved, and he was so far gone I didn't want to wait. One of Dad's sisters bought Shane and me tickets to fly into Green Bay. Our half-brother Chris picked us up at the airport and drove us to Stevens Point, near Plover, where Dad lived. We spent a week with him without the parole board knowing I had left the state, and they never found out.

Dad and I had a nice visit, considering he was dying. We said "I love you" to each other for the first time in decades. He was riddled with cancer and brave about it all; he chose not to get chemo treatments and planned to have home hospice care. He said he was proud of me for fighting so hard for my freedom and never giving up, and it meant a lot for me to hear that. He was also really impressed I had got a college education to better myself, even when I didn't know I would ever get out. I saw pride in his watery eyes as he said, "That took a lot of mettle."

We both avoided rehashing all that bad stuff from when I was growing up. I thought, what purpose would it serve but lay guilt on a dying man?

Some years earlier, when he visited me at Shakopee, he had joined A.A. I had hoped he had quit the booze forever, but he hadn't. During my visit, he would get up in the morning and drink coffee a while, but by noon he was drinking beer and smoking cigarettes and pot. My dad drank and smoked cigarettes and pot till the day he died. He was who he was. The fear of death didn't change that.

When his cancer got worse in March, Shane and I flew back to Wisconsin. I again didn't get a travel pass from the parole board. I just figured I had to go and I went.

A bunch of us had a celebration of his life while he was still living it. Chris was there; Dad's ex-wife and my old nemesis Cindy showed up, and she and I buried the hatchet. Her daughter Candi came, all grown up now. And we were joined by a couple of Dad's brothers and sisters, among the survivors of that big Shaw family.

Dad had never kept much weight on him, but he was splinter-thin now. He had a full-grown beard that made his gaunt face look fuller. As farm folks do, everybody told stories about Dad, about their childhood, and about funny things they remembered.

I had no more issues with Dad, but Shane still did. It was an old wound dating back to the day Dad kidnapped us from Las Vegas, when he told Shane he was "a little faggot tied to his momma's apron strings." He probably meant nothing by it, but Shane was young and impressionable, and it pained him all these years. So, I talked Shane into staying there when I flew home so they could make peace. They almost got into it again talking about it, but Dad did his best impression of an apology and Shane was good with it.

Less than two months later, May 3, Dad passed away peacefully at his home.

Life would go on, and I kept my nose clean, kept working six days a week. I got raises and promotions; I adopted more dogs, and my life was running on all eight cylinders.

Then came this really bizarre hiccup in my parole, and I got thrown back into that cursed prison.

69

Back to Prison

My nightmare began innocently in February 2011 and ended a year later with me back in prison for a violation that turned out to be a false positive.

I had got home from work and went to pick up a pizza when my car stalled on the exit ramp off the freeway. I wasn't there long till a police car drove up behind me, and a female officer got out and strolled up to the driver's window.

"Can I be of help, ma'am," she said. "What seems to be the trouble?"

"Thanks, officer. My car stalled. No idea why." I was still trying to start it, but by now it was flooded, so I gave up on it.

She leaned her head near my window and removed her sunglasses. "Can I please see your license and registration?" I handed both to her, and she took them back to her squad car. I knew she was calling it in for outstanding violations, but I didn't have any, so I wasn't worried.

But when she came back from her car, her once happy, helpful face had switched to a glare with a tight squint. "You had anything to drink?"

"No ma'am. I do not drink."

No doubt, when she called in my plates, she learned I was on parole.

"You mind taking a sobriety test . . . Miz Shaw?"

"Not at all." I assumed she would give me a breathalyzer right there. But she ordered me into the back of her cruiser and drove straight to the city jail. They gave me a breathalyzer test there and I blew 0.00. I told her, "Like I said, I haven't been drinking."

Her face tightened when she frowned and said, "Hold on a minute." She made me blow into it again, and I again registered 0.00. Then she went around the corner and returned with a nurse. "I think there's something in your system and you need to take a blood test." Had I been a bona fide citizen with actual rights, I could have said screw off and gone home. I legally didn't have to take a blood test once I passed the breathalyzer. But I was scared to start anything, so I took the blood test, and she let me go.

A full year passed, and I'd forgot all about that blood test. I knew I hadn't been drinking. Then, in February of 2012, not long after I'd got back from visiting Dad the first time, the police informed me my blood test results just came back and showed traces of PCP—*meth*. I was dumbfounded. I never smoked meth in my entire life. But that's what the report said. Why would it lie?

Meantime, during the year between the blood test and the results, I had been assigned my PO. From Hell. An ex-cop who told me all convicts on parole belong back in prison, and it was his *duty* to put them there, and that included me. As a parole officer, that was his sole purpose in life.

On May 31, 2012, not long after Dad passed, my PO had me come into the parole office and they arrested me there and took me to jail for a DUI. I was panicky. I called Mom and she called my work. I lingered in a jail cell for a whole month because they wouldn't let me make bail. If you were jailed on parole, they usually won't let you out on bail. That's when my PO decided to stick me back in prison for a parole violation. I am sure he was giddy about it. So on July 3, here I was, right back at good old Smiley Road, in the tomb from which I had been released five years prior.

I was terrified. I could barely eat and barely sleep. I didn't know what they were going to do to me. They said I violated parole; that's all I knew. I didn't know if I'd be there weeks, months, even years. They put me through Intake, just like when I was sixteen, and then I waited and sweated it out.

If I was in much longer, I would lose my job and the life I had worked so hard to build would be into the wind. I'd have to rebuild my credit and, worst of all, more of my life would be lost behind bars.

Back in prison, the familiar echoes of profanity and yelling were ceaselessly in the backdrop. A guard who had known me back when, who had whooped and shouted for me the day I made parole, saw I was back. He shook his head. "Jesus, Shaw, I didn't think you of all people would ever be back in here." I felt shame, yet I had no clue how they found PCP in my bloodstream.

When I had called Mom and told her I was in prison, she was so upset she could barely talk. She called my work, and it meant so much to me that everyone there was on my side. They all wrote letters to the parole board to support me. They would hold my job as long as they possibly could.

The State appointed a lawyer for me, mandatory for a revocation hearing. He advised me to plead not guilty, but I was an old hand at this stuff and I knew better than do that. It could take the court months to sort it all out if I pled not guilty, and they'd keep me locked up all that time.

Then, after lingering in prison forty-five days, I agreed to plead guilty to a DUI. I had not smoked PCP, but I admitted to it just to satisfy the court and put it behind me. I made up a story about how my cousin came into town and we smoked some. I pled guilty and paid a five-hundred-dollar fine so the cop who took me in wouldn't have egg on her face.

The next day, I was out of prison and back at my job, feeling like I'd just been shot at and missed. Another dispatcher was on her computer at lunch break and called me over. "Hey, Sandy, check this out." She pointed at her computer screen. She had found an FDA website and told me to read a paragraph: "False-positive blood and urine immunoassay screening tests for phencyclidine (PCP) and amphetamine have been reported in patients taking venlafaxine."

She knew I was taking a prescription anti-anxiety medication called Effexor. The main ingredient in Effexor is venlafaxine.

"Well, I'll be a son of a bitch," I said. "That's explains the whole crazy thing." I took my container of Effexor out of my purse, went to the bathroom, and flushed them all down the toilet. I never took another one.

Of course, me going back to prison went viral in the local press. The *Review-Journal* ran a story with the headline: *Killer Sandy Shaw Back in Prison*. I was embarrassed about the whole mess, but I was relieved to be out and back at work. I swore I'd never do anything, even accidentally, to let the bastards put me back in that place. The only good that came out of it was they switched me to a more reasonable PO.

70

A Week of Sorrow

There were several personal losses around this time. My grandmother, Marie Pronovost Fosteson, died near the end of that year, on October 12, 2012. She had been so caring and such a positive presence in my life. I still warmly recollect her helping me pull one over on Mom and signing my registration card when I forged my way into a different school after getting the boot for ditching. I vividly remember her consoling me during those dark days after I'd witnessed the murders at Jessica's house, and seeing the pain in her eyes when I got convicted. She loved all of us dearly and we had all loved her back. It was hard to imagine the world without her in it. Grandma was eighty-two, and though she had her ups and downs with her drinking, she conquered it and lived a full and interesting life.

My own life went back to its humdrum pace, but I treated myself to a nice ocean cruise down the Pacific coast of Mexico with my two sisters. We had a great time. But as we neared the bottom of Baja California, my thoughts turned momentarily to the city of San Miguel de Allende and my fanciful plan to escape prison all those years ago. If I had gone through with it and taken that leap, I realized I could still be living there.

Some three and a half years after Grandma died, March 3, 2016, my phone rang at four in the morning. I almost always kept it on silent, but for some reason, I had the ringer on. I was half asleep and barely heard Mom's voice on the line.

"Mom, what the hell's going on?" I was groggy and thought I'd heard her say somebody died. I mistakenly believed she said it was my brother Shane. "Oh, God, no," I said. "Shane *died*? How—"

She shouted into my ear, "NO, not Shane . . . *Oceania*. Killed in a car wreck."

I was in shock, and Mom was sobbing. I thought, God, no, not my sweet, kind niece Oceania, Nicole's oldest, only twenty-one. She had died a few hours earlier in a one-car crash, headed home down the mountain road from the Lee Mountain ski resort on Mount Charleston. An expert skier, she was a ski lift manager and worked till late. It was a two-lane road full of curves, and very dark, with no streetlights or reflectors to illuminate the road. The Highway Patrol said she was going way too fast, and the skid marks indicated she swerved, then overcorrected, and the car flipped. For some stupid or reckless reason, she didn't have her seatbelt on. She was thrown from the car and died instantly upon impact.

Jesus God, Oceania was still a kid, just getting her footing in life. I stumbled around in the dark to throw on some clothes and tore out of the garage so fast I hit the side of it and put a big gash in my car door as I headed for Mom's house.

Our whole family was taking it really hard, but nobody more so than Mom. She was inconsolable, and for the next few days, she wouldn't talk to anybody and didn't want to eat. I finally got her to drink a milkshake, and she asked if I'd come over the next day and spend time visiting with her. I said, of course I would.

Next morning, I'd just got out of the shower when Shane called, all upset, saying Mom was lying on the floor, unresponsive. He'd call the EMTs and they were working on her. He screamed into the phone, "You need to get over here. She's not moving, she's not even moving."

I sped over there and, when I was getting out of my car, two EMTs came out the door with an empty gurney. One of them turned to me. "I'm so very sorry, ma'am. We did all we could."

Tears poured down my face as I rushed in. I saw her bedroom door open and her head by the door. Her neck had been intubated, but she was dead. Shane was sitting on the bed, his head in his hands. I sat on the floor next to her and started crying, and for some odd reason, I started rubbing her head. I guess I didn't know what else to do. I was trying my hardest to make sense out of something that made no sense. She had not appeared ill.

The coroner took hours to get there. He had no real explanation other than her heart had simply stopped. To my mind, she died of a broken heart. Because of Oceania.

And so, my family mourned two more of its loved ones that week. Mom left the earth five days short of her sixty-third birthday. She was a rare, free, strong spirit and one of the hardest working people I've known. At her memorial service, I thought back to when I was a little kid, Mom hitching out to the lake in Wadena in freezing weather to work her waitress shifts. Just to keep food on our table when Dad had run off. Her strength and ability to get through each day, no matter what she was going through, had always amazed me. She had a truly kind soul and kept her door open to everyone.

I managed a smile when I recalled how hilarious she was, even when she would tell you the same story more than once! My rock was gone, the one person in my world who had never given up on me in the darkest hours of the darkest days of my life.

I vowed I would keep her spirit in my heart.

After that, I kept my nose buried in work, got promoted to head dispatcher, and got another raise. That was quite an achievement for an ex-con who'd come in there all those years ago with her hat in her hand. I continued working six days a week and was always too exhausted to get in trouble—even when I'd had a mind to.

My sister Leah was now married and raising two sweet boys. The pandemic came and went, and near the end of it, I played Sam Spade to rescue my fourteen-year-old niece Jocelyn, Nicole's youngest, from a situation where she had become the victim of some unspeakable acts.

I had learned one thing all those bleak years in prison—family is everything and you better do all you can to keep it whole. I soon learned Sheila Summers, who was like family to me all those years in prison, died of cancer in April of 2022. Such a brilliant, talented, witty gal. Her two daughters gave her six grandkids and twelve great-grandkids, and it warmed my heart to learn she had found a guy who loved her dearly to the very end.

As for me, I was still lugging around that ball and chain of lifetime parole. I took some satisfaction when I discovered how all the new defense lawyers taking the bar in Clark County had to take an ethics class. The early incoming lawyers had nicknamed it, "The Seaton Class," and it stuck.

It was absolutely *not* a compliment to him.

I finally made a genuine effort to get my case to the Pardons Board to seek a full pardon. I figured I was as good a candidate as anybody. Then the good news came; I was scheduled for a hearing, summer of 2021. But a few months prior, they canceled me to accommodate others who had applied before I did.

But soon, Nevada Supreme Court Justice Abbi Silver sponsored me to the board, and one year later, my case got to the docket of the Nevada Pardons Board on June 28, 2022.

And now, here I sit, sweating it out, terrified, waiting for Governor Steve Sisolak to rap his gavel for one final judgment of my life.

71

Judgment Day

The nine Board members finally stop shuffling papers and taking notes. Governor Sisolak wakes me from my daydreaming when he says, "We will now hear the case of Sandy Marie Shaw." My knees wobble and I can almost hear sweat trickling down my forehead. Jesus God, don't make me go first—my damn right foot's asleep.

An image flashes past my eyes of me stumbling to the podium on that numb foot and looking like a drunk.

My lawyer speaks first. Robert Langford. Good fellow, sharp lawyer, appointed and paid by the State. A former clark county deputy district attorney . . . mentored under Seaton, but when I learned he worked with the ACLU after that, I figured none of Seaton's dirt rubbed off on him. He's in his early sixties, tall, confident-looking, well-spoken, and likable.

He tells the court, "To say her home was unstable is a gross understatement of her young childhood." He reminds them how in spite of my dysfunctional home life, I was a cheerleader, a member of the school volleyball and softball teams, an honor student, popular, and socially adjusted before witnessing those murders.

He relives the murders I witnessed at Jessica's home, reminds them how I hid in fear for my life while bathed in Betty's blood and brain matter for over an hour. He then explains the shooting I saw at my school the next year and how by the time Cotton started stalking me, I was a basket case—"one foot in prison and one foot in the grave."

I fix my eyes on those Board members, glancing one to the other. I'm looking for a light of compassion. Langford recounts my bout with PTSD and brings up how I had incompetent counsel who got me to decline a deal that could have freed me in plenty of time to have a family and a normal life. He ends his address challenging the Board how the State might benefit by keeping me on supervision the rest of my life.

Now, it's my turn as I, oh so tentatively, maneuver to the podium to speak into the mic. How I dread this. I admit to them right off, "I'm nervous and I'm really, really scared. It's been a long journey."

I'm trying to defend my life, but inwardly I'm falling apart. My voice quivers, my hands tremble, and my legs shake. I'm a mess. I struggle to choke the words out about my childhood and what led up to that murder when I was fifteen. I look into their faces but can't tell if they feel my pain or think I'm a pathetic basket of nerves.

I draw a breath and try to slow down my breathing. It seems to help, but my legs are still shaking. I take comfort glancing at Justice Silver and seeing compassion in her face. I pretend I'm speaking only to her, that she's the only one in the room but me. My voice calms, and my knees stop shaking. But when I reiterate all that I lost because of that crime, I start crying. I tell myself, *Stop blubbering, goddamit. Get through this.*

Justice Hardesty cuts me off and asks the governor if he can ask me some questions. I tighten up, wondering what's coming.

"Ms. Shaw," he says, "you and your counsel have been re-litigating the circumstances of your case. I'd like you to focus on why you believe you should be taken off lifetime supervision."

I throttle my crying jag and pull myself together. I remind him I haven't had to report to my parole officer for two years; that I work six days a week, every single week, and live a quiet, humble life. I tell him I give back to the community, from helping a poor person pay their grocery bill when they are short of money at the store—I really do that—and often do volunteer work, even on my only day off. I am relieved when his voice softens as he thanks me for answering his question.

I'm waiting for more questions from the others, nervous my answers won't suit them. I pause a few moments then to my pleasant surprise, none of them have more questions. But then I wonder if that's good or bad, like when a jury is out only a short time and doesn't ask to review any testimony.

I thank the Board and sit down, relieved to be away from that mic.

Weeks in advance of this, a friend prepared copies of affidavits and key evidence in my favor and mailed a packet to each Board member. I'm hoping they read it.

Testimonials

Governor Sisolak opens it up for people in the courtroom to speak for or against me. My eyes pan the audience to see if Cotton's brother, George Thiede, is in the crowd. No sign of him, and I'm relieved. He hates my guts, blames me for everything that happened to his brother, and wrongly believes I set him up to be robbed and then shot him between the eyes.

My writer friend steps up first and tells the court how I pulled myself up by my bootstraps from the time I went to prison, how I did not come out of prison bitter but was determined to have a good life, and how he is proud to call me a friend. I am moved.

Crystal, the girl I saved in prison, now in her forties, living a good life and raising a family, goes next. She cries through most of it as she testifies what a bind she was in when she first hit prison, pregnant at sixteen. She describes her early anger, rebellion, and selfishness and says I intervened and took her under my wing. She tells the court, "Sandy Shaw saved me from total ruin." Her testimony touches my heart.

My sister Nicole goes next. She is a very well-spoken woman and reminds the court I have served my time for a crime that happened thirty-five years ago. "She has proven time and again that she has rehabilitated herself." She closes by saying I have always been her rock and have helped her through some of the most trying times of her life. I wipe a tear from the corner of my eye.

I'm stirred by what everyone is saying, but does this mean much to the Board? Are their minds made up? It takes five "no" votes and I lose my chance to have my conviction voided, my rights restored. No idea if or when I'll get another shot at this.

Much as anything, I want to clear my name. I want my good name back because it was taken from me in a courtroom by Dan Seaton and the State of Nevada and by the tabloid press. Other than a person's attitude and good name, what do they have of any value? They can take your money and you can get that back; they can take your possessions and you can replace them. But just try to get your good name back after they drag it through the muck for thirty-five years.

While I listen to everyone testifying for me, images start running through my mind like movie scenes. Things I lost out on, locked up all those years. I envision joyfully leaving the DMV with my first driver's license then dancing with some sweet boy at the prom walking around a lovely college campus, autumn leaves scattered on the ground, my arms loaded down with books then laughing with girls at a sorority party holding hands on a date and looking up at a big yellow moon on a football Saturday dressed in a business suit, first day on my first job then in a gorgeous white gown on my wedding day driving a couple of my kids to soccer practice an anniversary dinner with my kind, handsome husband.

My sister Leah is among those pleading my case. She was only a year old when I went to prison. In just four years, she will turn forty. "It may be hard for this Board to imagine someone in prison could be a role model," she says. "But Sandy was mine all the time I was growing up, always there to counsel me, guide me, teach me to care and teach me right from wrong." She tells the court she is working on her master's in criminal justice because my situation inspired her to help troubled juveniles.

Mike Flanery goes next. Leah's father. My stepdad and a great guy. He's been wonderful to me, always in my corner, even after he and Mom split. A caring, giving man. He tells the court, "Today, Sandy still dwells in the past because that's all she has. No future. I could go on hours talking about her character but everybody's pretty much covered that. Sandy would like to replace all her bad memories with good memories and have the freedom to finally create some. And this Board is the only ones with the power to do that."

My niece, Jocelyn, Nicole's daughter, slim and tall and confident, tells the court that today is her sixteenth birthday, but she's chosen to spend it here to support me. "I went through a horribly traumatic experience when I was fourteen," she says, "and it was only because of my Aunt Sandy I got through it. She means the world to me."

My brother Shane comes to the podium next and says, "As much as people may not want to believe an ex-convict can be a pillar of the community, she is exactly that. She made the best of an awful situation and has been nothing but positive since she got out. She has a golden heart and is the backbone of our family." I flash him a smile as he heads back to his seat.

My former co-worker Kathleen then speaks on closed circuit from Carson City. She is emotional, almost crying as she tells the Board how I advised and counseled her when her close relative was in deep trouble with the law. "Sandy is a kind soul and a good woman. She shouldn't have to live the horrible nightmares from her childhood the rest of her life. She deserves to be free."

Last of all, also from Carson City, Tanya Brown, Advocates for Inmates and the Innocent, pleads with the court to grant my pardon. "She deserves to spread her wings and fly, and experience what we have all had and she hasn't."

Then Governor Sisolak asks, "Do we have anyone in Las Vegas opposing her application?" A tall man, maybe in his forties, in a suit and tie, gets up from his seat, and my heart sinks. I have no idea who he is. Then I see he isn't coming forward to the podium but simply taking a seat farther in the back. A great relief washes over me.

"Anyone in Carson City opposed to this application?" the Governor asks. There is no answer at first, but Chief Justice Paraguirre asks the governor if he can ask a few questions of Parole and Probation before the Board takes a vote. He wants to know whether they think I am still a threat to society and need supervision. I shake my head and think, *Hell, I was never a threat to society in my whole life*. But I know if P & P say yes, and five justices sitting on the fence vote "no" because of it, my pardon goes down the toilet.

Natasha Koch, chief of the Division of Parole and Probation, whom I've never met and don't recognize, speaks for P & P. She says I have been reporting electronically and my last home visit was October, 2021. Then I see her eyes sort of draw tight and her mouth ease into a scowl. "We do not oppose commutation to time served. However, this Division opposes Sandy Shaw's petition for a pardon because of the egregiousness of the crime."

My heart drops, and I'm thinking, *Lady, you're the head of P & P. Didn't you bother to look at the facts of the case?* I have to get those five justices on my side so my chance at a genuinely normal life doesn't fly out into the breeze.

But then Justice Abbi Silver comes riding to my rescue. She asks for the floor, then leans slightly forward in her chair. "In light of that last comment and before we take a roll call, as long as I've been on this board we have seen at least three women who, after being convicted of murder at age fifteen, we granted pardons to *all three* of them. That includes a young woman who shot her stepmother in the face and killed her." She shakes her index finger. "And I'll remind this Board, Sandy Shaw did *not* pull the trigger. Having said that, I will note that we shouldn't give disparate treatment to any petitioner, and part of the reason we are here is to create balance in the justice system."

My emotions have been on a yo-yo all morning but now my spirits rise again.

Justice Elissa Cadish asks the Governor, "To clarify, is this vote to end lifetime parole or is it an unconditional pardon?"

"Unconditional pardon," the governor answers.

The Vote

Governor Sisolak pushes some papers aside and leans into his mic. "I'm now going to ask for a roll call." A "roll call" means the vote. My feet get fidgety under the table as I lean forward and wait.

The court reporter then begins polling the panel for their decisions.

"Justice Herndon?"

I cross my fingers under the table.

"Yes," he says.

"Justice Pickering?"

There is a noticeable pause and my heart pounds against my ribs. She answers:

"Yes."

"Justice Silver?"

"Yes."

Justice Cadish?

"Yes."

"Justice Stiglich?"

"Yes."

Justice Lidia Stiglich's yes vote was the fifth "yes." That is enough yes votes, except that if Governor Sisolak votes no, it doesn't matter that I got a majority. A no vote from him sends me packing and back on lifetime parole

"Justice Hardesty?"

"Yes."

Chief Justice Paraguirre.

"Yes."

Because he represents the state, I expect a no vote from Attorney General Ford. But he surprises me with a yes and then punctuates his "yes" vote by saying, "This act of mercy restores you to our society. " He smiles down at me. "And I'm happy to vote *yes*."

Now I hold my breath, cross my fingers, and say a quick, heartfelt prayer that the governor will not dash my hopes with a "no" vote. "I'm a yes," the governor says firmly.

The court reporter calls out, "Motion passes, unconditional pardon!" and the courtroom fills with applause. I want to join in that applause, but I put my face in my hands and cry like a baby. It's an involuntary reaction. I don't blubber long, just a few moments to release thirty-five years down a hard road. It then hits me. *Great God almighty, I'm finally free.*

I stand and shake attorney Langford's hand as I wipe my joyful tears away then head into the crowd to hug my friends and family members who came to speak for me and root me home. I will have a celebratory lunch with two friends and take the rest of the day off to let it all sink in.

I have calculated on the internet it has been thirteen thousand fifty-six days from the night Troy murdered James Thiede till this moment. But sometimes I think back, and it seems like fifteen minutes ago.

72

The Morning After

My boss gives me the next morning off, and I arrange breakfast with my brother Shane. As I sit near the living room window and wait for his arrival, I think about what a woman said to me in the courtroom yesterday after the vote: "All the happiness in the world is right on your doorstep now."

I smiled and thanked her, but I didn't correct her and say she was wrong. I'm a big fan of the happy ending in books and movies, but real life doesn't always roll that way. When I was a kid, before all the bad stuff happened, I was gregarious, almost extroverted, and absolutely optimistic. I feared nothing.

But now I fear most everything. What all those traumas and the PTSD and those twenty-one years in prison and fifteen years on parole did was change me inwardly, drastically, beyond repair.

Even though I'm off parole as of yesterday, I'm petrified to even go to a nightclub and have a little harmless fun. Because in the back of my mind, I'm scared somebody will do something and I'll get blamed, and they will throw me back in prison. I know it makes no sense, but that's what's in the deep recesses of my mind. I lost trust in people long ago and, more recently, in men who want to have a relationship with me. I can't do it because I know I can never fully trust them with my heart and emotions. I'm that gun-shy, though I really wish I wasn't. Living life all alone is a long ride down a lonesome road.

So, I avoid all that and cleave to a handful of close friends and family and fill other gaps with my two wonderful pit bull puppies—my "kids." All the happiness of the world is *not* at my doorstep or within my reach. Maybe it once was, but not anymore. It hit me the other day, I never really got to be a kid when I actually was a kid. I was either taking care of my sisters and brother or being a mom to my mom in her wild times. And then I got locked in prison.

Don't misunderstand me. I'm not holding a pity party. I don't solicit anybody's sympathy, including my own. Life is what it is. It's all in front of me now, and I intend to live it with all my might, given my limitations. In reference to what Mike Flanery told the court, I intend to replace those bad memories with good memories. And after all, there are plenty of people who have it way worse than me.

Shane texts me saying he's running late because traffic is bad. I text back: *No worries. Just chill. We got all morning.*

As I wait on him, I recall how he battled for me all those years. I had watched out over him as his big sister while he was a little boy, and then he did all he could to pay me back after I was in prison. When he was a teenager, so many times, he would march up to the newsroom of the *Review-Journal* or the *Las Vegas Sun* or the Channel 8 headquarters with stacks of papers and trial transcripts proving I got railroaded, hoping they would help me. He is truly a good soul and a great brother.

Finally, I see his car pulling into my driveway, and I go outside and greet him with a hug.

"Let's take my car," I say. "I know a short-cut to the café."

He has a copy of the Las Vegas *Review-Journal* in his hand. "Lemme show you somethin' first," he says. His smile falls into a frown. He places the newspaper flat onto the hood of his car and opens it to one of the inside pages. He points to my picture, one of many teary-eyed photos of me at one of my parole hearings. Then he taps his finger on the headline a couple times. The headline reads: "Show and Tell Killer Granted Pardon."

The byline is from a reporter named Katelyn Newberg, who must have attended my hearing. Shane's teeth are clenched, his jaw tensed. He seems even more upset than I am that she and her paper couldn't resist taking one last shot to tag me "The Show and Tell Killer."

"Hell," Shane growls. "You just got pardoned and your conviction got voided, right? And they're still calling you a goddam *murderer*."

I pat him lightly on the shoulder. "Yeah, well, you can't expect a whole lot from those people. Forget about it. Reality is reality. We won't let what's in the newspaper ruin our morning."

He folds the paper and sticks it under one arm as we head for my car, parked on the curb. We are the same height, about five-six, so as we walk, we can look at each other eyeball to eyeball.

"You were never no damn Show and Tell *nothing*," he grumbles. "Why don't they figure it out? All the shit's come down on you, you think they'd cut you a break."

We keep walking to my car. I reach around his back and put my hand lightly on his shoulder and look him in his eyes. "Little brother, once the bastards start on you, they never let up."

The only crime Sandy Shaw should have been charged with was conspiracy to commit misdemeanor assault.
—Det. Lt. David Hatch, Las Vegas Police Dept., Homicide Division

Index

Note: Page numbers in *italics* refer to figures.

abortions 10
alcoholics 9, 21, 35
Alcoholics Anonymous 52
All His Father's Sins 187
amphetamine 243
Angela 156–8
Angel (puppy) 15–17. *See also* fire
Anthony 91
anti-anxiety medication 243
appeal(s) 114, 163, 204, 225
    felony murder rule 175
    habeas corpus 216
    Sandy writing her own appeal 191–2
    Supreme Court denying 183–4
Aryan Brotherhood 164
Associate degrees 209
associate warden 179–81
at-risk youth 179–81
attempted rape 87–8
attorneys general 2
autopsy 67
Autry 172
Avants, Beecher 67

babysitting 77, 98
bail hearing 110
bank robbery 207
Bernice (babysitter) 27–8
Bertha 7, 27
Blackmon, Lonnie 205–6
blood test 242

breathalyzer test 241–2
Brown, Tanya 253
Buhman, Stacy 89–90, 105–6, 117–18, 122, 123, 227
Burns, Brenda 151, 160, 161, 206

Cadish, Elissa 254
Caesar's Palace 31, 35, 55, 57, 62, 84, 90
California 90
Candy 44, 45, 47–8, *145*
Caracappa, Stephen 221–4, 232
Carson City High School 209
Carson City prison 188
    at-risk youth touring 179–81
    being noisier and dangerous 153–4
    fights 153
    hooker parade 149, 150
    kitchen work 159–61
    movement to 135–8
    overcrowding 185, 186
    Sandy fighting Dolly the predator 155–8
    sexual predators 155–8, 163–4
    stealing 153
    winter in 185–6
Carter, Anita. *See* Woods, Cathy
casinos 111
Catholics 10, 14
Chamber of Commerce 181
Channel 8 News 235–7, 258

Christianity   164–5
Cindy   44, 45, 47–8, 50, 78, 79, 112, *133*, 212, 240
Circus-Circus   31, 83, 115–16, 125, 184
Clark County Jail   109–12
   all-female floor   109
   Cindi's love notes to Sandy   133
   inmates   109
   juvenile males   110
   solitary confinement   132–3
clinical psychologist   206–7
cocaine   226
college education   191, 209, 239
Conduct Disorder   206
Corrections Corporation of America (CCA)   218–19
Cortez, Tracy   189
counseling   74, 206–7
Cousins, Christopher   116
Crystal   207–8, 231
custody. *See* legal custody of children

deaths   245–7
Del Papa, Frankie Sue   217
Dennison   220
DiFiore, Betty   55, 57, 58, 61–4, 71, 101, 249
dispatcher   237
ditching   73, 74, 82, 87, 245
Division of Parole and Probation   253
Dolly   155–8
domestic violence   5–6, 10–12, 45
drugs   74
drug smuggling   226

education   179, 209, 215, 229. *See also* college education
Effexor   243
Egyed, Alex   53–8, 69, 71–4, 101, 206, 221
   autopsy   67
   Hungarian passport   67
   killing Betty, Virginia, Jack, and then himself   62–6
   plan   67

Elaine   143–4
enemy reconciliation   19–20
Eppolito, Louis   224
escape plan   199–204
extradition treaty   67

FBI   203, 222–3
fire   15–17
Flanagan, Dale   132
Flanery, Mike   2, 52, 71, 258
   testimonial at pardon hearing   252
Fletcher, Dave   101–2, 105, 106, 111, 117–19, 177, 235–7
Ford, Aaron   2, 255
Fosteson, Bill   9, 10, 20, 171
   death   194
Fosteson, Connie Jean. *See* Shaw, Connie Jean Fosteson
Fosteson, Doug   22, 33, 40–1
Fosteson, Marie   9, 10, *135*
   accident   51–2
   death   245
   felony   52

Gallego, Gerald   187, 188
gambling   35
German, Jeff   236
Gibson Middle School   73, 74
graduation ceremonies   209
Guinn, Kenny   223
gun   110
Gunnison County Jail   213

habeas corpus appeal   216
Hall, Annabelle   192–9, 206, 216, 217
Halloween   77–8
Hardesty (justice)   250, 255
Hatch, Dave   225, 228, 259
   letter to Nevada board of pardons   *139*, 225–6
homicide
   of Cotton (*see* murder of James Cotton Kelly)
   at Rancho Circle (*see* murders at Rancho Circle)

Howard Wasden Elementary 31
Hungary 67

illegal jury instructions 128
interviews 206

Jimmy 136-8, 143, 157, 205
job(s)
   as dispatcher 237
   prison 159-61
Jocelyn 2, 247, 252
   testimonial at pardon hearing 252-3
Jones, Raymond 82
jury instructions 128
juvenile hall 91

Kathleen 253
Kell, Troy 3, 37-8, 91-2, 163-4
   affidavit from *138*
   Aryan Brotherhood and 164
   death penalty trial (Utah prison murder) 205-6, 212-14
   imprisonment 38, 91
   killing Blackmon at Gunnison prison 205-6
   as neighborhood protector 37
   parents 37
   sentenced to death 214
   trial for Cotton's mrder 133
   troubled life 189
Kelly, James Cotton 3, 83-5, 89-91
   murder of 93-107
   stalking Sandy 89-92
kidnapping 29-30, 43-4, 47-8, 206, 212, 240
kitchen work at Carson City prison 159-61
Knapp, George 235, 236
Koch, Natasha 253
Kruger, Freddie 122

Langford, Robert 249-50, 255
Las Vegas 28-30
Las Vegas Sun 66, 236, 258
Laurent, Christopher 227-8, 230

law books 191
Leah 2, 77-8, 98, 175, 234, 247, 252
   testimonial at pardon hearing 252
legal custody of children 20
   court hearing of 21-6, 49
legal representation 191
legal separation 12-14
Levy, Jack 55, 57-9, 63, 65, 67, 75
library 166
lie detector test. *See* polygraph test
Lizard 145
Long, Miles 146-7
love notes 133
Lynch, Bill 21, 27, 33-4
   Carson City prison 164
   kidnapping Nicole 39-41

Mack, Joan 171-3
   suicide note 172-3
Mallin, Jennifer 53
Mallin, Jessica 31-3, 53-5, 58, 61-5, 67, 69-71, 73-5, 85, 91, 95, 103, 119-21, 125, 193, 234, 245, 249
Mallin, Stanley 31-2
Mallin, Virginia 32, 53-5
   Alex's plan to kill 67
   divorced Stanley 53
   fatal decision 57-9
McDonald's 89
McGuckin, Joe 103-5, 225
Mendoza (judge) 117, 120-1, 126, 128-30, 133, 173, 192
mental illnesses 192
Merritt, Billy 3, 95-8, 102, 104-6, 109-10, 113-15, 117, 118, 123, 127-8, 134, 216, 227
Miller, Bob 217-18
Miller, Mike 112
Minneapolis 19-20
mob and mobsters 111, 224
money laundering 226
Monica 151-4, 169, 175
Moore, Randy 132
murder of James Cotton Kelly 93-107
   bail hearing 110

Hatch's letter on   225–6
  Laurent's letter on   227–8
  police report   226
  Sandy booked for   103–7
  as tabloid fodder   111
  trial (*see* trial for Cotton's murder)
 murders at Rancho Circle   3, 61–6, 179
  aftermath   69–70
  plan   67
  terrors   71–2
  trauma   73–5

Nevada
  murder convict in   110
  stalking in   90–1
Nevada Board of Pardons   2
Nevada State Bar Association   194
Nevada Victims of Crime Program   74
Nevada Women's Correctional Center. *See* Carson City prison
Newberg, Katelyn   258
Nicole   2, 27, *146*
  rescuing   39–41
  testimonial at pardon hearing   251

Oceania   *137*, *140*
  death of   246
Oram, Christopher   114, 216, 218
Otter Tail Lake   7

Paraguirre (chief justice)   253, 255
Pardons Board   2, 4, 216, 221, 225, 227–30, 248
pardons hearing   2–5
  board vote   2, 254–5
  failed   223, 224
  governor's vote   2, 255
  judges   2–3
  roll call (vote)   2, 254–5
  testimonials   251–4
  unconditional pardon   255
parole/parole hearing   4, 197, 215–20, 231–7, 248, 258
  being tough and restrictive   233
  board members   230

  George Thiede attending   215–16, 220, 230–2
  jailed on   240–3
  visiting dying father while on   239–40
 phencyclidine (PCP)   243
 polygraph test   216
 Post-Traumatic Stress Disorder (PTSD)   8, 78, 101, 192–3, 206, 250, 257
 prison(s). *See also* Carson City prison; Clark County Jail
  as big businesses   166
  code talk   166
  education   239
  food   131
  guards   165–7
  jobs   159–61
 private prisons and detention centers   218
 PSI (pre-sentencing investigation) report   130
 psychotic intrusions   73–5, 191
 PTSD. *See* Post-Traumatic Stress Disorder (PTSD)

Rancho Circle   32, 53–6, 63, 65, 96, 101, 106, 125, 144, 179, 207, 208
Rancho Middle/High School   74, 81
Randy   87–8
rape   87–8
recidivism   212
Red Otter Supper Club   9
Regional Justice Center of Nevada Supreme Court   1, 2, 223
religion   164–5
Reno prison   186–9
Review-Journal   111, 184, 243, 258
revocation hearing   243
Roger, David   193, 196, 197, 227
Rohay, Ralph   112–21, 125–30, 163, 175–6, 183–4, 191, 226
Royal Canadian Mounted Police   226

Sandy Shaw v. Nevada   197
San Miguel de Allende   202, 204, 245

"Scared Straight" program   180
Schwartz, Nina   54–5, 57–9, 61, 63–5, 67
Seaton, Dan   110–28, 130–3, 176–7, 184, 193–4, 196, 198, 216, 226–7, 235–7, 248, 249, 252
self-help programs   206
sentencing   129–30, 197–8
separation. See legal separation
sexual predators   155–8, 163–4
Shakopee prison   211–12
Shaw, Chris   212, 239, 240
Shaw, Clara   165
Shaw, Connie Jean Fosteson   5–6, 8, *134–5*
  death of   246–7
  meeting Mike and get married   9–10
  memorial service   247
Shaw, Doug (Mike's brother)   22, 24, 25
Shaw, Mike   5–6, *136*
  cancer and death   239–40
  combat missions   8
  Connie and   9–10
  drinking   7
  farm work   7
  Vietnam war   7–8
Shaw, Shane   2, 10, 17, *137*, 246, 258–9
  testimonial at pardon hearing   253
Sheehan, Jack   235, 236
shooting   81–2
Silver, Abbi   248, 250, 254
Sisolak, Steve   2, 248, 249, 251, 253–5
Smith, Cindi   133, 150, 169–70
Sobel, Jeffrey   192, 197, 217
Society for Traumatic Stress Studies   192
Spinney, Joy   171–3
stalking   89–92
  laws   90–1
Stiglich, Lidia   255
suicide note   172–3
Summers, Sheila   132–3, 136, 145–6, 149–50, 155–6, 171–3, 175, 185–6, 191, 199–203, 207, 229, 247

Supreme Court of Nevada   132, 194, 216, 248
  denying appeal   183–4
  Regional Justice Center   1, 2, 223

terrors   71–2
Terry, Bill   114, *142*, 221, 223, 225, 236
Thiede, George   215–16, 220, 230–2, 251
Thiede, James. See Kelly, James Cotton
Thiede, Thomas Alfred   226
trauma   206–7. See also psychotic intrusions
  mental illnesses   192
trial for Cotton's murder   109, 110, 112–30
  Billy's testimony   115
  Fletcher's testimony   118–19
  illegal jury instructions   128
  Jessica's testimony   119–21
  Sandy's testimony   124–8
  sentencing   129–30
  Stacy's testimony   117–18
  Varela's testimony   122–4
  verdict   128–9
trial judge   112, 192
truce   49–50
trust   257

Utah Department of Corrections   212

Valium   74
Varela, Thomas   126
  apology letter to Sandy   *132*, 176, 177
  as a repeat offender   177
  testimony   122–4, 176, 177
venlafaxine   243

Walsh, John   203
Washington Continuation Junior High   74
Watters, Willie   112
Western High School   87, 89
Western Nevada Community College   191, 209
Williams, Charlene   187–8

Wilson, John P.   192–3, 206
Wilson, Tina   83–5, 89, 226
Wisconsin   43–5
Woods, Cathy   218–19

word code   200
write-ups   217–18, 221–2

Young (chief justice)   223
Yvette   81–2

About the Authors

Dan Gleason, the writer of this story, earned his Master of Fine Arts degree from Iowa University's celebrated Writers Workshop. A prolific magazine writer of award-winning fiction and non-fiction, Dan has also sold three books.

Sandy Shaw, whose life experiences provide the information for this story, became the youngest female ever incarcerated in an adult Nevada prison. After earning two college degrees in prison, the former honors student launched her valiant battle to win her freedom.